For my family, whose support made this book possible:
My parents, my children, and especially Deborah, my wife

Practical SharePoint 2010 Information Architecture

Ruven Gotz

Apress®

Practical SharePoint 2010 Information Architecture

Copyright © 2012 by Ruven Gotz

ISBN-13 (pbk): 978-1-4302-4176-8

ISBN-13 (electronic): 978-1-4302-4177-5

Trademarked names, logos, and images may appear in this book. Rather than use a trademark symbol with every occurrence of a trademarked name, logo, or image we use the names, logos, and images only in an editorial fashion and to the benefit of the trademark owner, with no intention of infringement of the trademark.

The use in this publication of trade names, trademarks, service marks, and similar terms, even if they are not identified as such, is not to be taken as an expression of opinion as to whether or not they are subject to proprietary rights.

President and Publisher: Paul Manning
Lead Editor: Jonathan Hassell
Development Editor: Louise Corrigan
Technical Reviewer: Fabio Claudio Ferracchiati
Editorial Board: Steve Anglin, Mark Beckner, Ewan Buckingham, Gary Cornell, Jonathan Gennick, Jonathan Hassell, Michelle Lowman, James Markham, Matthew Moodie, Jeff Olson, Jeffrey Pepper, Douglas Pundick, Ben Renow-Clarke, Dominic Shakeshaft, Matt Wade, Tom Welsh
Coordinating Editor: Tracy Brown
Copy Editor: Mary Bearden
Compositor: Mary Sudul
Indexer: SPi Global
Cover Designer: Anna Ishchenko

Distributed to the book trade worldwide by Springer Science+Business Media, LLC., 233 Spring Street, 6th Floor, New York, NY 10013. Phone 1-800-SPRINGER, fax (201) 348-4505, e-mail orders-ny@springer-sbm.com, or visit www.springeronline.com.

For information on translations, please e-mail rights@apress.com, or visit www.apress.com.

Apress and friends of ED books may be purchased in bulk for academic, corporate, or promotional use. eBook versions and licenses are also available for most titles. For more information, reference our Special Bulk Sales–eBook Licensing web page at www.apress.com/bulk-sales.

The information in this book is distributed on an "as is" basis, without warranty. Although every precaution has been taken in the preparation of this work, neither the author(s) nor Apress shall have any liability to any person or entity with respect to any loss or damage caused or alleged to be caused directly or indirectly by the information contained in this work.

Contents at a Glance

Contents

Foreword

In the early days of my involvement with SharePoint, back when it had the code name Tahoe and I represented Dell on Microsoft's Partner Advisory Council for Portals and Collaboration, I was always the lone voice in the room telling anyone who would listen that deploying SharePoint successfully is only a small part about getting the technology right and a very large part toward solving a business problem and the associated best practices that good business analysts have known for years. Ruven and I bonded over a shared passion about this topic—well, that and a blog post about my calling the TSA to find out if I could bring frozen brisket to my son at college in a carry-on bag! (The answer is yes, by the way, as long as it's frozen solid when you get on the plane.)

What began as a series of e-mail messages between two strangers with similar interests grew to a wonderful friendship that has enriched my personal and professional life immensely. When we first met in person, we sat down to show each other the tools and techniques we used to work with business stakeholders and to both elicit and translate the business outcomes into successful SharePoint information architecture designs. From that moment on, Ruven has been my "go to" guy when I need a new or different technique in my business analysis or information architecture tool kit.

In this book, Ruven shares his toolkit with the world—and does so in an incredibly "consumable" way. The book is really a master's class in how to be a good business analyst and information architect. In many ways, reading the book is like getting inside Ruven's head; he shares his thought processes and approaches for understanding as well as communicating and validating the information needed to design a successful SharePoint solution. And, despite the SharePoint focus, the tools and techniques are equally applicable for other technology platforms because they are about translating business objectives into a practical, achievable, and results-driven solution design. Understanding business objectives for portals and collaboration solutions is inherently hard because these solutions often involve new ways of working that are hard for business stakeholders to envision or articulate. If you want to get it right, you need the techniques in this book. Ruven himself is an amazing example of a continuous learner; he has documented approaches and practices that he's developed and refined over many years of continuous practice—and they really work. You are not going to instantly become a fantastic business analyst or information architect just by reading a book. These skills take practice to develop. You need a breadth of experience and lots of opportunities to refine your craft. Fortunately, Ruven has provided proven approaches, tools, and techniques in this book that will significantly accelerate your learning process.

If you are a business analyst or an information architect, Practical SharePoint 2010 Information Architecture needs to be on your bookshelf or e-reader. And, because Ruven is continuously learning and SharePoint is continuously changing, take advantage of the opportunity to attend a conference where Ruven is speaking, and he will share the latest approaches and techniques. He's a great storyteller on the printed page and even better in person!

—Sue Hanley
Portals and collaboration consultant
Co-author of *Essential SharePoint 2010 and Essential SharePoint 2007*
(Addison-Wesley, 2007)
www.susanhanley.com

About the Author

 **Ruven Gotz** is a senior consultant and SharePoint MVP based in Toronto, Canada. With over 25 years of IT industry experience, Ruven has spent the past eight years delivering award-winning SharePoint solutions for a wide range of clients. Working as a business analyst and information architect, Ruven is able to apply his eclectic education and varied experience in psychology, computer science, economics, software development, and training to get to the heart of complex problems. Ruven is a great communicator who is able to discuss technology concepts in language that is relevant to his audience, whether they are from IT or business. He has become a leader in the use of visual tools to help his clients and team members achieve shared understanding of problems and goals and shared commitment toward implementing a successful solution.

Ruven helps his clients understand that strong technical teams are necessary but not sufficient to deliver a successful result. A successful SharePoint project requires excellent planning, a good understanding of the client's corporate culture, and thoughtful change management.

When he wants to get away from computers, you'll find Ruven at the weeknight races on Lake Ontario, sailing his keelboat *In the Groove*.

Ruven's blog is at http://spinsiders.com/ruveng and you can follow him on Twitter at @ruveng.

Contributors

Sarah Haase: Sarah is an information architect and corporate librarian with more than 15 years of knowledge management, technical writing, and business process reengineering experience. From building wikis and other online knowledge bases to supporting content management system implementations, Sarah has focused on using technology to enable efficient information storage and retrieval. In her current role as a collaboration and search engineer, Sarah relies on SharePoint to drive online collaboration and optimize business processes. To date, her efforts have netted more than $750,000 in annual cost savings.

Michal Pisarek: Michal is a Microsoft SharePoint MVP with experience in development, infrastructure, requirements analysis, training, and implementation. Focusing on the business side of SharePoint, with a deep technical understanding, his goal is to make sure that all his clients discover the incredible business value the platform offers. As the founder of the popular SharePoint blog SharePoint Analyst HQ and contributor to other well-regarded SharePoint-related publications including *CMSWire* and *NothingButSharePoint*, he approaches SharePoint from a business angle, ensuring that business goals, technical solutions, and effective change management are all considered in a pragmatic manner to deliver value to any organization.

About the Technical Reviewer

Fabio Claudio Ferracchiati is a prolific writer on cutting-edge technologies and has contributed to more than a dozen books on .NET, C#, Visual Basic, and ASP.NET. He is a .NET Microsoft certified solution developer and he lives in Milan, Italy. You can read his blog at Ferracchiati.com.

Acknowledgments

I have had many teachers during my career, too many to name here. But I do want to mention some people in the world of SharePoint who have helped me form many of my ideas (and who have called me out when I would go off the deep end). My top three idea people are Paul Culmsee, Susan Hanley, and Richard Harbridge. Over the past five years or so, I have had innumerable conversations and discussions with them, and many of my best ideas have taken shape while talking with them. I am glad to count them as friends. I can't go further without also thanking the SharePoint community that I have come to know via Twitter, Facebook, and conferences. I have made so many good friends and learned so much from them all.

I am very lucky to have had great bosses, past and present. Val Prendergast is everything that you'd want in a boss and a wonderful human being. Gord MacLeod (in addition to his sardonic sense of humor, which I love) has given me the backing that I need to apply the approaches I advocate. I very much appreciate his support.

I have had some really great coworkers and mentors over the years, but one who must be named is Joe Markus. He listened to me talk about the issues I was having communicating navigation and taxonomy to clients. He demonstrated MindManager to me and suggested that I try it. There are many other reasons too, but even if it were just these things, I will be forever in Joe's debt.

Getting the technology right is essential but not sufficient for success. My essential "getting the technology right" guy is Brian Lalancette. He has helped me in many ways over the past few years, answering my dumb SharePoint technology questions and helping me appear to be smarter than I am. He also came through with some crucial support during the writing of this book.

People who have generously contributed material to this book include Jeff Conklin, Paul Culmsee, Marcy Kellar, Dave Snowden, Erik Swenson, and Sadalit Van Buren. My thanks to them for helping me make this book better.

Everyone who writes about writing a book puts in what sounds like obligatory thanks to contributors and the editing team. Only those who have actually written a book know how real those thanks are. I need to start with my contributing authors: Sarah Haase and Michal Pisarek. When I realized how daunting writing a dozen chapters was going to be, I reached out to my two first choices and was thrilled when they each agreed to take one chapter off my hands. They came through wonderfully with great content. Without them, I really could never have finished this book.

Special thanks to the Apress editing team led by Jonathan Hassell. I want to thank Jon for first getting in touch with me after reading my session abstract at a conference. However, the day-to-day work of making this book happen fell primarily to Tracy Brown and Louise Corrigan. From my point of view, Tracy's main job was to let me know that I was behind schedule every single day for the past six months, and also to be my therapist when I felt like I just couldn't do it. She is the prime driver behind the delivery of this book. and it would not have happened without her tenacious (but friendly) pushing. Louise appeared to be nice, but she has an iron fist inside that velvet glove. She would gut me with her comments, but after I would calm down, I realized that she had helped me make the combination of words and images flow so much more smoothly for the reader (and she *is* actually really nice). There were others on the Apress team who had a go at my words: technical editor Fabio Claudio Ferracchiati and copy editor Mary Bearden, who each made suggestions and improvements to the text.

Finally, I'd like to acknowledge you, the reader. I thank you for taking the time to read this book. I hope you will try out the tools you learned about and I'd love to hear from you if you find any of it useful in your daily work.

Introduction

Practical SharePoint 2010 Information Architecture is not just for people whose job title is "information architect." It is also for business analysts, project managers, IT managers, or business managers who have been tasked with delivering a SharePoint 2010 solution.

If you are thinking of reading this, I want to make sure you have picked the right book for the right reasons. This is ultimately a practical book based on what I have learned in the practice of delivering successful SharePoint projects. This book is not going to be a deep dive into the theories of taxonomy and ontology. If you are a library science graduate, you will not find anything here to stretch your understanding of those subjects. It is also not a deep look into user experience and usability. Finally, it is not meant to be a reference book, with hundreds of SharePoint facts and features you can look up. What I am hoping is that you will find this to be more of a handbook: One that you can read fairly quickly that is full of practices you can learn rapidly and then apply to your next project. I did not include a ton of SharePoint screenshots here, because this book is less focused on detailed SharePoint features than it is on preparing the way for a great SharePoint deployment.

The reason I wrote this book is that over the past five years, I have discovered a small collection of tools and techniques that are quite easy to learn and have made a *huge* difference in the way I was able to communicate with my stakeholders. I have found that these tools can make a major difference to the chances a delivering a successful project.

The methods and software I describe are all centered on the concept of using visual abstractions that can be employed interactively during meetings and workshops with stakeholders. I have especially focused on tools that work well in these types of interactive sessions. It is true that if you plug your computer into a projector, almost any software could be used interactively; you could just project a Word document on the screen as you take notes, but that would not be as powerful as the mind mapping, wireframing, and process mapping tools explained in this book. The products I use amplify shared understanding through their use. As I will explain, getting to a shared understanding is the most important factor in getting to a successful result.

I have used these tools and techniques on projects that employ SharePoint for public-facing web sites, for team collaboration, for application development and integration, and for corporate portals, but my experience is that they are most directly applicable to the development of corporate portals that include a web-content management tier for sharing information widely throughout the organization and a collaboration tier that facilitates teams who work together on a day-to-day basis.

I have been speaking about these tools and techniques for the past four years at conferences around the world, and I often hear from attendees who tell me that they have applied what I have shown them and found it to be incredibly helpful for them. I hope you will find what you learn here useful for your projects.

Point of View of the Author

I am writing this book from the point of view of someone responsible for SharePoint projects at a high level. I am a consultant who uses the titles business analyst (BA) and information architect (IA; more on that in a minute). I am involved in projects from the beginning to the end, helping to define what the stakeholders' goals are and what the scope and budget for the project should be. I am intimately involved in designing the site structure, navigation, and taxonomy. I work closely with the project manager, the architect who leads the development and deployment effort, and the infrastructure architect who specifies the hardware and installs and configures SharePoint. I am involved in the branding process, working with the designer to ensure that the design complements the goals and vision for the project. I provide oversight to the teams who do training, governance planning, and communications planning. I then consider it my responsibility to be the representative of the customer during development, deployment, and migration, to ensure that the original vision I helped to define is what gets delivered to the customer.

My point of view for this book is of a person doing the job I have just described. I am assuming that you own all or part of this process, and the tools I describe and techniques I explain are meant to help you accomplish all of this successfully.

Naming the Players

In this book, I will variously use the terms customer, stakeholder, team member, and user.

When I say customer, I am referring to the people you are building the solution for. It can be an external client if you are a consultant, or it could be your company as a whole or another department within your organization. When you are working on a SharePoint project, the people you work most closely with to design and implement the solution are the SharePoint team, and they may include people from within the customer team as well as team members from other departments or a consulting firm.

Another type of customer is the end user (or better, information worker or knowledge worker) who does not necessarily have a say in what was developed. All these groups from users through senior executives together make up the stakeholders in the overall project and the delivered solution.

What Is an Information Architect?

What is my actual job? I don't have a great name for it, and neither does anyone else. I sometimes used to call myself a business analyst. One definition of that job, from the International Institute of Business Analysis (www.iiba.org) is:

A business analyst works as a liaison among stakeholders to elicit, analyze, communicate and validate requirements for changes to business processes, policies and information systems. The business analyst understands business problems and opportunities in the context of the requirements, and recommends solutions that enable the organization to achieve its goals.

Okay, that does cover quite a lot of what I do, but my job is a bit more specific than that because I work specifically on SharePoint projects. Also, I do more than "recommend" solutions; I design and build stuff as well.

But I'm also not entirely happy with the definition of information architecture from the Information Architecture Institute (iainstitute.org), who defines information architecture as:

1. The structural design of shared information environments.

2. The art and science of organizing and labeling web sites, intranets, online communities, and software to support usability and findability.

3. An emerging community of practice focused on bringing principles of design and architecture to the digital landscape.

Well, I do a bunch of that, but it's more too. I hesitate with this title partly because it seems that most jobs that I see for IAs are more focused on the design aspects, meaning the artistic use of color, font, and layout, which, to me, leans more in the direction of usability and user experience design.

So, with all that, I'm not really sure exactly what an information architect is, but I had to pick a title, so 70 percent of the time I say I am an information architect and about 30 percent of the time I say I am a business analyst. This is my definition of what I do as an IA:

I work with stakeholders to understand their business and the issues they are having concerning information creation, sharing, processing, and management. We work together to achieve a shared understanding of the problems we are going to try to solve and then we collaborate on navigation, content taxonomies, and workflows that facilitate information sharing and findability.

I know this sounds pretty pretentious, but I decided to call this book *Practical SharePoint 2010 Information Architecture* because it covers the work of an IA as I have just defined it.

Why Is SharePoint So Hard?

You wouldn't start building a house without a blueprint. But what would you do if you're not really clear on the concept of what a "house" is? The blueprint only makes sense to someone who understands what it represents. What may surprise you is that a lot of people are sold on the concept of SharePoint as a relatively low-cost, easy to implement solution that will solve a bunch of business problems with very little work. The actual truth is that most organizations who agree to buy SharePoint don't really know what it is. Part of the problem is that no one can sum up in one sentence what SharePoint is or what it does. Many have tried, but SharePoint is unlike other Microsoft server products like Exchange (e-mail) or SQLServer (database), or IIS (web). These products can be thought of as if they were picture puzzles: They are not easy to put together, but you know ahead of time what the result will look like when you're done, and you have a pretty good template to guide you. SharePoint is more like a huge set of Lego blocks with no instructions: If you open a container of Lego and ask "What do I do with this?" the only answer is "What do you want to do with it?" Lego lets your imagination run free; it can be used to build almost anything. For some people that freedom is liberating, for others it can be frightening.

SharePoint is a platform with a broad and powerful set of tools that requires careful planning, architecture, implementation, and maintenance to make it useful to a business. The past ten years of SharePoint implementation have often been of the "Ready, Fire! Aim" variety, resulting in implementations that don't deliver the magical results that were expected. In the past few years, we have started to see a groundswell of new writing and presentations about governance and other concepts, many of which have become buzzwords, that attempt to address these issues. The reason for this rapid "buzzwordification" of SharePoint planning and governance concepts is that a lot of people see the potential for the SharePoint platform, but they don't want to invest the resources (time and money) required to get the full value. What they are really looking for are shortcuts via a collection of so-called best practices that will do the job for them.

The problem with SharePoint is that in addition to it being an inherently powerful and complicated system, the people who buy it and implement it often don't have a clear picture of the business problems they are trying to solve. You can't just dump the Lego container out on the floor, stick a random bunch of pieces together, and say "Wow; that looks great."

This book will show you how you can apply visual tools that will help you to clarify the scoping and planning, as well as build the structures and processes you will need to implement your SharePoint projects.

Planning your SharePoint deployment is a complex, multistep process involving multiple groups of stakeholders. In many cases, the stakeholders are not exactly sure what SharePoint does or how it works, so you, as the information architect (or business analyst, or project manager), must help them articulate their pain points and design a solution that will meet their needs.

Because of this lack of clarity between the business that needs a solution and the team that is building that solution, there are many places where poor communication can make the project less successful than it otherwise could have been or, in the worst case, a total failure. I recognized this to be a problem during my early years of SharePoint consulting, so I made it part of my job to find solutions to the communication problem. I have been lucky enough to find some really great tools that have literally changed my life as an information architect. These tools are easy to learn and use and make a huge difference in the likelihood of success for a SharePoint project.

More recently, I have come to understand more about why these tools work so well.

How Can We Make It Easier?

Whenever you are dealing with a complex problem that has a lot of social complexity issues (e.g., political factors, diverging goals, differences in levels of understanding), you cannot hope for success unless you get a shared commitment to the goal by at least most of the stakeholders. Without a shared commitment, the project will be pushed off course, mired in endless bickering, or just die through lack of drive to invest the time and energy required to see it through to the end.

Before you can get to a shared commitment, you must achieve shared understanding. There is no way someone can commit to a project that is going to take up valuable time and energy without a clear understanding of its goals. At a more detailed level, getting signoff for a navigational structure or a content taxonomy requires an understanding of what is being designed and, as importantly, trust that the team building the solution understands the problem deeply and well.

Working with diverse teams who have diverse motivations, the information architect has to combine enthusiasm, storytelling, and some psychology to help everyone see the carrots (benefits) and sticks (results of project failure) that await them. As Sue Hanley states, you need to be able to answer the "What's in it for *me*?" question.

What Is In This Book?

In this section I will briefly describe what is presented in each chapter of this book.

Chapter 1: Planning for Successful Outcomes

This chapter builds the basis for the key personal skills you will need to cultivate to be successful as an IA or a BA: confidence, humor, and honesty among them. We then talk about how to run successful workshops and how to use them to build your own understanding of the issues within the organization that SharePoint could be applied to. We then cover the concept of building road maps for planning your project phases.

Chapter 2: Introduction to Mind Mapping

This is the first tool I discovered that led me on the path I am now on. I will show you how quickly you can learn mind mapping as a technique for visualization that will instantly make your meetings more compelling, useful, efficient, and fun.

Chapter 3: The Magic of Metadata

Having a clear understanding of metadata and being able to explain it clearly to your project stakeholders are essential for success. This chapter begins by explaining the metadata concepts and then build on them to an understanding of taxonomy, content types, and exploration of the "f-word" (that's "folders"). We talk about how to gather the metadata you will need for your project and how to build interactive taxonomy maps using mind mapping tools.

Chapter 4: Site Navigation and Structure

One of the most political elements of building a SharePoint site is getting agreement on the site navigation. There are multiple competing interests who want their area to be highlighted or who don't understand why just replicating the organization chart won't work. We again use mind mapping to work interactively with the stakeholders to solve this efficiently. We talk about card sorting techniques to validate the structures, and talk about the differences between portal areas and collaboration areas.

Chapter 5: Wireframing for SharePoint

Wireframing was never something I enjoyed doing until I discovered a tool called Balsamiq, which had just the right mix of simplicity and power. This chapter will cover the approach I take to wireframing and demonstrate how to use Balsamiq. I also talk about Microsoft Visio for wireframing as well as usability testing and content strategy.

Chapter 6: Complexity, Wickedness, and Dialogue Mapping

Getting to a shared understanding of what it is you are actually going to accomplish with your SharePoint project is probably the single biggest factor that will govern your project's success or failure. This chapter will introduce the IBIS grammar for mapping, as well as the compendium software used to build these types of maps. I will show you real-world examples of how I have used these maps to rapidly achieve agreement about project goals and scope.

Chapter 7: Business Process Mapping

Business information is not just static, it flows. So just discussing the structures for storing information leaves out a big part of the story. The mapping of information flows as part of business processes is an important part of planning for SharePoint because of the workflow capabilities that it brings. This chapter covers the use of Microsoft Visio and BizAgi software for modeling business processes.

Chapter 8: The Art of Creating Business Process Solutions

In Chapter 7 we covered tools for mapping business processes. In this chapter, Sarah Haase writes about how to actually build solutions that implement business processes and—very crucially—talks about how to measure the return on investment (ROI) for these types of solutions. The ROI calculation is one that will matter to anyone who needs to prove the bottom-line value of any investment you have made.

Chapter 9: Success with Search

In this chapter, Michal Pisarek writes about how important good search is to the success of your SharePoint project. He talks about establishing search requirements and then how to take advantage of SharePoint search features such as facets, best bets, and reporting to ensure that your users get the best search results possible.

Chapter 10: Governance, Adoption, and Training

Governance, adoption, and training are concepts that are deeply intertwined. After your SharePoint site is delivered, it is these elements that will determine if you have built a viable, long-term solution or something that will either die from lack of use or become chaotic and unmanageable.

Chapter 11: Practice and Testing in the Cloud

Our work often requires us to test new concepts and potential solutions. Because SharePoint is so large, we can't know all of the parts of it, and when our colleagues or customers ask us whether something is possible, we need to have access to an environment that gives us free rein to test out ideas. This chapter will compare the services I have used for this purpose: CloudShare, Microsoft Office 365, and Amazon's Elastic Compute Cloud.

Chapter 12: Conclusion: Putting It All Together

I conclude by taking you through the lifecycle of a SharePoint project, put together everything you've learned throughout the book, and emphasize the key tools and when and how you would apply them.

CHAPTER 1

Preparing for Successful Outcomes

Everything should be made as simple as possible, but no simpler.

Attributed to Albert Einstein

SharePoint projects are notorious for their difficulty. The seeds for a successful project are sown in the early days of the project, when you, as the project consultant, have to rapidly integrate yourself into an organization, build trust with your client stakeholders, and gather the essential information you will need to be able to deliver a successful solution. You are doing more than just listening and learning in this phase: You are educating your clients and often shaking them to their core by forcing them to rethink their approach to technology solution implementation. You push toward simplicity and maintain your focus on business outcomes rather than simply gathering lists of requirements. You do this knowing that the simpler solution is much more likely to be successful, and that it will be the foundation upon which more complex and sophisticated solutions may be built.

The Soft Side of Successful Projects

Around the turn of the 15th century, Niccolò Machiavelli would have said something like the following about SharePoint projects:

> *It must be considered that there is nothing more difficult to carry out nor more doubtful of success nor more dangerous to handle than to initiate a new SharePoint project; for the project team has enemies in all those who profit by the old portal, and only lukewarm defenders in all those who would profit by the new portal; this lukewarmness arising partly from the incredulity of mankind who does not truly believe in anything new until they actually have experience of it.*

Okay, so he wouldn't have been specifically talking about SharePoint, but it certainly rings true today. In my experience, pretty much everyone hates the current intranet portal: They can't find stuff and they don't know if they can't find it because it's not there or because it's hidden. And once they do find it, it's hard to tell if the material is still valid. Even so, there's a lot of resistance to the new portal project because cynical disbelievers don't trust the team to get it right this time either. As good old Niccolò says, they do not "truly believe in anything new until they actually have experience of it."

It is into this environment that you are about to enter when you take on a SharePoint project. You are going to have to navigate your team off the path of hope (which always proves to be a false route), over the rise of optimistic excitement, and through the valley of despair. It's a steep climb at the end to reach the plateau of the desired future state. The other problem with the valley of despair is that there are dangerous predators who live there: creatures who would be happy to derail your project because they want to implement a different solution or who have other political purposes for causing your project to be reduced or to fail. Figure 1-1 shows this variation of highs and lows or, as I like to call it, the dangerous path to success.

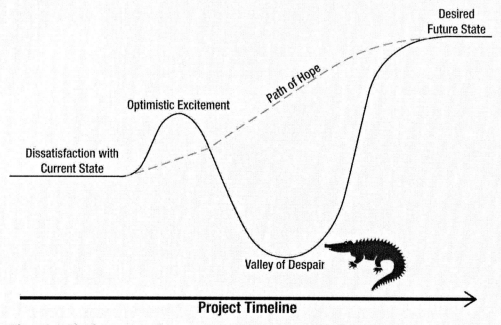

Figure 1-1. The dangerous path to success

As tough as it is to navigate the dangerous path to success, if you or your sales team has oversold the project and set the desired future state too high, there's a good chance you'll never get there. You always have to be honest with your client about having reasonable goals that are achievable. Figure 1-2 shows how to set up multiple phases toward the eventual future goal, rather than trying to reach that peak in one step, because it is only once you start the journey that you will discover the issues and roadblocks that are going to make the project much harder than it seemed at the start.

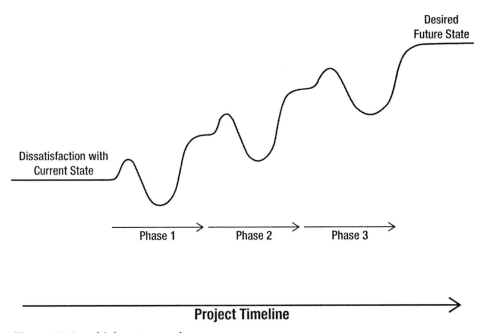

Figure 1-2. A multiphase approach

At the end of each phase is a milestone or subgoal that demonstrates success and provides the scaffolding for the following phases.

■ **Note** Even though it is useful to break the project into phases, it is very important that you do your initial planning with the ultimate goal in mind so that you don't paint yourself into a corner by designing a solution that gets you to the end of phase 1 or 2, but that needs a lot of rework or workarounds to reach the true, final goal.

To conduct successful projects, you need to be able to quickly build rapport with the team, make them feel heard, and guide them along the path to success. This is not an easy task; it requires a good mix of psychology, SharePoint technical knowledge, business knowledge, confidence, honesty, humility, and humor. The process can be stressful, but when you get it right it is a tremendously enjoyable experience to know that you have heard your clients and helped to guide them toward a solution that will work for their unique needs. So, let's examine the elements that we need to master in order to get to success.

Building Confidence

It is essential that the people you are working with (customers, stakeholders, team members) have confidence in you as a leader of the process. You need to project an air of knowledge and experience that helps them feel you are leading them along the correct path. You also need to be able to do this without appearing arrogant or dictatorial or you'll just turn people off.

Being confident is not the same as pretending you know all the answers when you really don't. Don't be afraid to say "I'll need to think about that and get back to you" or "I'll need to do a bit of research and get back to you." Getting the balance right can be tough. If you answer every question with uncertainty, you'll lose the confidence of the team. There is also nothing wrong with answering a question confidently when you feel you are likely to be right, but if you have some doubt, do the extra research and don't be afraid to come back to the next meeting and admit you've changed your answer based on some additional work.

You need to be willing to embrace the fact that despite a lot of conferences and books that talk about SharePoint best practices, there are very few cut-and-dried solutions to the problems you are trying to solve for your customers. You are there to help them navigate a path that is just one of a large number of possible paths, each with its own pros and cons, many of which can bring them to a successful destination.

Your goal is to use your experience and knowledge to keep your customers moving in the direction of the goal, making adjustments as obstacles and new information come your way. Find a balance of strength and humility. Don't put yourself in a difficult situation by refusing to consider alternatives because you don't want to deviate from a previous statement.

▦ **Tip**   One of my favorite bloggers is Bob Sutton of the Stanford Design School. In one of his posts he writes about Paul Saffo of the Palo Alto Institute for the Future who taught that leaders must have strong opinions. Weak opinions are uninspiring and don't motivate people to test them or argue passionately for them. But, it is also important not to be too strongly wedded to your ideas, because it prevents you from seeing or hearing evidence that contradicts your opinions. So to be a strong and wise leader you need to have strong opinions, but you need to be ready to move off those opinions when the evidence requires it. This is summed up in the phrase that you should take to heart: Strong opinions, weakly held.

Listening

You need to listen to your customers or you will miss important information. If you are conducting a workshop, you are there to facilitate and gather information, not to impose your vision. You have to be mindful and in the moment. You need to eliminate all possible distractions. This means you turn off or silence your phone, close your Twitter client (yes, I've seen people check their tweets during a workshop!), and close or silence e-mail (it can really throw a meeting off track when an e-mail "toast" notification pops up on the screen while you're working).

There are a number of books and blogs on how to improve your listening skills. Search the Internet for "active listening" or "mindful listening." Choose a book or a program and then practice these skills.

It is very important to fully hear what is being said without focusing on what you are going to say in response, because once you start to think of your response, you're not listening anymore and there may be valuable additional information you are missing.

Some of the techniques discussed later regarding the use of visual tools to capture information can make it easier to ensure you've really heard what the users have said (and in a way that allows them to verify your understanding).

It can be very helpful if you have a scribe (a person there from your team solely to take notes) at the meeting. It is much more helpful if your scribe is someone who is more than just a clerk, but rather someone who understands the problem space you are working in, so that the notes are not just a verbatim transcript, but rather a narrative of the essential elements of the conversation.

Humor

Workshops can be stressful for everyone involved. Your customers are taking time out of their busy days to attend this workshop. They don't want you to waste their time and, at first, they may not really trust that you are going to use their time effectively. You are under the gun to deliver a successful workshop, and you need to keep the meeting focused, but you can also keep it a bit light by using humor. This does not involve telling jokes, but rather making light of certain situations—especially if you are the target. It takes a pretty good level of trust and familiarity before you can make a joke at the expense of one of your clients, and this is dangerous territory—I have seen it backfire (on me!).

Here is an example of light humor in a workshop: We were talking about who would be the editor-in-chief of the portal and I nominated someone in the room to be the "Queen of the Portal." Everyone laughed (I know, you had to be there), but from then on, she referred to herself (as did the rest of the team) as the Queen of the Portal, and it served to lighten the mood of the room.

Brutal Honesty

You need to be brutally honest about yourself. As I said above, if you don't know something, say so. People can tell when you're faking—either immediately or later when they find out you didn't really know. People will rely on your integrity, and once they trust you, they will believe you when you argue that a particular choice or course is the right one. A place where it can be tougher to be brutally honest is when it involves the politics and hierarchy of your stakeholders' organization. If you are working on a project where choices and decisions are being made, you have an obligation to voice your opinion and explain your reasoning and the consequences of the path being taken. In many cases that's the best you can do. You have to realize that there are many competing interests, many competing projects, and a lot of complex things going on that you may have no idea about. When you come into an environment like this as just one consultant (or part of a small team), it can be really risky to stick your neck out to do what you believe to be the right thing. Here is an example of a project I once worked on where things worked out well. I won't guarantee that this approach will always work, as I know I could have had my ideas shot down (or worse), but I feel confident about my choice to speak up.

▓ **Tip**   Being brutally honest is no excuse for being rude. The people you are working with are for the most part trying hard and giving their best. Don't call out people in a way that will embarrass them. Don't snap at an idea or roll your eyes. Don't insult work done by the previous team or the previous consultant (I know, we just can't help doing that one!). Being brutally honest means being scrupulously honest, not being brutalizingly honest.

A Large Conglomerate—let's call it ALC—wanted to migrate from its old, out-of-date portal to a brand new SharePoint portal. The migration had to be completed on a very aggressive schedule because the old portal had to be phased out by a certain date for a bunch of reasons. When I joined, many months had already been spent identifying content owners and inventorying the documents on the old portal. A new site had been designed (information architecture [IA], wireframes, mock-ups, prototypes) and the migration/implementation was proceeding to go live in four and a half months. The go-live day was scheduled for the same day that the old portal was to be shut down.

Now, here's the wrinkle: ALC had decided to use SharePoint as the front end to the portal, but all documents would be stored and managed in a dedicated enterprise content management (ECM) system from another vendor. ALC had purchased the ECM/SharePoint connector, but it would not be implemented in time for the go-live date. The migration plan was to migrate all documents from the old portal to the ECM and link to them from SharePoint. What it didn't address was all the content that existed on web pages within the old portal (i.e., all the context for the documents). The plan called for, but did not leave enough time for, the design of a new taxonomy to assist with findability on the new portal, but the new portal didn't account for a collection of nonstandard sites that had been created by many teams (some internal, some hosted externally).

This project train was headed down the track at full speed and the brakes weren't working. The operative phrase from the project manager was "it won't be ideal on day one, but we'll fix it up later." Within the first few days after I joined the project, I started to get the big picture of what was going on and I had a very bad feeling. The project manager (from a very large, international firm) who was leading the project was working effectively and forcefully to deliver an on-time/on-budget solution within the constraints he had to deal with. This was a highly visible project with a multimillion-dollar budget, but it looked to me like it was going to crash and burn. I had a couple of options: put my head down and produce my deliverables, or look for a way to save this thing.

I used my issue mapping skills to produce a map of options along with the arguments pro and con for each of the alternatives. I then converted those arguments into a slide presentation complete with semi-amusing images, like the one in Figure 1-3, to represent the likely adoption failure that would result from the current approach.

Figure 1-3. Getting the message across

I presented my PowerPoint deck to the business owner who was then able to tell the story to the steering committee and project sponsor. The net result was that we were allowed to scale back to a manageable set of deliverable solutions for the go-live date. The steering committee agreed to extend the deadline for decommissioning the old portal so that we would have time to work with the various content owners to design a functional and usable portal for them. We didn't just move all their documents into a new place with the same old unworkable structure, but took a phased approach that allowed time and resources for the proper design, implementation, and migration to the new portal.

Of course this new solution had its costs as well: We did not meet the initial goals (and timelines) for the project. This had a political cost for the sponsors. We also required that the old portal would continue operation for many months beyond the initial phase-out date. This had a licensing impact and caused problems for other, related projects. Finally, by extending the timeline, the implementation costs were higher (but not greatly, as we were able to create a much more efficient team and project plan). These are all factors that had to be carefully weighed. Ultimately, the risk of the portal project failing outweighed the other factors.

So, do I recommend that you "blow up" a major project starting less than a week after you join? Not always, and maybe not even most times. I was taking a major risk, calling foul on a project plan that had been created by one of the biggest consulting firms in the world and that was heading for a finish line that had been very firmly set. But if the project is looking like it will be a train wreck and you can offer alternatives that will avert the disaster, and (very important!) you can capture and organize the issues, create a well-articulated message, and present it well, then your brutal honesty will be taken for what it is: a way for the client to avoid a disaster that costs time, money, and morale.

Now that we have looked at some of the soft skills that are essential elements to be successful at the performance art that is called a workshop, let's look at the types of workshops that need to be run and how to make them effective.

Understanding Requirements Gathering

My three rules of SharePoint are:

1. Simplicity

2. Simplicity

3. Simplicity

SharePoint is a giant toolset that lets you do almost anything. The downside of this is that your client probably doesn't understand the range of possibilities and how the choices they make will impact their business and how they do their work. And frankly, you don't understand these things either (yet).

Designing complex, large-scale solutions to complex problems is a very high-risk proposition that often leads to tears.

If you can find a way to implement a reasonable subset of the functionality, either as a pilot project or even as a full-blown solution, the client will be able to start using it, find the holes, and get it enhanced sooner. Over time the solution may evolve and grow or may even be scrapped in favor of a more complete or sophisticated toolset. But that evolution will be the result of a detailed understanding of the problem space and how technology may or may not be able to solve that particular problem.

The process of evolving toward a great solution is called *opportunity-driven learning*, which you can read about in the book *Dialogue Mapping: Building a Shared Understanding of Wicked Problems* by Jeff Conklin. In this process, the understanding of the real, underlying problem grows as candidate solutions are designed and put into use.

In *Dialogue Mapping*, Jeff describes an exercise in which engineers had to design a chip that would act as the control system for an elevator. Our normal model for this process is one where the engineer has to gather specifications, analyze the data, formulate a solution, and then implement a solution. The reality is that the designers thought about the problem briefly and then immediately dove into designing the solution. As they created their solutions, they realized that they had left something out and had to rethink their understanding. They would then start over or modify the design. This process of jumping back and forth between thinking more deeply about the problem and then designing the solution reflects the reality of complex problem solving.

The reason I push for simplicity is that no matter how careful you are with your requirements gathering process, it is not until the users see the solution in action that they will be able to tell you whether it works or not. If you design simple solutions, they will be less costly and time consuming to implement, so you will be able to see how they work in the real world and then adjust as you learn.

In this section, I will describe my process for the requirements phase of a SharePoint project.

The SharePoint Chicken and Egg Problem

Here is how many SharePoint conversations start:

> *Analyst*: I'm here to help you to implement SharePoint.

> *Customer*: Great! What can SharePoint do?

> *Analyst*: Lots of things: What do you want it to do?

> *Customer*: Um, I'm not sure . . . maybe you can give me a demo.

> *Analyst*: Sure: Imagine that you are a bicycle manufacturer in the Pacific northwest.

> *Customer*: But we aren't a . . .

> *Analyst*: Isn't this feature cool? It has a bike as a background image.

This type of conversation happens all the time during the early stages of SharePoint projects. The client/stakeholder doesn't really understand in detail what SharePoint is or how it works, and the analyst is very excited to demonstrate all of SharePoint's "cool" features using canned demos (often created by Microsoft and seen before by the client). The result is either confusion (my team will never figure all that out) or an unrealistic expectation of how easy it will be to solve long-standing problems within the organization (I want it *all*: Turn everything on for launch).

I call this the SharePoint chicken and egg problem—What comes first: the solution or the requirements? Well, you can't build a solution without requirements, but I can't describe my requirements until I see the solution.

"Requirements" Is the Wrong Word!

What makes something a requirement? After all, is your client holding a gun to your head saying "include this or else"?

One of your most important jobs as an analyst/architect is to manage the demands of your clients and stakeholders. They often have preset notions of how the solution should look and work, even before any real investigation has been done to understand the capabilities of the tool being used or thinking though the real business needs that should be analyzed and understood before you start building a solution. It is not *really* about requirements, it *is* about business outcomes.

If a client were to tell you that they have a business need to travel to headquarters on a monthly basis, and that it is a requirement that the vehicle that carries them there has four wheels, what would you say? Can you see the absurdity here? We must work to understand the business need more deeply and, at first, we need to ignore the stated "requirement." This customer cannot visualize a solution that will get them to the head office that does not have four wheels, and they are willing and able to argue with you at length why that requirement *must* be included in the contract.

You must show the client that you are working to understand the true business issues that have led them to make an investment in a new technology, and that you are designing a solution that will focus on delivering a successful outcome that meets that business need. Focusing on requirements (at too low a level) is a recipe for failure: You may meet the terms of the contract, but you will not deliver a successful outcome.

▓ **Note** There are some things that are actual *requirements* that would not be adjusted or eliminated, no matter what the cost. An air traffic control system has a requirement that aircraft not collide in midair. That is an absolute requirement that cannot be modified due to budget constraints.

What Makes Something a Requirement?

What is it that makes something a requirement? By definition, it is an element that is required for success. Without this required element, the tool or project will be a failure.

So what would happen if someone told you that something was a requirement, and you said "Fine, we can accommodate that requirement for $10." The client would tell you to go ahead. But what if you said "Um, okay . . . we can do that, but it's going to cost a million dollars or it will add a year to the length of the project." The client might stop and pause and say that they may be able to live without that bit of functionality or start asking you for ideas for workarounds or alternatives.

If it turns out that the item was not really required, or that an alternative would suffice, then it's not really a requirement. Or maybe it was perceived to be a requirement, but the focus changed. The reality is that without understanding the underlying goal of what is to be accomplished, it's hard to tell the difference between what's really a requirement, what is nice to have, and what is just someone's idea of something cool or leftover from an old process but has no real applicable value.

A lot of the time what we are really talking about are *feature requests*, not requirements. Let's consider some factors that can impact feature requests.

Considerations for Feature Requests

A lot of the time, people have experience with information-technology [IT] –related projects that makes them want the jumbo jet solution upfront. It often has taken a long time to get it on to the IT department's agenda, and they know that it may be three years or more until they can get it on to the agenda again, so they want to cram every possible feature (in their mind, requirements) into the project now. But jumbo jet solutions are very difficult to get right on the first pass. The reality is that a giant, all-encompassing solution will have so many risks that can lead to failure. For example, as a project progresses, or in the time after the launch, the ground changes under your feet: the company may get reorganized, a new business is merged in, a division is sold off, new regulatory requirements may come into play, or new product lines may be developed. In fact, there are so many moving parts in a business that building a giant, monolithic, and hard to change solution means that a lot of what gets built may be out of date on launch day or very soon thereafter.

The result is that you end up with lots of components that never get used but that need to be carefully considered in maintenance planning, and when it comes time to upgrade to the next version of the platform, the entire monolith needs to be upgraded at once. This makes the solution more expensive, both upfront and throughout its entire lifetime. So let's consider some alternatives.

Can we solve the problem with a really lightweight solution that is low risk, fast to implement, and will meet a pretty good chunk of the desired outcome? It is far better to underdesign the solution, hitting the key goals with a deliverable that is as simple as possible, and then expand the functionality in later phases. The alternative—a jumbo jet—is going to cost a fortune and much of the functionality may not be used. Or the project may fail outright because it is too complicated to get all the parts to fit together properly or it's too hard for the users to figure out how to use it.

One of the major advantages of SharePoint is that many solutions can be built in in a more agile way: Use the out-of-the-box capabilities to deliver 60 or 80 percent or maybe even 90 percent of the initially desired functionality, and put it into the hands of your users. At that point, they will see where the holes are and where the initial set of requirements was lacking or overspecified.

Another alternative to consider is whether this path has been cleared before. You need to ask if you can buy a prepackaged product that may not work exactly as you had planned, but which can get you to your destination in a low-risk way at a reasonable price.

The goal here is to step back from the specific requirements and look at the outcome that is to be achieved and examine simpler, faster, and cheaper alternatives.

It's Outcomes That Matter

The message that I hope you come away with is the shift in focus from requirements to outcomes. You really need to hammer away at your stakeholders. They will tell you that they understand their business and that the requirements they are giving you are the ones that are . . . um . . . required! And, in a worst-case scenario, you may have to live with that. But I am telling you that you can fight against that trap and really convince your clients and stakeholders that you have a much better chance of delivering a successful solution if you can understand the real business objectives first and then add in the details of how that is to be delivered later.

▒ **Caution**   Just to share a cautionary tale here, a number of years ago I saw with my own eyes a project in which the stakeholders were interviewed (by their own IT department) for the requirements of a new system that was to be built for them. We were forbidden from speaking directly to the stakeholders, so using only the requirements documents, a $200,000 custom application was designed, built, tested, deployed, and documented. Training and knowledge transfer was completed and the final payment was made as the completed project was handed over to the client's IT team. A year later, we had the opportunity to look at the database that held the content for this application and saw that it held only the original test data that existed at the time of the handover. It turned out that the real end users of the tool found it to be useless for their needs, despite meeting the requirements they had dictated. Was this project a success or a failure? (Hint: Despite doing our best and getting appropriately paid, we viewed this as a complete failure.)

Running Discovery Workshops

I hope that I've now convinced you that you are not going to be gathering requirements. Rather, you're going to be working to discover what the real pain is in the organization and understand the underlying business issues. In this section I will cover the details of how you accomplish this.

The Discovery Workshop

You are now about to meet with a group of people so that you can listen and learn. These are not sessions to sell users on the various SharePoint features that you love; this is a time for you to hear what real business problems these teams are having. You will then be able to use your understanding of the business, their pain points, and how SharePoint works to craft a roadmap for them. The roadmap will lay out a proposed solution and phased deployment plan that will allow the users to learn how SharePoint works so that they can take advantage of the powerful features that have been deployed and then enhance and expand on those features to fill gaps or enhance functionality.

Workshop Planning

Planning your workshops can be tricky. It is essential to get the right mix of people in the room. You don't want to be in a room with just managers, because often they don't know, or have forgotten, what the frontline people really do each day. Getting line staff into the meeting is essential; only they can truly tell you what the pain points are in the day-to-day activities of the business. Getting this message through to the powers that be can sometimes be difficult and highly political.

On the other hand, you don't want to have *only* line staff in the meeting. You need to have some serious leaders or executives there who have enough clout to take action or approve budgets for programs that relate to the pain points brought out during the workshop.

■ **Note** Sometimes it is hard to adjust the point of view of a senior manager. I was working on a project where I described my approach to the project owner (the company COO). He said "I can see that your approach is good, and it would work at any other company, but it won't work here: Our staff will just lead you down rabbit holes and you'll never move forward. I will tell you what needs to get built." I finally convinced him to let me have just one workshop, where he could sit in and observe. After that, he saw the value of my workshop and let me run one for all the other teams as well.

I plan these workshops to run for an hour and a half each. In reality, I expect to need about an hour to get through everything I want to do, but sometimes an hour is not quite enough, and I don't want to cut off a good conversation just when things are getting interesting. Also, many times key people are late or get called out during a meeting.

Some people like to schedule these types of workshops for half a day or even a full day. I find it is almost impossible to schedule a group for such a large chunk of time. However, if you get enough lead time, an hour and a half is quite doable.

Another great thing about this idea of about an hour or an hour and a half time slot is that if we wrap up a bit early (as I almost always do), then everyone has a small chunk of unscheduled time in their day, and *everyone* loves to have that tiny chunk of time to grab a coffee, a smoke, or just catch up on e-mail. So I've found this to be a great practice that gets people into a good mood about the project.

A few days before the project, I send the meeting slide deck out to the people who are going to be attending, so they have an idea of what we'll be there to talk about and that they can gather their thoughts.

■ **Note** Sometimes, due to scheduling conflicts or time constraints, you will have to run all-day or half-day workshops. In those cases you need to find the right balance between serious work and taking breaks for more social conversation. No group of people can be focused hard on a complex process all day long and continue to be effective throughout that time.

Workshop Size

There is no perfect number of people to include in the workshop, but I find that it works best if there is somewhere between 4 and 12 people. I've had it work with up to 15 people, but then it's hard to hear from everyone, and it allows for some people to dominate the conversation. Having less than about four people doesn't quite provide the critical mass that helps people bounce ideas around. Sometimes someone will say something and it reminds someone else of something similar that happened to him or her. That type of idea amplification only seems to happen when there are enough people in the room.

Who Should Attend?

It is important to try to see each team separately. If, for example, you had a meeting with human resource clerks and finance managers at the same time, half the time the meeting would be relevant and interesting to only one group. This cannot always be avoided, but you should try to make these workshops as granular as possible.

Your Team

It is always helpful if you can have someone from your own team in the room with you to act as a scribe (i.e., the person taking the notes). I have run many workshops where I was both the facilitator and the note taker, but it's easier if someone else takes the notes. Even if you are using dialogue mapping to capture the details of the workshop, it can be helpful to have a scribe who is taking down some of the narrative detail that may be missed by the mapping process.

It is best if the person taking the notes is not just a clerk, but is rather someone who is familiar with the customer and the problem space, so they can take better, more useful notes.

The Workshop Plan

The plan I am about to share with you is only slightly abstracted from the actual plan I use when I work with my clients. It contains all the same elements and sections. Sometimes though, the plan does need to be adjusted to match the specifics of the type of project or client that I am working with.

Let's go through the plan.

Setting the Scene

We always want to start with the agenda (Figure 1-4). These workshops hinge on setting the right expectations and then following through.

Agenda

- About the Project, Our Team, and Goals
- SharePoint Overview
- Department and Role
- Document Collaboration
- Document Storage and Search
- Compliance, Records Management, and Off-line Access
- Questions

Figure 1-4. The agenda

Because the workshop participants have already seen the schedule and the presentation is not very complex, I don't spend a lot of time on the agenda. Its role is to act as a table of contents for the person looking through the schedule for the first time or for attendees who never opened the attachment when it was sent to them (a not uncommon occurrence).

Next, we move on to the slide that introduces the project, the team, and our goals for this session (Figure 1-5).

About the Project, Out Team, and Goals

About this Project

- Determine the requirements and scope for a SharePoint implementation at ABC Corp.

Our Team

- Alison Andrews   – Project Manager
- Bob Baker   – Technical Architect
- Carol Conrad   – SharePoint Analyst
- Don Drummond – Infrastructure Analyst

Workshop Goals

- Set expectations
- Gather your input
- Keep it to an hour (+ optional half-hour for further questions)

Figure 1-5. Introducing the project, team, and goals for the session

Everyone thinks they know what requirements are and why they're needed, so I humor them and use the "R" word on this slide. At this point I usually haven't had enough time with the customer to explain the difference between requirements and business outcomes, so I play along. Don't be fooled though: This workshop is all about discovering pain points and business goals.

Introduce the team that will be working on this project, even if they're not there in the room with you. This helps the attendees feel that there is a team that is going to implement a solution and that their words won't be wasted.

Reviewing the workshop goals is crucially important. I really want to set the proper level of expectations with the participants. I tell them that I want to hear *all* the details of their pains and what they'd like to see changed. But I explain that any project we initiate will not be able to address all their issues. The result of the workshop will be a set of recommendations, but then it is up to management to choose which recommendation to follow based on strategic and resource-driven priorities. I tell them that this project will likely be implemented in phases, and that something that seems to be very important may become part of the solution, but perhaps not in the first phase or not ever. My goal is to be brutally honest about what I am asking of them: Tell me everything that hurts, but I can't guarantee a fix.

I make sure to also tell them that (even if there is a representative of IT in the room) no one expects them to hold back with their discussion on what works and what doesn't. They don't need to worry about hurting anyone's feelings, as we are all there to work together to build better solutions. I also tell them at this point that we will probably finish in less than an hour and a half, but that we have the flexibility to use the whole time if required.

13

Introducing SharePoint

The next slide is a SharePoint overview, and for this I use the widely hated pie (a.k.a. donut) diagram from Microsoft (Figure 1-6).

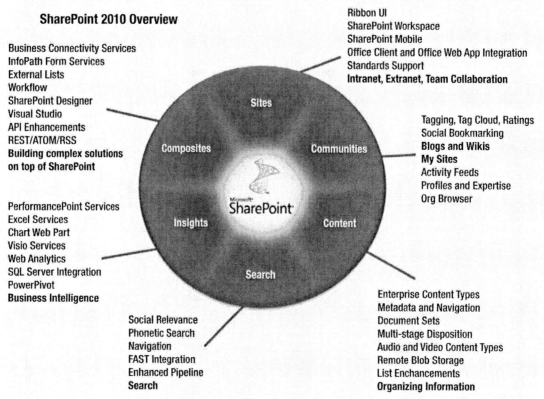

Figure 1-6. The SharePoint pie

Many people dislike the image in Figure 1-6 because the terms are mostly very abstract and hard to map onto business problems to be solved. I agree with those people; as a diagram to hand off to someone, it may not provide much value. But I find it useful for one main thing: to set the scope for the types of problems that we can work on together. When I ask the participants to tell me of their day-to-day pains at work—mostly to do with technology—I need to let them know that I can't help them with their telephone system or with issues with security badges not working in the elevators. So I use this diagram to let them know roughly the types of problems that I can work on. I do *not* go into detailed explanations of all the features of SharePoint, and the amount of time that I spend on this diagram may be just a minute or two for knowledge workers who don't really know SharePoint or maybe up to 10 or 15 minutes for IT team members who are involved in a SharePoint upgrade. Depending on the audience and the initial project scope, I may highlight different elements in the callouts.

Starting the Conversation

The next slide is really the most important one in the schedule (Figure 1-7).

Department and Role

Please introduce yourself:

- Name
- Department
- What is your role within your department?
- How do you interact with technology to do your job?
- How does the current technology help you (or hinder you) from doing your job?

Figure 1-7. Getting people talking

The first three questions on this slide set the scene for me in terms of understanding who is in the room and what the pecking order is. It's important to understand who manages who and to judge how far you can push people. If there is someone trying to dominate the meeting when you want to ensure that everyone gets heard, understanding who's who can help you manage the egos in the room.

The key questions on this slide are the last two, and it's possible to get through a discussion lasting over an hour just by staying on this slide. As people talk about their issues, others pipe in with their take on a comment, which leads the conversation to be further expanded by another person.

Managing these discussions is a bit of a tricky balancing act: You don't want to stifle conversation by saying things like "Okay, let's move on" or "I think we're finished with that topic." The worst thing that can happen is if you make someone upset about not being heard, so that he or she clams up and doesn't contribute any further.

On the other hand, you *do* have to keep things from wandering out of bounds or allowing people to get wrapped up in a specific deep issue that may be political or for some other reason doesn't continue to add new information to the issue at hand. It can take some practice and it's a bit of an art to find the right balance. You have to remain aware of the type of information you are trying to elicit, and if the conversation appears to be stuck on only one topic or area, or if people seem to have run out of things to talk about, the next slides can help steer or stimulate the conversation.

Extending the Discussion

The next three slides open up the conversation (Figures 1-8 to 1-10) by focusing on specific areas that need to be explored. These questions can be modified or expanded upon, depending on the type of project you are working on or which direction you want to take the conversation.

15

Docoment Collaboration

- **Do you work on documents with others?**
  - How do you collaborate (e-mail, shared drive)?
- **What document types do you create?**
  - Which programs do you use?
- **Do your documents require multiple reviews and edits? Is approval required?**
  - How do you implement the required workflow?
- **How do you get the final information out to the audience that needs it?**
  - Do you publish PDFs?
  - How are they distributed/posted?

Figure 1-8. Issues around document collaboration

Document Storage and Search

- **Can you find the documents that you need, when you need them?**
  - Does your shared drive folder hierarchy work well?
  - How long does it take to find a document? At what point do you give up?
- **When you create a document, do you know where it should be saved?**
  - Are documents saved in more than one location to ease' retrieval?
- **Does search work well?**
  - What features would you like to see in search that would make it better for you and your team?

Figure 1-9. Findability and putability concerns

Compliance, Records Management, and Offline Access

- **Do you have any regulatory requirements that you need to meet?**
  - ISO 9000
  - Sarbanes-Oxley – Bill 198

- **How are records management policies implemented?**
  - Are there specific policies for document retention and destruction?

- **Do you have a need for offline access?**
  - Do you travel offsite for your work?
  - Do you need to work when you are disconnected from the network?

Figure 1-10. Regulatory issues and offline work

Sometimes you have an engaged and chatty group, and you never even get to the last couple of slides, except at the very end, to ensure that you haven't missed anything. Sometimes you have a quieter group that needs a bit of prompting. The questions on these last three slides serve the purpose of prompting the participants to open up about the key business processes that impact the way they work and where they struggle.

The final slide (not shown) is the traditional "Any further questions/Thank you for your time" wrap-up slide. There are hardly ever any further questions, because they have already been hashed out during the session.

How Many Workshops Should Be Run?

As I stated at the start, you get better results if you run more granular sessions, where all the people in the room are from the same team or related teams. This can lead to having a large number of workshops (I have run as many as 21 sessions at one company). The interesting thing is that after you have run about three workshops, you have learned about 90 percent of what you need to know about the pain points within the organization. As the workshops continue, you get increasingly diminishing returns in terms of new and useful information. However, I still strongly advocate that you continue with the workshops for two reasons. First, you *do* continue to learn key things that could make the difference between success and failure with a particular department or team. Second, and I think more importantly, you get the participants committed and excited about the potential of a solution to many of their daily problems.

Many SharePoint projects are prone to issues of adoption: How do we get the people that we built this solution for to actually use it? My answer to that question is to build the commitment and excitement upfront by telling people you want to hear their pain and you want to work with them to build a solution. The value of involving a core group of people in this phase of the project is huge in terms of the value that you will get out of them when the project is actually delivered.

▓ **Example**   On one project I worked on, I ran 21 workshops involving over 150 people. Instead of demonstrating SharePoint, I listened to their pain, learned their terminology, and tried to understand their business processes. After the workshops were complete, we build a very simple day-in-the-life demo, without any branding except for a color scheme and the company logo. We invited all the participants for a pizza lunch and a demo and almost 60 showed up. The excitement level of the attendees at seeing a different way of working that addressed so many of their key issues raised an incredible level of excitement, which they then spread to their coworkers. Instead of having to *sell* SharePoint to this organization, the demand started growing from the grass roots.

After the Workshops: Roadmapping

When all the workshops are complete, you will need to compile the information (much of it redundant) into a gap analysis document. Much of what you hear during workshops is about the current state and how things work now. You also hear a lot about a desired future state. For example, here is the detail of one small element of a project that I worked on:

> *Current state*: Job offers and employment contracts live in various e-mail boxes, shared drives, and physical files. When we need to put our hands on the document that was given to the employee, we often scramble to search for the actual version that was used.

> *Desired future state*: A single, managed location for all job offer documents and employment contracts that can be easily searched by position name or person and which indicates which version of the document was eventually used.

The gap analysis does not specify how the gap is to be bridged (i.e., the solution); it just identifies places where the current state and desired state differ.

After the gap analysis is complete, there will need to be a prioritization exercise to determine which problems will be worked on first. This process is covered in the next chapter. Once the priorities are set, we create a roadmap document that lays out rough blocks, the timing, and dependencies of various initiatives. See Figure 1-11 for a roadmap example.

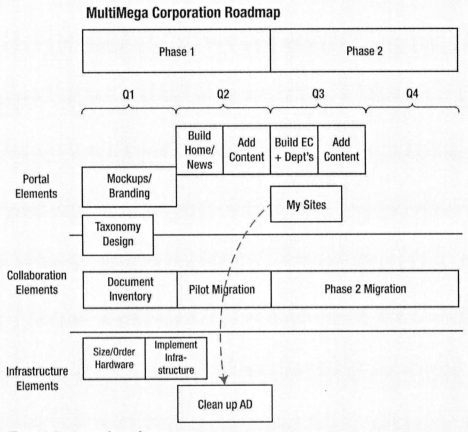

Figure 1-11. A sample roadmap

This roadmap is not a project plan, and it does not have final and exact start and end dates for any element. This is just a rough guide of all the things that can be done over the short, medium, and longer term. The roadmap also illustrates dependencies (items that cannot start until another one is finished).

A real roadmap would be much finer grained than this. I've created maps that list each numbered item from the gap analysis document onto this map. While the roadmap itself is not a project plan, it is an overview document from which key decisions get made. It then acts as a guide for the creation of detailed project plans.

Summary

This chapter detailed the skills you will need to work on to be able to manage the people side of running workshops and meetings. We then dug into the details on how to plan for and schedule a collection of discovery workshops. Finally, we proposed how to organize and share the information that has been gathered in the form of a gap analysis document and a roadmap.

CHAPTER 2

Introduction to Mind Mapping

What do you call what we just did there? That was amazing!

More than a few of my clients on more
than a few occasions after a workshop
where I used mind mapping

This chapter will introduce you to the tool that really changed my life as a consultant: mind mapping. After my first few experiences applying it during working sessions with clients, I realized that visual tools are incredibly powerful when you are working on complex issues. This has led me down a path to a number of other tools and ways of working. In my talks at SharePoint conferences around the world, I often demonstrate mind mapping and I hear back later from attendees that it really helped them as well.

I initially started using mind mapping for taxonomy design, but I soon found that it could be applied to many different aspects of SharePoint projects. In this chapter I will be showing you the essential elements of how mind mapping works and how to use MindManager software for mapping. I will then use a real-world example to illustrate how I use it for prioritization and brainstorming. In Chapter 3 you will learn how interactive mind mapping can be applied to taxonomy design for SharePoint projects, and in Chapter 4, you will see how you can apply mind mapping to building the navigational hierarchy of a SharePoint site. Finally, in Chapter 6, you will see how a different type of mapping called dialogue mapping can help you think through difficult problems and make decisions.

Introduction to Mind Mapping

The classic form of a mind map starts with a central idea surrounded by concepts that expand on the central topic. These maps make use of curving, tapered lines, concept words, color, and small, illustrative images. They have an organic structure that is meant to reflect the mental process of having an idea and then "exploding" that idea into a collection of related ideas (Figure 2-1).

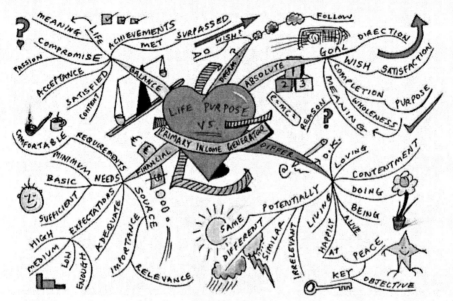

Figure 2-1. Paul Foreman creates beautiful and expressive mind maps. Visit his web site to see many more examples.

The origin of using this method of expanding and illustrating a concept is actually centuries old; examples from the third century illustrating Aristotle's ideas have been found. More recently, in the early 1990s, British popular psychology author Tony Buzan started writing books about, and developing a system for, creating mind maps. These mind maps were, in many instances, works of art: hand-drawn posters that artfully expanded on a central idea. The use of this creative approach for brainstorming and creative problem solving has grown, but, until recently, it has remained mostly a niche tool.

My first exposure to mind mapping occurred when I was telling Joe Markus (at the time, my mentor at Ideaca) that I was having a lot of trouble building and communicating a taxonomy design for a client. Joe showed me a program from Mindjet called MindManager. I downloaded the trial version and I was immediately hooked. Two hours later I was using it in front of my client.

Buzan's fluid and artistic mind maps are well suited to his method of taking a central concept and exploring it in any direction that your mind leads. He always starts at the center and then uses images and colors to evoke thoughts and emotions as part of the process. The work I do with mind maps is also exploratory, but a bit more rigid in structure. Usually I'm not looking to explore "wherever your mind takes you," but rather to dig into a specific problem and then organize the elements that are involved, for example, menu choices in a SharePoint site or potential values for an item of metadata. Because of this difference in goals, Buzan would probably not call what I do mind mapping, but my application makes use of similar concepts and tools. In the next few pages you will see how the tools I use are not quite so organic, but how they serve the purpose of what I am trying to accomplish.

I came to understand that the key to this approach is that people seem to be able to comprehend complex concepts, and especially to see the relationships between them, when they are presented visually like this.

In the examples I will show you in this chapter, I use software called MindManager, which is produced by a company called Mindjet. There are other options when it comes to mind mapping tools. There is a company that makes Buzan-style maps, called ThinkBuzan, that has really cool tools for easily making those organic and fluid styles of mind mapping with lots of color and images. I have used other paid-for and open-source mind mapping tools as well, including XMind (which is free for the basic version) and FreeMind. All of these implement the same core tools for building mind maps, and all of them have advantages and deficiencies.

At the company where I work, we are experimenting with the Pro version of XMind, which at the time of this writing cost $50 per user license. Ultimately, I find that MindManager has a greater level of control over the look and feel of the topics, the expanding and collapsing of branches, and the options for output that make it a tool that works for me. Also, it's the one that I have been using for over four years, so I may be biased just because I am used to it, but at over $300 per license, it is also one of the most expensive options for creating mind maps.

Using MindManager

MindManager is available for a variety of platforms: Windows, Mac, iPad/iPhone, Android, and the web. The versions for iPad/iPhone/Android are free. The Mac/PC versions are available for download with a

free 30-day trial. Obtaining MindManager is simply a matter of visiting mindjet.com (or the AppStore) and downloading the appropriate version.

Mindjet also has a web-based tool called Connect, which is available by subscription, that allows teams to collaborate over the web to build and modify maps. Connect also allows round-trip support between the desktop product and the web-based tools.

▓ **Note** XMind is available for free download from xmind.net. You will be able to experiment with the basics of mind mapping with this tool, and for $49 per year you can upgrade to the Pro version, which has additional features for export and import, printing, and so forth.

Creating Your First Mind Map

This section will walk you through the creation of a very simple map that builds a small taxonomy of animals. We will create groupings for mammals, reptiles, and insects and then add some examples of each type. We will see how to add elements to the map, how to move them around, and how to change the look and format of the map.

When you start MindManager, you will see a screen that looks very similar to a typical Microsoft Office 2007/2010 application (Figure 2-2). It has the modern Microsoft-style ribbon, with tabs that follow the Microsoft standard. This look and feel leads many to believe that this is a product developed by Microsoft. Although the use of the Microsoft standards does make it easier to learn, Mindjet is an independent company.

In the center of the screen is a box that says Central Topic. We call these boxes *topics*. This topic is currently selected, which you can tell because it has a blue box around it, with a narrow blue bar at the top.

It is important to know when a topic is selected because you want to be sure that the next action you take will be applied to the correct topic.

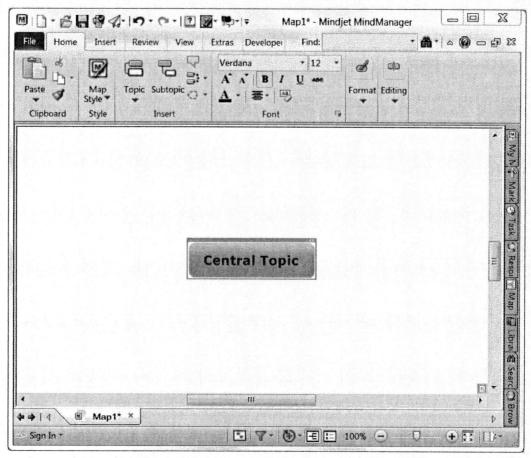

Figure 2-2. The initial MindManager starting screen with a default central topic

Although there may seem at first to be an overwhelming number of icons and menu items on the screen, a really powerful thing about learning mind mapping is that you only really need to know three things:

- How to change the text within a topic.
- How to create a topic at the same level as the current topic.
- How to create a topic below the level of the current topic.

Changing the Text Within a Topic

When a topic is selected, just start typing. The default text in the topic (e.g., Central Topic) will disappear and your text will appear as you type. When you have finished typing, press the Enter key on the keyboard to indicate you have finished entering text into this topic. (Note: Some people call the Enter key the Return key.)

If the topic is too wide because your text is too long, you can drag the right edge of the topic box left to force the box to wrap the text. If the text has been autowrapped for you by MindManager, drag the edge to the right to unwrap it if you desire a long, single-line box.

Creating a Topic at the Same Level as the Current Topic

Clicking the Topic icon on the Insert area of the ribbon will insert a topic at the same level as the current topic (Figure 2-3). A much faster way to do this without taking your hands off the keyboard is to press the Enter key on the keyboard.

■ **Note**   You can't add a topic at the same level as the first Central Topic box on the map. It is the only topic that can *only* have subtopics.

Creating a Topic Below the Level of the Current Topic

Clicking the Subtopic icon on the Insert area of the ribbon will insert a topic at the level below the current topic (Figure 2-3). A much faster way to do this without taking your hands off the keyboard is to press the Insert key on the keyboard.

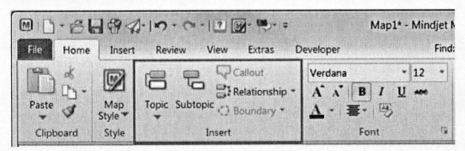

Figure 2-3. The Topic and Subtopic icons on the Insert section of the Home tab in the ribbon

Now that we've covered the three essential things you need to know, let's move into the steps and create our first mind map.

■ **Note**   For the rest of this section, I will be giving instructions for adding topics using only the keyboard. This is the way I normally work, because it is much faster than clicking the icons on the ribbon every time you need to add a topic.

---

1. Normally there is no need to select a topic when you first start because Central Topic is the only item on the screen. However, if it is not selected, click this box. Type Animals and press Enter. You will see that the Central Topic has now been renamed Animals (Figure 2-4).

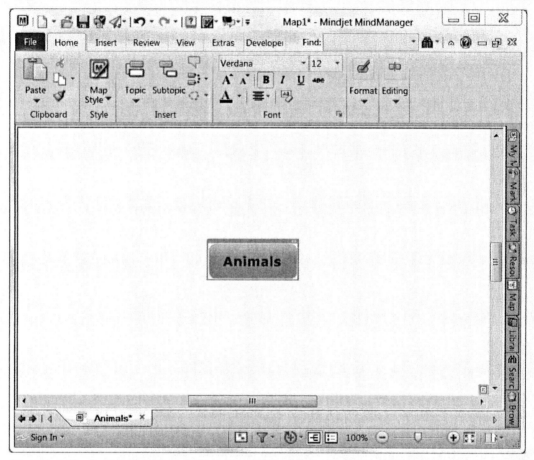

Figure 2-4. The Central Topic box, visible in the middle of the screen, edited to have the title Animals

░ **Note** While building the rest of this mind map, I will just show the topics and omit the surrounding application except when it is useful to show the whole window.

2. Now press the Insert key to get a new subtopic box. It is labeled Main Topic by default. You will see that a line connecting the new topic to its parent is automatically created and that your new topic is already selected so you can immediately type a new label for it.

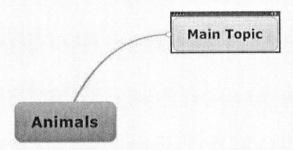

3. Let's change the text in this box to Mammals, simply by typing the word and then pressing the Enter key.

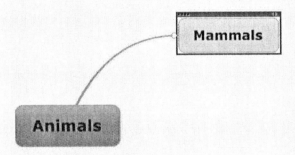

4. We are going to add a subtopic to Mammals by pressing the Insert key again. This node is named Subtopic by default. It will be already selected so that we can type Cows and press the Enter key. Notice that there is a line connecting the node to its parent, but that this time there is a circle with a minus sign in it. You will also see that the formatting (font size, background) is different for these topics. We'll discuss the reasons for this a bit later.

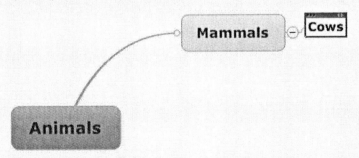

5. We are now going to do a slightly different action. Instead of pressing the Insert key to get yet another subtopic, we will press the Enter key to get a new topic at the same level as the currently selected topic. Type Pigs into this topic and press Enter.

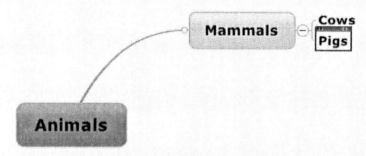

6. We now want to create a new subtopic for Animals. We can do this two different ways: We could select the Animals topic and press the Insert key, or we could select the Mammals topic and press the Enter key. Let's do it by selecting Mammals and pressing Enter. Now, type Reptiles and press Enter twice (once to finish typing, and again to create a new topic at the same level). Now type Insects into this new topic and press Enter.

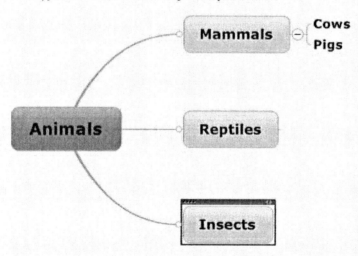

7. At this point, Insects is selected, but we want to add subtopics to the Reptiles topic. So use the mouse to click the Reptiles box. You also could have used the Arrow keys on the keyboard to move up to the Reptiles topic box. (Getting used to using the Arrow keys will take a bit more practice, so we'll stick to the mouse for selecting topics.) Now, press the Insert key to add Alligators, press Enter to finish typing, and then press Enter again to add a new topic and type Sea Turtles. Press Enter to complete the typing and your map will look like this.

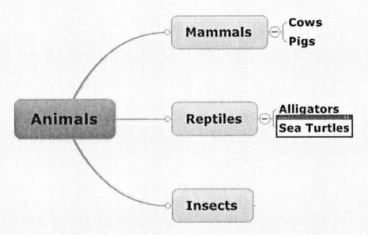

8. Let's finish off the Insects section by selecting it, pressing Insert, and typing Mosquitos then pressing the Enter key, then Enter again to add a new topic and type Snakes and press the Enter key.

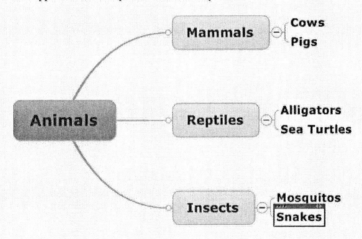

9. Now I may be a computer consultant and not a biologist, but even I know that, as shown in the diagram above, "Snakes" is in the wrong category. With MindManager, you can move topics easily by dragging them to another location. You click and drag the topic in the same way you would with other Microsoft Office application. As you drag, you will see nearby topics light up with a red border and a red line, indicating where your topic will be attached when you drop it. It will take a bit of practice to find where to place topics so they connect with the right parent topic, but it's not too hard to figure out.

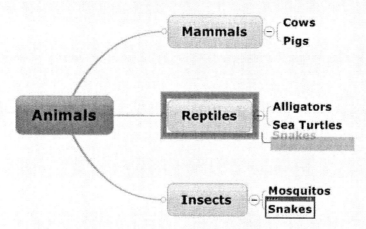

10. When you release the mouse, the topic will now be in its new home.

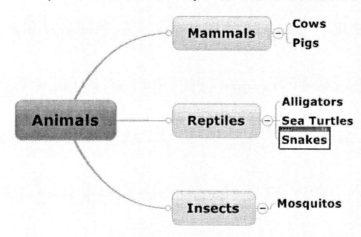

11. Let's take this just one level deeper (you can go to arbitrary levels of depth with MindManager). I won't give the instructions in quite such explicit detail this time. Let's add three types of snakes by selecting Snakes with the mouse (if you are following directly from the instructions above, this topic should already be selected). Press the Insert key to create a subtopic for Snakes and type Boas. Now add Pythons followed by Vipers. For the last two topics, you should have just pressed the Enter key and typed the name.

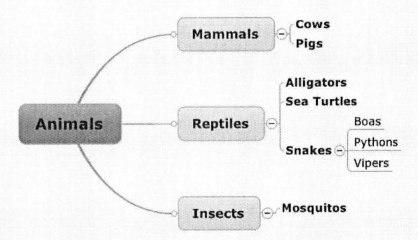

So now you have a nice map, representing the hierarchy of animals that you wanted to classify. When using MindManager, you can create this map in about a minute. This is amazingly fast compared to a diagraming tool like Visio. I would never be able to build a map interactively in front of a client with Visio. Although Visio gives you much more fine-grained control, I find it difficult to operate smoothly. Lines sometimes connect where I expect them too and sometimes they don't.

There are limitations to what MindManager can do. For example, you will note in the map above that the topic boxes for Mammals and Reptiles are not exactly the same length. This is something you can't really change easily in MindManager, so if you are concerned about the exact shapes that your topics use or you want to incorporate sophisticated text and shadow effects, then you'll need to consider Visio. But to me, the true benefit of a mind mapping tool is the freedom it gives you to focus on the stuff that matters coupled with an interface that is fast and easy to learn.

Formatting Your Mind Map

Some of the other features that MindManager provides do allow for some fairly sophisticated formatting. For example, you can change the layout of the map to an organizational chart (or org-chart style) by clicking the Growth Direction icon on the Format area of the ribbon (see Figure 2-5).

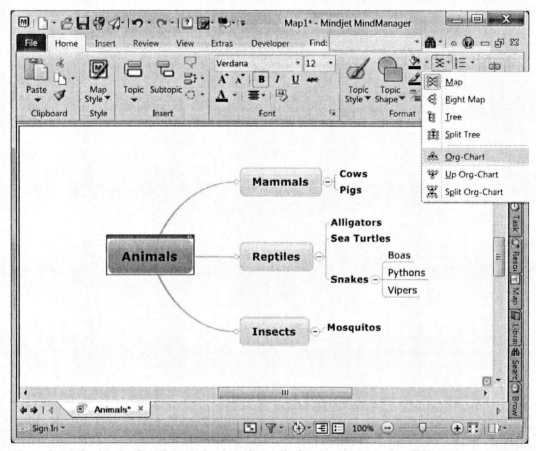

Figure 2-5. Selecting the Org-Chart option in order to display the mind map in a different layout.

The Org-Chart option is what I use most often, as it is ideal for representing hierarchies for navigation and metadata (Figure 2-6).

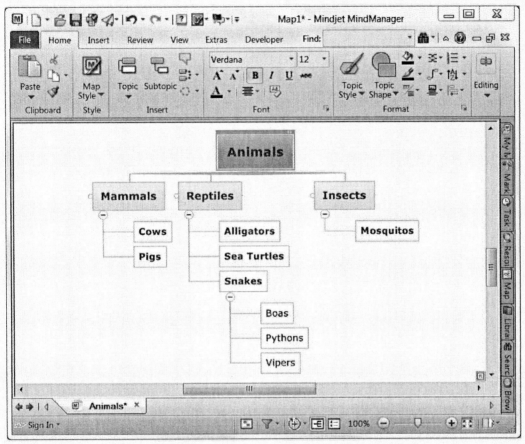

Figure 2-6. Changing the layout to an organization chart will result in a map that represents hierarchies in a familiar style.

MindManager will also allow you to style the topics and text in a number of ways. In Figure 2-7 I have applied shape and background colors to the Mosquitos topic, as well as made the font italic instead of bold.

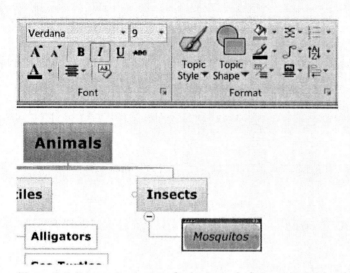

Figure 2-7. Formatting options for topics include fonts, styles, border colors, and shades.

As you saw when I was adding topics at various levels, they looked different from one another, with the fonts getting smaller and the background color of the shapes changing. This is accomplished by creating a Map Style, which defines the formatting for each level and element (see Figure 2-8 for an example of the style sheet editor for the default style—the one we've been using so far).

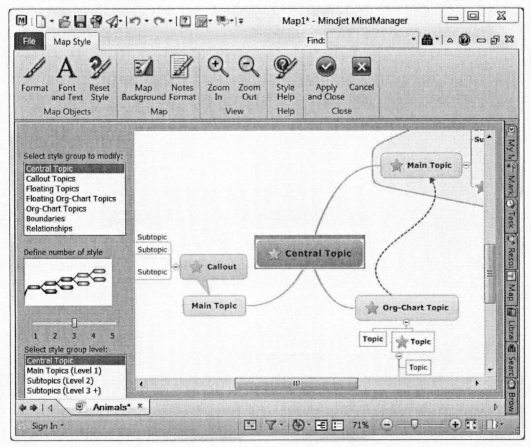

Figure 2-8. The style sheet editor. Modifying these styles is an advanced step that you don't need to worry about when you are first learning MindManager.

The style editor is accessed via the Map Style drop-down in the ribbon (Figure 2-9).

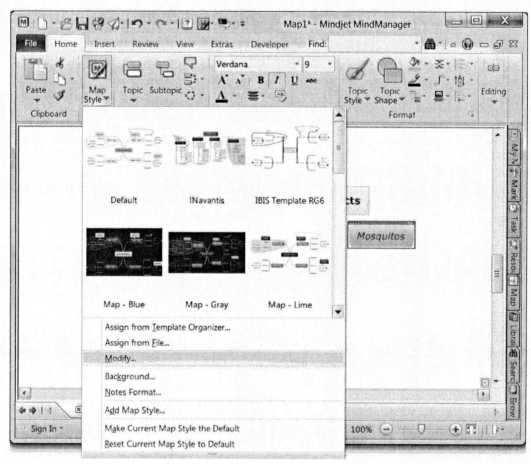

Figure 2-9. *The Map Style icon is used for selecting preexisting styles or modifying one of your own.*

If we apply a custom style that I have previously created (the top center one in Figure 2-9), our map will now follow that style (Figure 2-10) and all new topics we add from now on will follow the format defined in that style.

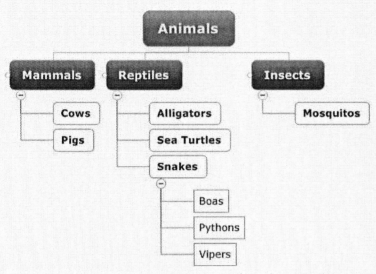

Figure 2-10. The same map with my custom style applied.

One of the most powerful capabilities that MindManager (and most other mind mapping tools) has is the ability to focus on one part of the map by collapsing other parts. The minus sign in the circle I pointed out earlier is how you manage the expansion and collapsing of various map sections. If I want to focus just on Reptiles, I can click the Minus signs to collapse the other main topics (Figure 2-11).

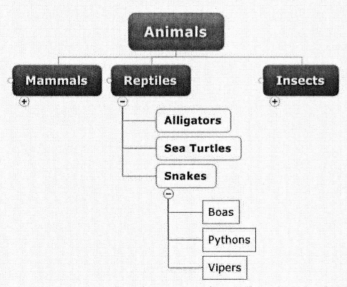

Figure 2-11. Mammals and Insects have been collapsed. Notice the plus signs below those topics. Clicking them will reexpand them.

Alternatively, we may want to focus on just the first few layers of the map and hide detail that we may want to ignore for now. In Figure 2-12, you will see that I have expanded Mammals and Insects, but collapsed everything below Snakes. The map is now simpler and less cluttered.

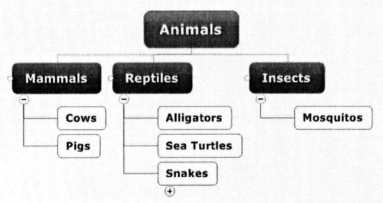

Figure 2-12. Subtopics below Snakes have been collapsed.

You can expand or collapse whole sections of large maps by clicking the Expand icon at the bottom of the screen (Figure 2-13). The Expand and Collapse options apply to whichever topic is currently selected (in this case Reptiles). By selecting appropriate topics and using this menu, you have a great deal of control over what parts of the map you can show or hide to meet your needs.

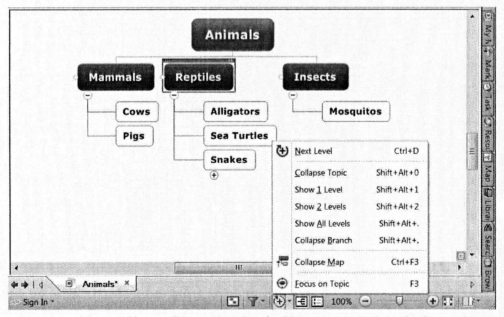

Figure 2-13. The Expand button showing the expand/collapse options available for the Reptiles topic.

MindManager has many other features and options that are worth investigating. They include the ability to use topics as project tasks and assign resources and durations, as well as various types of other formatting and presentation tools. There are help files and tutorials on the Mindjet web site that will help you dig in to some of these other features. Of all the remaining features, the three that I use most commonly, are Icons, Callouts, and Relationships.

Icons can be used to draw attention to topics in various ways. For example, suppose I want to flag dangerous creatures with red flags, annoying ones with yellow flags, and then use green flags for the rest. By selecting a topic and then clicking the Icons button on the Insert ribbon tab (Figure 2-14), I can apply the relevant icon to the topic.

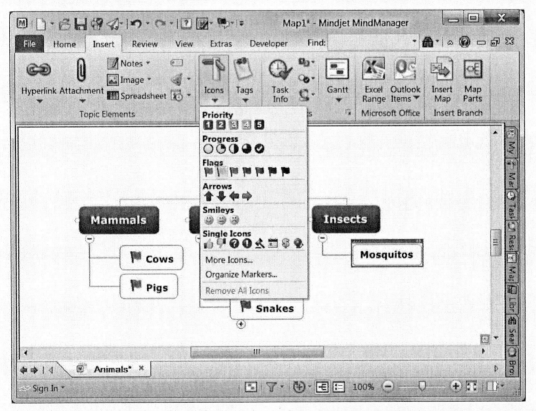

Figure 2-14. Adding the yellow flag to the Mosquitos topic.

The Relationships button on the Home tab prompts you to click on any two topics, which are then connected with a dotted line. There are options that allow you to set the thickness and color of the line, as well as the type and shape of the arrow heads (Figure 2-15). The Callouts button allows you to add comments or to point out specific details about a topic or relationship. You just select the topic and then click the Callout icon. See MindManager help for details on how to customize these elements.

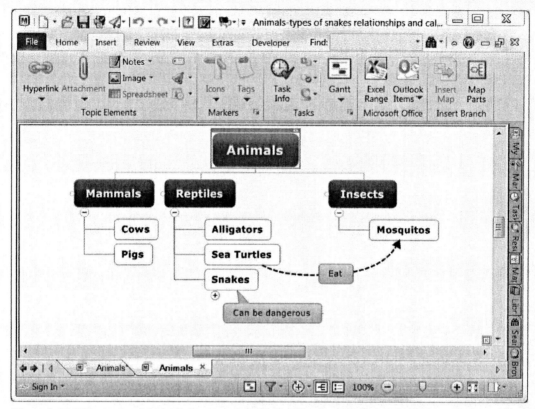

Figure 2-15. *I have put a red highlight around the Callout (top) and Relationship (bottom) icons in the ribbon. The yellow callouts and red dotted relationship line illustrate how these look in a map.*

Now that you have seen how mind mapping can work, let's walk through some scenarios where I have applied it successfully on SharePoint projects.

Mind Mapping for Project Brainstorming

SharePoint is *not* a product that is a solution to a problem. It is a toolset that lets you build solutions to problems. Unfortunately, many organizations have been sold on the idea that SharePoint is the solution without really understanding how or why it works. If you are going to have any chance at success with these organizations, you will need to tell them what kinds of things you can build with the SharePoint toolset and then help them figure out which ones they need to build, based on their own unique issues and goals.

I was faced with this situation on a project where the decision had been made to implement SharePoint without the client having a clear understanding of the goals to be accomplished. The customer decided to fly in all the senior executives from across the country for a brainstorming session. They wanted our team to facilitate the workshop.

The customer's executive team had already been given a full SharePoint capabilities demo by Microsoft, so we started off with a brief discussion to remind the group of the types of solutions SharePoint is suitable for (making use of the hated pie slide described in the previous chapter).

We then let people talk. As they talked, we started to build a mind map. This was an interactive process with the mind map being projected onto the screen at the front of the room.

We had preconstructed the first layer of a map and showed the key divisions that were represented at the workshop, along with the names of the executives from each division.

As the team members talked, we captured their thoughts in the map (as you can see in Figure 2-16).

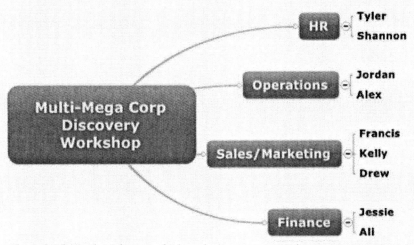

Figure 2-16. The initial map, which we had preconstructed

You can see in Figure 2-17 that Shannon from HR cared about performance management, linking with benefit suppliers, on-boarding, e-learning, and a host of other initiatives.

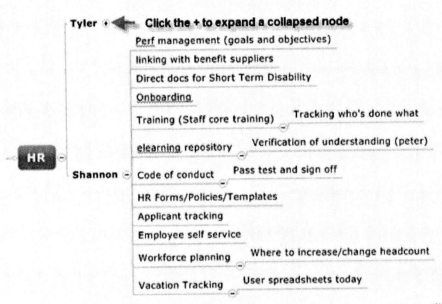

Figure 2-17. Showing the ideas that Shannon came up with during the session. You will notice that there are a number of spelling errors (shown with red underlines). While in a mapping session, I don't focus on spelling or grammar, it is most important to just 'get the map built' without distracting the speaker by pausing to fix the actual words.

▓ **Note** As described earlier in this chapter, one of the powerful features of most mind mapping software is the ability to get whole sections out of the way by clicking the little Minus sign next to a topic. Clicking the Minus collapses all the branches of a topic, getting them out of the way so you can see the important parts of the map. Clicking the Plus sign expands that section again.

Once we had spent the morning working through everyone's ideas, we reconvened in the afternoon to work on prioritizing all the ideas. We used the Icons button on the Insert tab in MindManager to associate a priority icon with each topic (Figure 2-18).

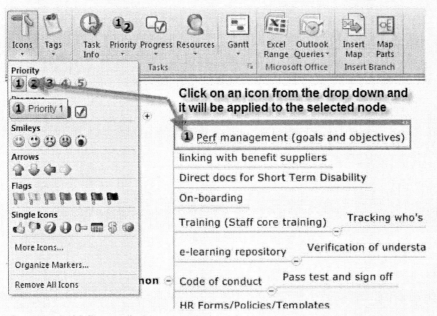

Figure 2-18. Adding a priority icon to each topic

We then took most of the afternoon to work through the entire map, discussing and marking the priorities for the team (Figure 2-19).

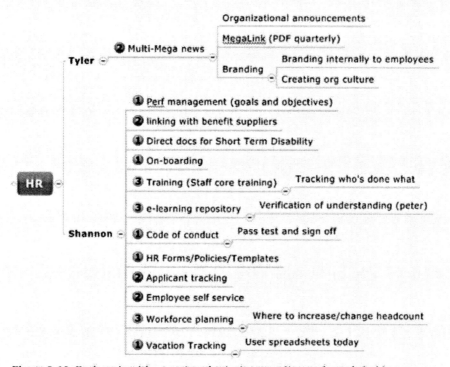

Figure 2-19. Each topic with an assigned priority according to the stakeholders

The final step was to roughly approximate the difficulty of each item, where by difficulty we mean complexity (and therefore cost) of implementation (Figure 2-20). We used flags to denote:

- *Easy/Green*: Accomplished with out-of-the-box functionality.

- *Medium/Yellow*: Some additional work required.

- *Hard/Red*: Needs deeper investigation or custom code. (We also used orange for "requires further discussion," but I prefer to avoid that if possible.)

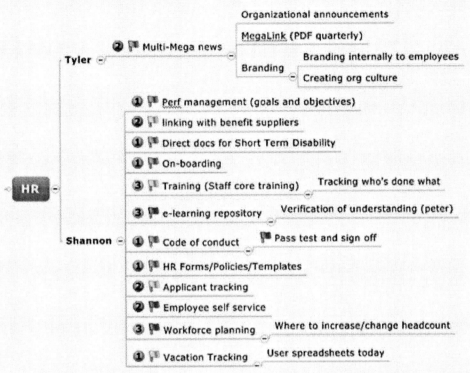

Figure 2-20. All topics flagged with both priority and complexity icons

The result is a map that shows how the executive leadership team prioritizes all the different potential initiatives that have come up during brainstorming, along with how simple or complex that function will be to implement.

You have probably heard the expression "pick the low hanging fruit" for initial project success. This means do the things that have the highest value, and are the simplest, first. This is a great way to start a project because it shows the rest of the organization that the product can solve real problems and show real value with relatively little risk. Our current map will let us pick that low hanging fruit because it exposes those high-priority, simpler initiatives. To make it even simpler to display this combination, all we need to do is filter the topics to show only the priority-one items that fall into the easy category and we have a pretty good first cut about what a phase-one implementation could look like. We use MindManager's filtering tools (Figure 2-21) to accomplish this.

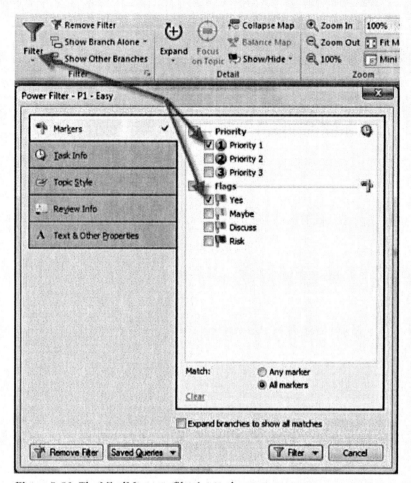

Figure 2-21. The MindManager filtering tool

This leaves us with a reasonable subset of items. (Note: This is just for one area: HR.) We did the same for all divisions (Figure 2-22).

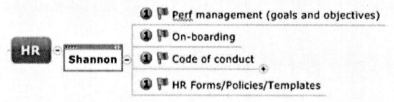

Figure 2-22. The low hanging fruit: High priority, low complexity.

Our clients loved this approach, because after a lot of talking and discussion, a clear set of goals emerged, giving direction to the project. When we use this approach, we often convert these maps into roadmaps that help our customers to plan a phased approach to implementing SharePoint in a way that leads to initial success at a relatively low cost.

Summary

My journey as business analyst and information architect has been immeasurably enhanced since I learned how to use mind mapping tools. The benefit of working with a system that visually and interactively captures thought processes and structures and then reflects those processes and structures back to the people you are working with is its incredible efficiency compared to taking notes and writing those notes into a document that few people read thoroughly or carefully (or at all!), which then requires follow-up meetings to clarify misunderstandings. Facilitating shared understanding is a critical step to getting to a shared commitment to a course of action, because without shared understanding and commitment, the probability of succeeding with a complex project is dismal.

Making mind maps is also more fun than the standard approach, which makes meetings less tedious and encourages workshop attendees to participate more. It even gives them something that holds their focus, reducing the amount of e-mail checking that typically goes on.

The key concepts I have shown you cover how to use mind mapping for capturing hierarchical structures. We will be using these techniques in later chapters on taxonomy and navigation. In the second part of the chapter I have given you an example of a nonhierarchical, free-form, brainstorming approach for using mind mapping, another very useful and powerful application.

This chapter has presented the basics of how to start mind mapping with MindManager, but it is interesting to note that most of the keystrokes and functions presented for this particular software work similarly in other software packages. What is even more interesting is that the basics I have shown in this chapter cover 95 percent of the features I use in my mind mapping work. With a minimal amount of practice, you too will be able to take advantage of mind mapping tools.

CHAPTER 3

The Magic of Metadata

If it walks like a duck, quacks like a duck, looks like a duck, it must be a duck.

—Proverb

The single most important task of a SharePoint system is to find information. You may be looking for relevant news about your organization, the policy document that describes the process for hiring a new employee, or the proposal you wrote last year that you now desperately need to find because the customer has decided to move forward with the project. In all of these cases, quickly and easily putting your hands on the information you need so you can do your job is the key driver behind almost all the SharePoint projects I have worked on.

We have some pretty sophisticated tools for the creation of content—programs like Microsoft's Word, Excel, and PowerPoint. We also have a number of powerful ways of communicating with one another (like e-mail, Twitter, Yammer, Lync, etc.). But because electronic files seem to breed like rabbits and we have such a deluge of them, we have always had trouble figuring out how to organize our documents so we will be able to find them when we need them.

If you've been alive long enough, you'll remember the color-coded labels we used to label floppy disks and the disk organizers we used so that we could find the one we needed when we were looking for a particular file. We then graduated to hard disks that held many thousands of files and we learned the metaphor of the filing cabinet: The drawer is the drive letter (e.g., "C:") and the disk file folders held documents. When each person had a separate "C drive," we were the only ones who had to navigate our folder hierarchies and, given time, we could often (not always) eventually find the document we knew was in there. We would share documents with others by "sneaker net," which meant copying the document to a floppy disk and delivering or shipping it to a recipient.

Then the world of the networking was created, and groups of people were networked together and would share a common hard drive. Productivity was enhanced (no more sneaker net), but the world of document management became infinitely more complicated: People could create their own folders that were named and nested differently from what others were using; two people could attempt to update the same document at the same time, with the person saving last overwriting the work of the previous person, with no way to get the previous version back. The result was a mess—and it's been that way ever since (and getting worse) as the number of documents explodes and the methods for figuring out how to organize them has not moved forward.

This chapter will discuss metadata: what it is and how it can be part of the solution to document findability.

What Is Metadata?

This question has a very simple answer, one that many people are familiar with: Metadata are data about data. A more rigorous definition can be found in Patrick Lambe's book *Organizing Knowledge*: "We define metadata as the collection of structured information about a document or a piece of content" (p. 37).

When I was first trying to understand metadata in the context of the SharePoint projects I was working on at the time, these types of definitions were just not very helpful. I couldn't see how to apply them to my SharePoint projects. I have since found that I was not the only one feeling confused about this: A lot of people have trouble understanding how the basic definitions of metadata apply to SharePoint.

Metadata Metaphors

I have found that this can be made a bit easier to understand if we use metaphors, so let me ask you a few different questions: What sound does a cow make? What sound does a chicken make? What sound does a duck make? (Go on, answer out loud; don't worry about what the people around you think.) Now that you're done mooing, clucking, and quacking, I want to point out that these barnyard animals do not *consist* of the sounds they make, but that these sounds are *attributes* of the animals that allow you to distinguish one from the other. Even a four-year-old can point to the correct animals based on their sounds. This seemingly frivolous task of naming animals by their sounds is a serious attempt at explaining how important the attributes of something are when it comes to distinguishing one object from another.

Let's move on to a more serious example. If you are of a certain age, you may think that Prince's *Purple Rain* is one of the top pop/rock albums of its era. If I were to ask you "What does someone who likes this album really care about?," I think the correct answer would be "the music." The music is the essence of this object; its songs are the *data* that a fan of this artist care about. (For those who answered "frilly collars," you're wrong.) There is more than just the music associated with the album. We know the *year* it was created, the *genre* of music, the name of the *artist* (though that was in some dispute for a while), among other things. The interesting thing about those attributes is that while we'd never say that any of them replace the music, they are useful for organizing a music collection.

The issue with a physical collection of CDs is that they are physical objects that need to be organized into one (and only one) physical arrangement. You may have separate shelves for musical genres: rock on the top shelf, classical on the bottom, and jazz/funk fusion in the middle. Within each shelf, you may sort the CDs by date produced, by the artist name in alphabetical order, or by cover color. And, once you have them nicely ordered, you tell your friends or kids "don't touch them," because you don't want anyone messing up your carefully constructed organization that lets you put your hands on any disk in just a few seconds. The collective attributes of the albums are the metadata: It is the data about the data that help you organize and find your music.

Let's review one more metaphor for the organization of physical objects. Imagine that you had a collection of unlabeled tin cans. The only way to know what the cans contain would be to open them. I think you'll agree that this is not a very efficient strategy. Now, imagine you had a disorganized pile of labeled cans. In this example, you still have to pick each one up to examine it, but you do have labels that tell what's inside without opening each can. The fact that the labels may be in a language we can't read is another issue that we may have to deal with, but we are still in a better situation than with no labels. Finally, let's push the limits on this metaphor and take it to the next level—the supermarket—where cans are all grouped into aisles and organized on shelves. We are now in tin-can heaven: We know exactly where to go for our canned veggies because all of them are located together, and there are signs at the top of each aisle that tell us which section they're located in.

We still have some slight difficulties to deal with, however: Because the objects are physical, we may have to duplicate some of them. For example, the canned chili peppers are in the vegetable aisle, but they also live in the ethnic foods aisle. This is not the worst problem, but it can lead to issues when a customer goes to the ethnic foods aisle, searches for a can of chilis, and is disappointed to find that there are none left, when in fact there are 50 cans sitting untouched in the veggie aisle.

We will talk more about taxonomy later, but I want to point out to you that a supermarket has a taxonomy of food items organized for easy search and retrieval. Once you learn how your store is laid out, you can dash in quickly for some milk, eggs, and flour and know where to go with a minimum number of steps. Visiting a store you've never been to before is a challenge, because it is laid out differently from the one you frequent and you have to learn its particular organizational structure.

So, through expanding on the more formal definitions, I hope the metaphors presented here have helped you to see how the concepts associated with an item (an animal, a can of food, or a music album) can help with the organization of those items. This is, in general, what metadata is used for. Let's look more specifically at what metadata give us in the context of SharePoint:

- *Findability*: Being able to find a document or item of information easily.

- *Policy*: We can construct our records management policies so they act on metadata values.

- *Process*: We can use metadata to track the state or status of a business process (e.g., not started, in process, complete, approved, rejected).

In order to understand how metadata give us these capabilities, we have to look at the organization of electronically stored objects. So far, in all the examples in this chapter, we have been working on the organization of *physical* items and we've seen the trade-offs that have to be made, including:

- Duplication to help with findability (the chilis).

- Choosing a rigid physical layout and making sure that no one messes with it (the CDs and the supermarket aisles).

Now it's time to move on to metadata in the context of document management.

Document Organization and Folder Hierarchies

As discussed earlier, we've always had problems with organizing and find our electronic files. Part of the reason for this is that the organizing principles we use for electronic documents are based on the physical construct of a filing cabinet. The drawers represent disk drives, the hanging folders are the first level of hierarchy, and folders are next, and the documents are found in the innermost folder. (The one place that the model breaks down is that the computer allows us an essentially unlimited nesting of subfolders within folders, which makes for a very large filing cabinet, but also one in which a folder within a folder essentially becomes invisible until you open the outer folder so you can see whether it contains documents or just more folders.) As difficult as this approach is to manage, this filing cabinet–based metaphor has been around for so long that we rarely question it. It is a standard that everyone growing up with computers since the Apple Macintosh in the early 1980s has learned (Figure 3-1).

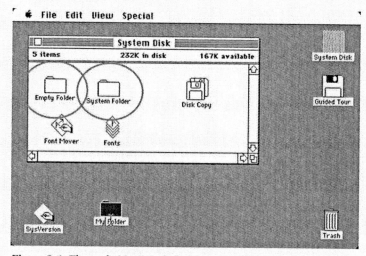

Figure 3-1. *The early Macintosh desktop with file folders (and a trash can!)*

The problem with this system is that it imposes the constraints of physical objects onto items that are not physical. Let's look a little bit more deeply into the constructs of file organization in the computer to see why this is true.

If you were to see a collection of files that had meaningless names (as in Figure 3-2), what would you compare it to?

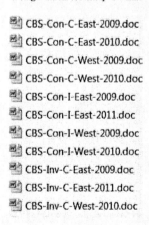

Figure 3-2. A collection of files with meaningless names

To me, this is the same situation as the unlabeled tin cans: The only way to know what's inside these files is to open them one by one. A set of files that use a rigid naming convention (as in Figure 3-3) makes things substantially easier.

📄 CBS-Con-C-East-2009.doc

📄 CBS-Con-C-East-2010.doc

📄 CBS-Con-C-West-2009.doc

📄 CBS-Con-C-West-2010.doc

📄 CBS-Con-I-East-2009.doc

📄 CBS-Con-I-East-2011.doc

📄 CBS-Con-I-West-2009.doc

📄 CBS-Con-I-West-2010.doc

📄 CBS-Inv-C-East-2009.doc

📄 CBS-Inv-C-East-2011.doc

📄 CBS-Inv-C-West-2010.doc

Figure 3-3. Files that follow a strict naming convention

We can see a lot more order in these filenames, but they still have a number of weaknesses: You have to understand what the layout and abbreviations mean; you can't sort them by anything other than alphabetical order from the left-most character; you have to follow the naming convention religiously to make it work.

Let's look at a more advanced approach, where folders are used as well in a nested folder hierarchy (as shown in Figure 3-4).

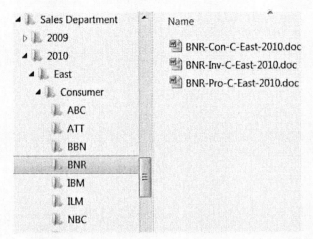

Figure 3-4. A snapshot of a file system on a shared drive

You may not realize it at first, but this is logically equivalent to the supermarket. The files are all grouped appropriately, and the folder names act as headers that help with the organization of the information.

But what happens if you hire an intern and ask him or her to upload a bunch of files? Your poor intern may open a bunch of nested folders, give up on finding the right location, and just create a new folder to put the files into. The result is that now, whenever you have to look for a file, you have an *extra* location you have to remember to search. This is how a nicely structured folder hierarchy can very quickly start to fall apart.

■ **Example** I once ran a discovery workshop with a team of engineers from a large manufacturing company. They told me that their folder hierarchy was "perfect" and that after a bit of training to get new staff up to speed, it really worked out well. I told them that I was impressed because they had succeeded where pretty much everyone else fails. A week or two later, I was talking with one of the engineering managers about issues with search and I asked him: "What does an engineer do when he can't find a document he's looking for?" The manager said: "Easy, he just e-mails the engineering group asking 'Who's seen the X-file?' It happens all the time." I was floored. Can you imagine the wasted time and effort; e-mailing all 100 engineers every time they can't find a file? I don't think their folder hierarchy was working as well as they indicated it was.

Another issue with this nested folder hierarchy is that if you need to find a group of files that are split into multiple branches of the folder tree, you need to do a lot of clicking. For example, your boss wants to see all invoices for the ABC Company over three years. The only way to do this in a shared drive is to expand each node of the hierarchy and check what files are in there, and then copy them out to a new location or to an e-mail.

As bad as this process of hunting through nested folders is in a shared drive, the experience of doing this inside SharePoint is even worse! It is a much slower and more painful process to drill down and then come back up again via the browser interface. I think that some of the people who hate SharePoint the most have to deal with this scenario.

Findability and Putability

The problem that we are facing is one of asymmetry: You are willing to invest quite a bit of time searching for a file that you really need. You know that it will cost you a lot of effort to re-create it or that it's not possible to re-create it (e.g., the scanned, signed employment contract for a key employee who is now suing you). Depending on how desperate you are, you will not give up until you find that crucial item.

On the other side of the equation is the task of figuring out where to save a file. You will look at your folder hierarchy for a bit, trying to decide whether there is a logical place to save a particular file. This search won't last very long though: If you can't find somewhere obvious to save the file, you'll just create a new folder. C'mon, admit it, we've all done it. Often, the thought when we do this is "I'll remember where this is later, when I need the document." I think we can also all admit that this usually turns out to be a lie.

The concept of *findability* (which in my opinion is a useful term, but not really an English word) encompasses how you'll find an item in a system. It includes browsing to an item, finding a shortcut to it, or using full-text search. The concept of *putability* (even less of an English word) captures the idea of the amount of effort it takes to find where to *save* a file.

When I talk about a fundamental asymmetry, I am talking about the amount of time people will invest into finding a file (quite a bit) versus the amount they will spend figuring out where to save it (not much). One of the things that the magic of metadata can bring us is an improvement (often a great improvement) in findability, but, more importantly I think, it can help with putability as well. The impact of better putability is found every time someone wants to find a file. A bad job while saving can cost effort for every single user, every time someone looks for an item.

■ **Note** Although findability and putability are not English words, I first heard them from Bill English (http://sharepoint.mindsharpblogs.com/Bill), so in that sense, they are "English" words.

As we look further into metadata later in this chapter, we'll see how we will be able to solve both the findability and putability issues by eliminating the rigidity of the folder hierarchy. I will show you how the structures we are so familiar with for physical objects do not have to apply to electronic file organization.

Understanding Taxonomy

Taxonomy is the classification of physical or conceptual objects into a hierarchy. When I showed you how to do mind mapping in Chapter 2, we built a small taxonomy, and in this chapter our folder hierarchy is another type of taxonomy.

Let's now dive into a more complex biological hierarchy in preparation for explaining how taxonomy applies to SharePoint projects. To show you an example, I'd like to begin with Roborovski hamsters (Figure 3-5).

Figure 3-5. We can use Roborovski hamsters to show taxonomy in action.

If you want to understand how these animals relate to other creatures, you would need some type of classification hierarchy. Fortunately, a man named Carl Linnaeus created just such a hierarchy in the 18th century. The structure shows us the location of this hamster in the animal kingdom (as shown in Figure 3-6).

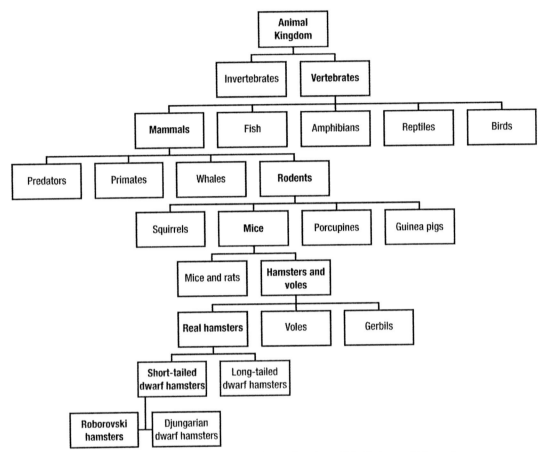

Figure 3-6. *The part of the animal kingdom that shows the place of the Roborovski hamster*

You can see that the Roborovski hamster has a definite location in the animal kingdom. Now, what if we made a change to this hierarchy to make it relevant to our situation? In Figure 3-7 we show the hierarchy for the sales and marketing team of the Industrial Soap Division of MultiMEGA Industries. MultiMEGA has a wide client base that falls into a hierarchy of categories.

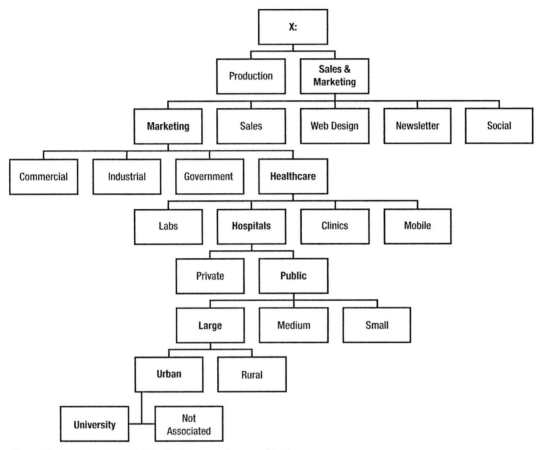

Figure 3-7. The typical "X drive" with many layers of folders

As you can see, this structure, which models the shared drive in most organizations, is an exact replica of the one shown above it, yet its structure is the source of a lot of daily pain in business life. The question is: What is the difference between the complex animal kingdom map and the chaotic X-drive map (other than the obvious subject difference)? The answer is *governance*. The map of the animal kingdom changes only rarely, and when it does change, it requires agreement among a large number of leading scientists, who meet at conferences and (maybe) scream at one another about why their adjustment to the taxonomy makes sense, while the other guy's suggested change is idiotic. The bottom line is that it is *very hard* to change the structure of this taxonomy. Another important factor is that every zoologist learns about the animal kingdom in college, and its structure is very well known and understood.

Now, think about how hard it is for someone to change the X-drive taxonomy. If someone on the sales team decides to give up looking for where to save that file regarding a large university hospital and that person just creates a new folder thinking that he or she will "remember later" in a location that makes sense to that person at that time, you'll end up with a taxonomy that has now become inconsistent, confusing, and chaotic (Figure 3-8). The taxonomy we use to store our files on the X drive is not known by every person who joins the company and, even if it were, it's just too easy to change.

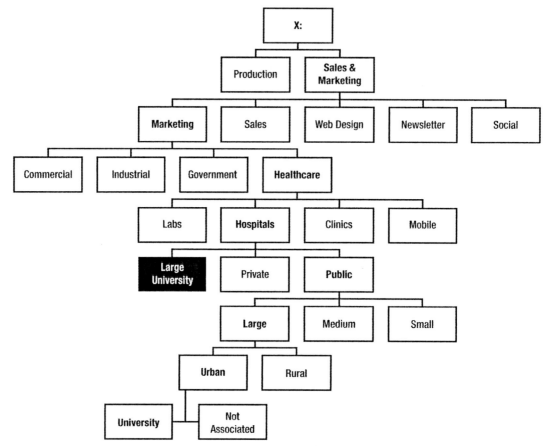

Figure 3-8. *After someone adds a folder to suit his or her particular needs, the structure is now chaotic, with more than one place to find the same types of files.*

The key point I want to make is that just because a hierarchy for organizing information is complex doesn't mean that it can't work. The taxonomy that helps you find Roborovski hamsters is structurally identical to the file storage taxonomy in the example X drive. The difference is that if a complex hierarchy is not deeply known and understood by its users, and if it can be easily changed without careful consideration and communication, chaos will ensue. And that is the situation in which most organizations with shared network drives find themselves.

Taxonomy in SharePoint

Now let's take a look at how taxonomy can help us do a better job with document findability and putability in SharePoint.

If we compare the diagram in Figure 3-9 to the original folder structure presented earlier in the chapter, we'll see much similarity. We have a top level "root" followed by a level that includes "Sales" and

"Marketing." Below marketing, we have places (in this case, SharePoint libraries) that will house documents for commercial clients, industrial clients, government clients, and health care industry clients.

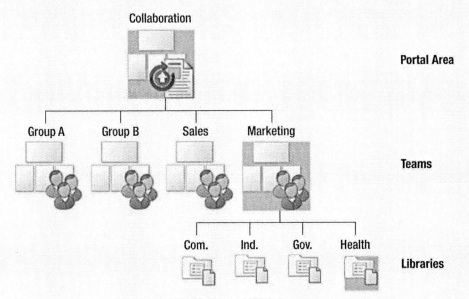

Figure 3-9. A SharePoint hierarchy of sites and libraries

Logically, they are identical structures, but the true difference between this structure and the folder structure we looked at earlier comes down to governance. In a well-managed SharePoint environment, not just anyone can create a subsite or a document library. These levels usually have at least some management so they can only be created by someone with a bit of oversight or authority over the structure. The result is that we don't get crazy and arbitrarily change multilevel nested sites. Now, it is true that you could get a similar benefit by carefully governing the creation of folders and subfolders on a shared drive, but in practice, this rarely happens.

There is also a "weight" associated with sites and libraries that mere folders don't have. It's like the difference between giving directions to a destination just by listing all the roads you have to follow, compared to describing the city you are going to, followed by the district, and then the road directions. The name of the city and district act to "chunk" the details of the location into items that are memorable. If you are looking for a store named Bloomingdales, you'd get a better idea where to go if someone said "go to New York City, and in Manhattan, navigate to 59th Street and Lexington."

Once we get down below the major grouping units (sites and libraries), the next few levels are treated differently: Unlike folders, which would just continue to nest the hierarchy into ever deeper layers, we use metadata to capture the distinguishing information we associate with each file. In Figure 3-10 we see that we have values for Customer Type, Sector, Size, Location, and University attachment. We will use those attributes to set up metadata for this document library.

Customer Type	Sector	Size	Location	University
• Lab	• Private	• Large	• Urban	• Yes
• Hospital	• Public	• Medium	• Rural	• No
• Clinic		• Small		
• Mobile				

Figure 3-10. The list of metadata fields that we will use and their values

This information is captured in a pop-up dialog box similar to the one seen in Figure 3-11.

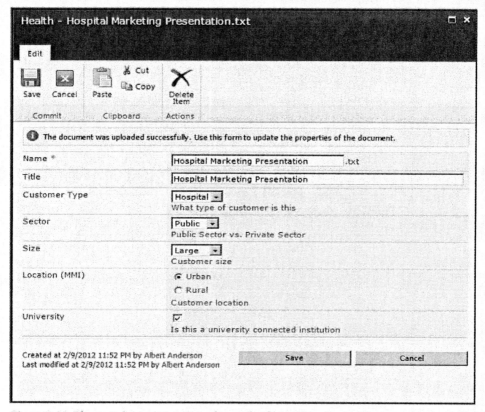

Figure 3-11. The metadata entry screen when uploading a new document

As you can see, there is no free lunch when it comes to saving documents: You either have to find the right folder to save it in or you have to enter the relevant metadata. Later we will talk about how much metadata you can reasonably ask a person to provide.

The result of entering that metadata is that you have made findability and putability so much simpler: When it comes to saving a document, if it belongs to the marketing department and it falls into the health category, you know that it lives in this document library. From there, you just enter the correct metadata. When you need to find a document, you go to that library where it is very easy to create views to show you just "hospital" or "private hospital" or "urban hospital" documents.

How Much Metadata?

Deciding how many metadata fields you will ask your users to fill in every time they add an item to SharePoint is not obvious. You want to add as many fields as are necessary to make the content easy to find by the people who will be using it. The issue is that if the people uploading documents don't (or won't) fill in the correct metadata, your documents become very hard to find. One way to ensure that metadata get entered is to enforce entry by setting the fields to be "required." The required setting is an option for every piece of metadata you create. If you set this value to "Yes," then an item cannot be saved within SharePoint unless that field has a value entered for that field (Figure 3-12). But this can backfire if people enter incorrect information just to be able to move on. A particularly insidious problem is allowing the use of "miscellaneous" or "other" as a metadata entry. This will result in all your files falling into the "other" category, which is as useless as leaving the fields blank.

Additional Column Settings	Description:
Specify detailed options for the type of information you selected.	Which product does this material apply to
	Require that this column contains information:
	○ Yes ● No
	Enforce unique values:
	○ Yes ● No

Figure 3-12. Setting a field to be required (the default is "No")

The best way to get the correct metadata entered is to make it as simple as possible and to ensure that everyone sees the value of entering that information.

■ **Example** I once had to enter documents into a library that had a dozen metadata fields, none of which made any sense to me and that had only one required field, which was "Date Created." Ninety-five percent of the time the right value would have been today's date, but there was no default set for it. This complete failure of design really bothered me, so—in protest—I never entered anything into *any* of the metadata fields except that one required date field and hardly anyone else did either. I felt sorry for the people who took the time to figure out what metadata to enter, because the fact that most of the rest of us did not meant that the metadata were useless for finding information and so their efforts were wasted. When choosing metadata, if you want to have a successful result, you have to consider the users who will be entering the data to ensure that their task is as easy as possible. If necessary, you will need to also educate them on the value of the metadata and how they will be used by others to find the content they enter.

I have heard Sue Hanley say in presentations that you have to "tune into the radio station called WIIFM: What's In It For Me." For each person, what's in it for that person will be different from any other person. In some cases, getting the right metadata entered means keeping your job. But for most people, the metadata you input help you or your colleagues with findability and therefore allow people (including you) to do their jobs better and more efficiently when the correct information has been entered. The result is that the right amount of metadata may be just one field or it may be over 20.

As an example of an extreme number of metadata fields, I worked on a project for the legal team in a midsized corporation. The two legal assistants were used to spending one full week each month preparing reports for the vice president. When we created their information architecture, we worked closely with the team and came up with over 20 items of metadata for each legal document. Normally that would be considered excessive, but this team was highly invested in entering correct information because once we implemented the solution, the result was that the one week spent creating reports was cut down to just half an hour per month by making use of SharePoint views and exporting the data to Excel.

Another way you can get the benefits of additional metadata without requiring users to have to enter too much information is by setting default values that are location based. For example, if each document needs to have the name of the department that created it added as metadata, you can make sure that the metadata are automatically set: When you create a site or a library that is for the exclusive use of a particular department, make that department's name the default value for the department field, thus saving the user from entering it.

Later in this chapter we'll cover another way to help people get their metadata entered in a less painful way when we look at how we can leverage folders to set default values for metadata.

■ **Caution** If you define a metadata field at the root of your site (usually a good practice) and then modify the default value within a subsite somewhere, you have to be careful about modifying the parent in the root location because doing so can overwrite your locally modified value when you save changes if you select "Yes" for "Update all list columns based on this site column?"

Another consideration for how much metadata to collect is how they are going to be used to help with findability. If you can filter a collection of documents down to about 20 results, which can be displayed on a single page, then adding an additional piece of metadata to refine it further may be a waste of effort. Just ensure that you can limit the result set down to one page that's easy to scan. Because inputting metadata adds workload to the people creating documents or list items, it can be counterproductive to be overly granular with your metadata.

So, how much metadata is the right amount? People used to say "about six items," but like most canned answers, it's not that easy. You need to carefully examine how much metadata you *really* need to do the job, while also considering the issues of asking someone to enter information that is annoying or poorly understood. No matter how good your information architecture is, if the items don't have properly entered metadata values, it's all wasted.

Running Metadata Workshops

Now that you understand quite a bit about metadata, you will need to be able to convey this information to your stakeholders so that you can work together with them to build out the metadata for their sites. The way I normally do this is to run a preliminary educational workshop where I use a PowerPoint presentation to explain what metadata are to my stakeholders. It is not my goal for them to have a full understanding of all the intricacies of metadata, but rather just enough for them to do the homework I will be assigning.

The attendees for this presentation can come from all different departments and roles. They are not going to be giving me feedback during this session, so it is not necessary to split the teams up.

▓ **Note** On the web site for this book, you will find the PowerPoint deck that I use to explain what metadata are to my stakeholders. It's essentially a more graphical version of this chapter along with a bit of mind mapping.

After the presentation, I give each of the attendees a blank document-type inventory spreadsheet to use for homework. I instruct them to go back to their desks and look at their existing content and list all the different types of documents they work with. I also ask them to list all the possible metadata items they can think of (Figure 3-13).

	A	B	C	D
1			**Document Type Inventory**	
2		Customer:	MultiMEGA Industries	
3		Department:	HR - Hiring	
4		Name:	Ann Anderson	
5		Date:	January 24th	
6				
7	Document Details	Metadata	Example	Notes
8	Job Applicants	Last Name	Gates	
9		First Name	William	
10		Phone Number	416-555-1234	This is for North American hiring only - 10 digits
11		Email	billg@hotmail.com	
12		Resume		Attach a resume
13		Source	Newspaper	One of: Newspaper, website, direct, Internal referral, externa
14		Position Applied for	HR Administrator	Selected from a database of job titles
15		Date Applied	24-Jan-12	
16		Interviewed by	Arlene Martin	Select from internal employee list
17		Interview Date	28-Jan-12	
18		Interview Score	7	Number between 1 and 10
19		Interview Comments	Great potential	Multiple lines of comments
20		Recommend for hire	Yes	Yes or No
21		Hire Date	31-Jan-12	
22		Postion Hired For	HR Administrator	Selected from a database of job titles
23		Manager	Percy Chan	Select from internal employee list
24		Start Date	14-Feb-12	

Figure 3-13. The filled out document type inventory sheet

I remind them that I want only one example of each type of document. (I once had someone fill in the metadata details for every document on his hard drive. There were about 400 of them and it must have taken the poor guy ages to fill out the spreadsheet.)

I do not ask them to limit themselves to a reasonable amount of metadata; I don't want them to self-censor before I've had a chance to evaluate what is important. So I tell them to include the metadata items they can think of, even if they are not sure whether they are valid. Later on, if necessary, I eliminate or consolidate the metadata items they have listed.

I then schedule a follow-up workshop, which has to be highly segregated by team and role. It would not make sense for the human resources team to be describing their documents and metadata while the engineering team sits around waiting. These groups need to be split up for these workshops.

When we meet for the follow-up taxonomy workshop, I ask them to bring their homework and I set up my mind mapping software and a projector so that we can work interactively.

In this example, using the homework from Figure 3-13, I start by building the mind map (Figure 3-14).

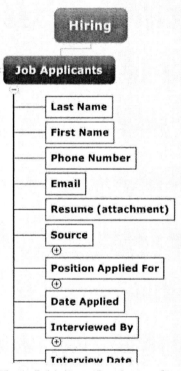

Figure 3-14. Capturing the metadata in a mind map

As you can see, I have simply listed the details from the homework. Now, as I continue to work with them, I ask about the phases of the hiring process: What comes first? They tell me that the process has three phases. First, the applicant is added to the system with just their basic information, their résumé, and which position they have applied for. Oh yes, and the source for the job information—newspaper, web site, or another. Second is the interview process, and finally, the hiring process.

Given that information, I modify the map. Finally, I abstract the metadata that should really be common across all three phases and produce the map shown in Figure 3-15, which shows the common metadata among all three phases (contact information and résumé).

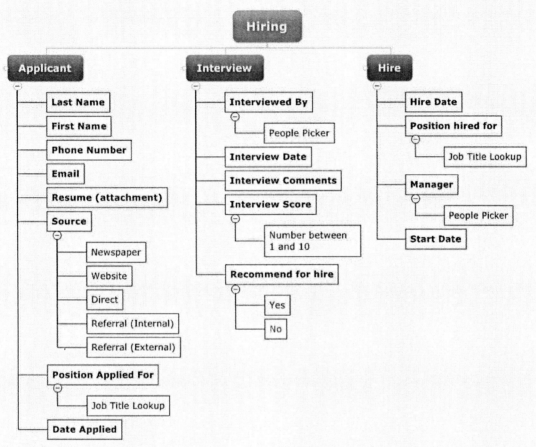

Figure 3-15. The metadata split among three phases

At the end of the workshop, I convert this map to PDF format and send it to the team members so that by the time they get back to their desks, they will have a copy of what was decided (Figure 3-16). I would also print a poster-sized image of each map and paste it to the wall in the project room. This can be very useful, because later on in the project, when other groups go through this same exercise, we will be able to spot overlaps in content and metadata between teams.

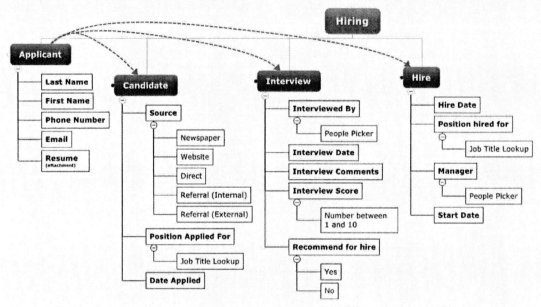

Figure 3-16. The final map showing the groupings by phase and the key applicant metadata

If you were to think of this as a paper process, you may think that there would be a form for applicants to which the résumé would be stapled. Then there would be a separate form for interview notes and hiring recommendations. Finally, a further document would exist to track the people who were hired. In SharePoint, we use content types to take the place of the forms. Let's investigate how we would use them here.

Understanding Content Types

I have found that when I explain metadata to people, they generally get it; they see how it works and the value it provides. Content types are harder to get a handle on, but this is a very useful concept that can help with content organization and with metadata entry.

The easiest way to envision content types is as if they were paper forms with different fields. We are used to filling in lots of paper forms. Things like vacation requests and benefits reimbursement at work, medical history at the doctor's office, permission slips for the kids' school, and many others. Each of these paper forms is made up of a collection of fields to be filled out. If we think of each field as metadata and each form as a content type, we can see how this maps onto SharePoint information architecture.

Let's continue with our example using the MultiMEGA human resources department. They want a place to keep track of people who apply for jobs, those who get invited for an interview, the results of the interview, and the hiring information if that person is hired.

One interesting attribute of content types is that they are built with a parent–child inheritance relationship. All of SharePoint's built-in content types are part of an inheritance hierarchy that we must inherit from. When you create a content type for a document library, it inherits from the built-in "document" content type. In Figure 3-17, you can see a subset of the SharePoint built-in content types (white boxes) and how our new content types fit in to this hierarchy.

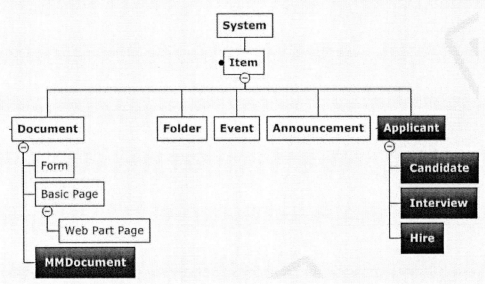

Figure 3-17. Some SharePoint built-in content types along with five new ones we have created

It is an important rule that we should never modify the SharePoint built-in content types, but let's say that we have a business requirement to include a "confidentiality level" field for every uploaded document. This field defaults to "internal only" but can be overridden to be either "public" or "confidential." At MultiMEGA, we can inherit from the built-in document content type. Now, any further document content types that we create will inherit from this content type instead of the built-in one, and all future document content types will automatically contain the confidentiality metadata field. Note how we have created our own MMDocument (for MultiMEGA Documents), which inherits from "Document."

We are allowed to take advantage of this hierarchy with our own content types. This structure lets you do things like create an applicant content type that contains a résumé attachment and the name, phone, and e-mail metadata.

Another useful aspect of content types is that workflows can be defined to run against specific content types. So, a drug reimbursement form can have a different approval process than the vacation request form. This makes a lot of sense, as you would expect these two forms to have different steps for approval. Records management policies are also applied to content types.

The concept of what content types are and how they can be used is one of the most difficult of the SharePoint information architecture elements to understand. Let me give you one more way to think about it: A library is created to hold documents of one type or another. You can make that library more useful by adding metadata. For example, a library that holds invoices may benefit from metadata like invoice number, customer name, and due date. Creating these metadata fields allows you to sort the library by invoice numbers or group it by customer names. If we now define a content type called "Invoice" and add those same metadata fields, we can tell that library to use the "Invoice" content type. Now we can say that the library holds documents of type "Invoice." In essence, nothing has changed; the library still works the way it always did, but we can now apply workflows to the content type called "Invoice" or set specific records management policies to it. We can also add a content type called "Payment" to that library. It contains slightly different metadata (say "Amount" and "Payment Date"). Now we can add both invoices and payments to the same library, but treat them differently and have them display different metadata. The proper application of content types can make your SharePoint libraries and lists more useful and powerful.

When to Use Folders

I have shown you a few reasons why folders are problematic: They hide content and structure in layers that remain invisible until you actually dig down into them; they are easily added, but remembering where you have stored them can be hard; they impose a rigid structure, like a supermarket's aisles, which doesn't let you change the way you group information for different purposes; and they can be hard to govern. However, folders can be useful in certain circumstances.

▓ **Note** When I present about metadata, I like to joke that we are going to talk about the "f-word": Folders. I explain that the number-one rule of folders is never, *ever*, use them . . . (pause for dramatic effect) except when it makes sense to do so. This contradictory sounding rule usually gets a bit of a laugh. The message I am trying to send is: Start off trying to avoid the use of folders, and then—if there is a compelling reason to do so—go ahead and use them.

There are three main instances where it makes sense to use folders:

1. *Security*: It's easy and powerful to apply permissions to a folder within a library (you should almost never apply permissions to individual documents or items).

2. *Ease of use*: With SharePoint 2010, you can now automatically assign metadata to a document based on the folder it is saved to. This allows you to make use of your user's comfort with the use of folders to help them organize their information.

3. *Dividing a large dataset*: A SharePoint list or library will have performance problems if you try to return 5,000 or more items in one view. By dividing your documents into folders, each one holding less than 5,000 items, you can avoid this limitation.

Let's expand on these three areas. First, security. Imagine that you have a document library that has human resource forms and employee handbooks for three different office locations in three different countries (Toronto, Los Angeles, and Hong Kong). You would like to put these three documents into one library in the employee center, but you don't want to confuse your users by making the handbook for one country visible to employees in another country. In fact, you want to keep those secure because there are human resources rules and benefits that don't apply from one country to another and you'd prefer not to share that.

The solution is to create three folders, one for each location, and then assign permissions based on groups (SharePoint groups or Active Directory groups) to each folder (Figure 3-18).

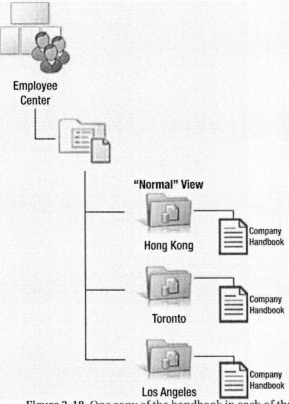

Figure 3-18. One copy of the handbook in each of three folders

This library has three folders, and each folder holds the location-specific files (in this case, just showing the different company handbooks—all having the same name). You can now change the view to show the documents without folders (Figure 3-19).

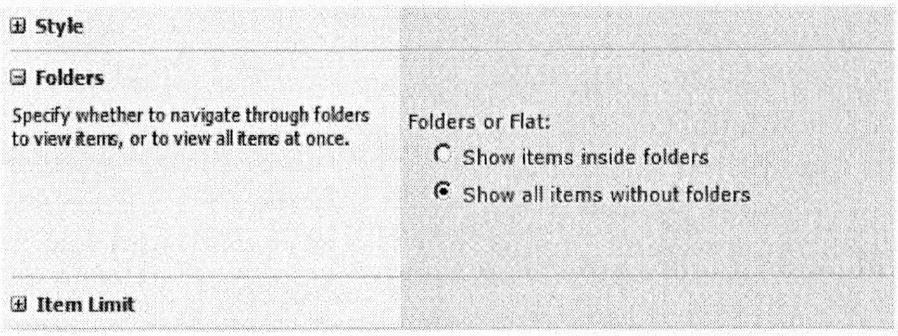

⊞ **Style**

⊟ **Folders**

Specify whether to navigate through folders to view items, or to view all items at once.

Folders or Flat:
- ○ Show items inside folders
- ◉ Show all items without folders

⊞ **Item Limit**

Figure 3-19. Modifying the view to show items without folders

Now, when regular users navigate to the Employee Center, they will see only those documents that they have the right to (Figure 3-20). In fact, they will not even be aware that there is a folder with their city name on it or that there are other handbooks out there.

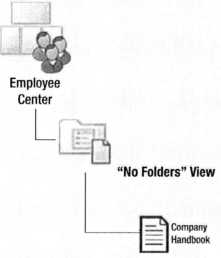

Employee Center

"No Folders" View

Company Handbook

Figure 3-20. The "No Folders" view hides the folders as well as the documents that are secured by those folders.

Human resource administrators have the right to see all documents in all of these folders. If they were to view the documents in this view, it would look as if there were three documents with the same name. So, for their use, they would use a different view that has "Show items inside folders" selected. This also makes it very easy for them to add new documents and ensure that only the right people will see them: Just drop them into the right folder when uploading (Figure 3-21).

The other way to take advantage of folders is to use one of the new and very useful features of SharePoint 2010: It is now possible to configure folders so metadata values are automatically assigned to a document when it is added to the folder. This allows the user to get the familiar "folder experience," but it doesn't force the rigid folder structure on the content because you can always view the files in a "No Folder" view that flattens out the folders, allowing you to use metadata to organize and filter the content.

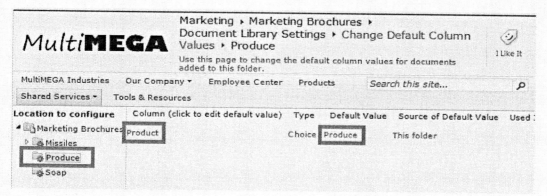

Figure 3-21. Dropping a document into the "Produce" folder will automatically set the "Product" metadata field to the value "Produce."

Now, let's add a document to the folder "Produce" (Figure 3-22). Note that the "Folder" value shows

/Produce/. We could have selected that here, but it is there for us automatically because we had navigated into the "Produce" directory first.

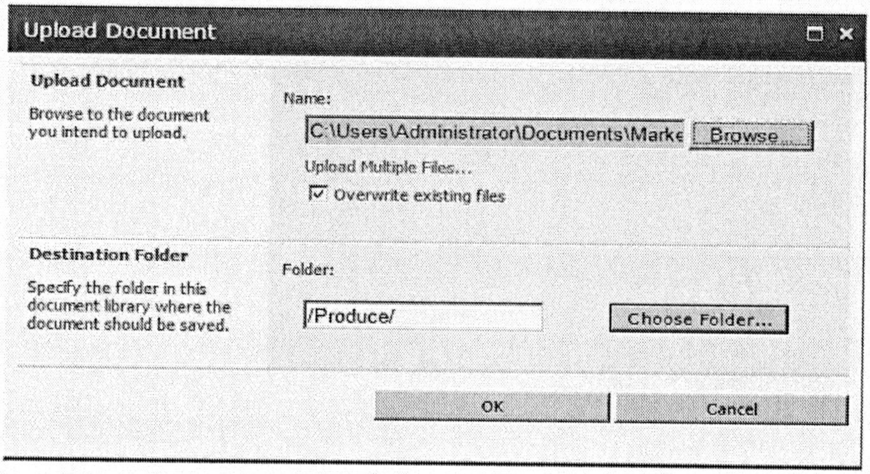

Figure 3-22. Uploading a document into the /Produce/ folder

When you click "OK" to upload, you will see (in Figure 3-23) that the "Product" field has been prepopulated. (I did not do anything to select that drop-down.)

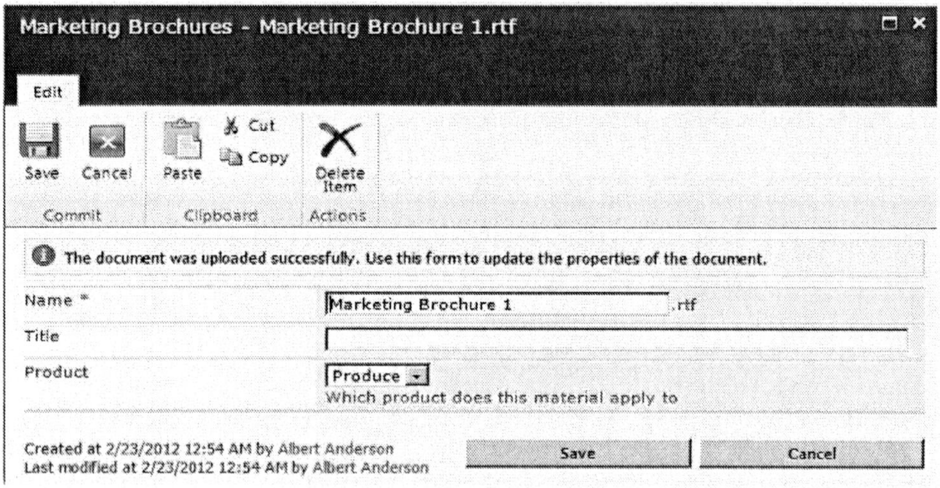

Figure 3-23. The prepopulated "Product" field

Now, create a view using the "No Folders" view. To access the "No Folders" view in SharePoint, create a new view and then expand the "Folders" setting in the view creation screen and select the "Show all items without folders" option (Figure 3-24).

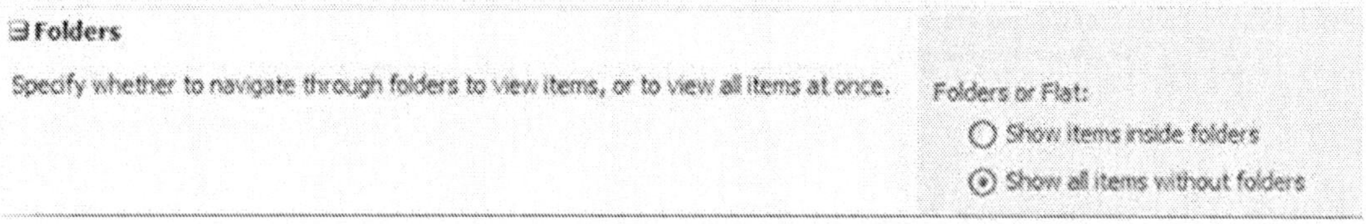

Figure 3-24. Set the "No Folders" view (i.e., "Show all items without folders")

Now, when you view the library with the "No Folders" view, you will see that "Produce" appears in the "Product" metadata field, even though we never typed it ourselves (Figure 3-25).

Figure 3-25. Showing the library without folders

The final way to use folders is to divide SharePoint content into folders (and even subfolders). This can be *very* problematic for the same reason as folders on the shared drive are problematic: It is hard to find the stuff when you need it. But if you have large volumes of content (exceeding 3,000 to 5,000 items), dividing them into folders can dramatically speed up retrieval.

Summary

This chapter started by presenting some metaphors to help you understand the meaning and value of metadata and how it can be applied to document organization. We discussed the findability and putability issues that make metadata superior to a hierarchy of folders (the magic of metadata!), and we saw how to work with stakeholders to gather the metadata that works for their content and how to use that to build the metadata map that will drive the construction of their SharePoint sites.

Even if you understand the value of metadata, it can still be hard to convince others of its value. Hopefully, some of the material in this chapter will assist you in educating others. The key elements to understand are:

- *Metadata*: Attributes or fields that add information to your content that you can use to sort and filter.

- *Content types:* Named collections of metadata that you can apply workflow and policies to.

- *Taxonomy*: The hierarchical ordering of information to support findability and putability.

You then need to explain these concepts in terms that your users will understand and then use the taxonomy homework sheets to allow people a chance to consider and collect their own metadata. Using mind mapping software, you can work interactively with the users to build taxonomies that support their business requirements. Finally, we talked about the instances when folders can be useful, but we always start with a healthy desire to avoid them unless necessary.

To really get value out of SharePoint, you just have to understand how to apply the concepts of taxonomy, content types, and metadata. Simply using SharePoint as a shared drive with a bunch of nested folders is really not taking advantage of what SharePoint has to offer and in fact offers a worse experience than what it is intended to replace.

CHAPTER 4

Site Navigation and Structure

I may not have gone where I intended to go, but I think I have ended up where I needed to be.

Douglas Adams

Building out the navigational structure of a SharePoint site can be one of the most politically difficult parts of your project. The reason for this is that the site navigation is not something you want to change very often, and it has to be agreed upon by a fairly broad collection of people.

Why do you have to try to get this right up front? SharePoint is a flexible platform that is easy to modify; you can change the navigation once a week if you like, just by shuffling the order of pages or how subsites are nested. But people don't like change very much, especially if they have invested time in learning something they need to use for their daily work. Just because it may be technically easy for you to change the main site navigation later, you really don't want to do this very often, so you must invest the right level of effort and involve the right people in an exercise that a lot of people are going to have to live with for a long time.

You will often find that when you're working on a corporate intranet project, the navigational structure is driven by the political agendas of the various groups that make up the project team. Most commonly, the key owners (and drivers) include marketing, corporate communications, human resources, knowledge management, and IT personnel. Each group sees the company through a different lens, and each has different priorities.

The natural tendency people have when working on their initial pass at the navigational structure is trying to match it to the organization chart. This is a bad idea for a number of reasons. It is very common for companies to reorganize from time to time. Sometimes the change is driven by an acquisition (or having been acquired), sometimes it is driven by a change in the business model, and sometimes it's to implement a new strategy (or just to shake things up a bit). Changing the navigational structure of the intranet is—as I said above—painful and annoying. Avoiding the organization chart trap will help prevent that from happening.

Another reason to avoid the organization chart structure is that people have to try to figure out how responsibility is divided before they can figure out where to find things on the intranet. An example that was told to me by Eli Robillard (http://weblogs.asp.net/erobillard/) is of a client of his that had a problem with their staff finding out how to get a parking pass that would get them into the office parking lot. When someone new would start at the company, that person would naturally start looking in the human resources intranet site for parking passes. Then the person would start hunting all over, trying to find where this information could possibly be stored. It turned out the finance department paid for the parking spaces and issued the passes. You can see how a departmentally driven navigational structure did not help new employees of this company get up to speed very quickly.

If building an intranet site based on the structure of the organization chart doesn't work, what is the alternative? Later in this chapter, we will look at how to develop a navigational model that is more efficient and easier to work with. We will see how the use of mind mapping can help you to get to a shared understanding with your stakeholders for this particular task. As we do this, we are going to be looking at SharePoint–centric examples—after all, this is a book about SharePoint—but the issues we are going to cover apply to any platform you use to build an intranet.

Establishing Who the Site Is For

Before you can figure out what you are going to build, you have to get a handle on why you are building it. We covered some of this in Chapter 1, and in Chapter 6, we will learn a bit about how we can use an Issue-Based Information System, or IBIS—a special mapping language—to figure out what the business goals for the project are and how to make sure you have alignment among the stakeholders. For the time being, let's assume that we have a well-established goal and we understand what it is we are trying to build. The first thing we need to get a handle on is who the site users are and how they are going to use it.

There is a whole category of work in the field of user experience (UX) and site design involved in creating personas. These are fictional characters that are meant to represent the typical user of a certain type.

The development of a persona can include finding a representative picture, and then giving the persona a biography. For example: *Samantha is a 38-year-old legal secretary. She is a single mother of a teenage daughter and she has worked for the firm for over 15 years. Samantha has risen in stature in the firm as she has worked for the same lawyer since he started, right out of school. "Her" lawyer is now a senior partner. Samantha is very good at her job, but is resistant to new technology or any change that may make her feel less than fully competent, especially compared to the younger people (mostly women) who look up to her . . .* That is just the introduction of a bio that could go on for a full page. These personas can become quite detailed and, throughout the life of a project, they can almost come alive: Project team members may describe a feature by saying "Samantha would hate that."

I don't believe it is necessary to devote that level of time and effort to create these types of fictional character personas. I am more interested in understanding the different groups or audiences who will be using the site and understanding what they are meant to accomplish. In Figure 4-1, you can see a very simplified list of personas that I use, really split by role more than personality type, that gives the main priorities for those roles and what they expect SharePoint to provide to them.

MultiMEGA – Personas

Persona	Group	Site Priorities/Goals	Details
	Everyone	Contact Information - Name/Role/E-mail Effective search Pulse of the company (news)	We have 15,000 employees, 10,000 of which are information workers who have daily access to a computer
	Member of the Board of Directors	Relatively limited use Collaboration space for meeting minutes and material to prep for next meeting	Outside the corporate network most of the time

	Manager	Pulse of company
		Creating the messages to lead the team
		Tools & Templates
		Human Resources
		  - Staff Management
		  - Hiring/Forms
		Project collaboration	

	Administrator	Team collaboration workspaces Policies Human Resources Easy to search material	

Figure 4-1. A snapshot of a list of personas for our example company—MultiMEGA Industries

There are a number of ways to build the persona list. The best is to interview people from across the organization. In Chapter 1, on conducting requirements-gathering workshops, you saw how to interact with a good cross-section of the organization, and you can often draw your personas from those meetings. If you don't have the opportunity to meet a broad swath of the organization, you will need to rely on your project team and stakeholders to fill you in on the details of the various groups of people who will be using the system.

Imagine that, as the IA for MultiMEGA Industries (our example company), you are working through the process of designing the intranet site structure and navigation. You will need to keep the persona list handy so you can determine how each person will navigate the site and which personas will be making use of each area. You will actually be adding to the persona list and refining it as you go because certain roles may not become apparent until you determine this information. Remember, it is important that everything you do in your IA design process aligns with the people who will actually be using the system. Without that, you may not build something that suits them, and then it is all just a big waste of time, money, and your reputation.

You now have a persona list (or are evolving one) that tells you who you are building this site for. The next step is to understand the concepts that the people in this organization use on a day-to-day basis. In the next section, we'll discuss the process of gathering these concepts and getting users to organize them to help you design the structure of your site.

Card Sorting

Card sorting is a simple tool for helping to design a navigational architecture. I think this quote sums it up best:

Card sorting is best understood not as a collaborative method for creating navigation, but rather as a tool that helps us understand the people we are designing for.

That quote is from the best book on the subject, *Card Sorting* by Donna Spencer, a freelance IA,

writer, and speaker (`http://bit.ly/dscardsort`). This is a comprehensive and inexpensive resource, but you can also find a lot of the important information from Donna's article on the web site

`boxesandarrows.com`.

The thing to take away from that quote is "understand the people we are designing for." The site structure and navigation *must* serve the people who will be using it. Imagine a library that has books organized by color, size, and thickness. This clearly will not help someone who is looking for a particular title or work by a particular author.

How Card Sorting Works

The basic process of running a card-sorting exercise is to ask people (working individually or in small groups) to take a collection of concepts that are written on cards and then organize those concepts into groups. There are two main types of card sorts: open and closed.

In a closed card sort, you supply the participants with the concepts along with the grouping categories. You then ask the users to sort the concepts into the categories. In an open card sort, like the one shown in Figure 4-2, you ask the participants to organize the concepts into groups and then to name the groups with a category label.

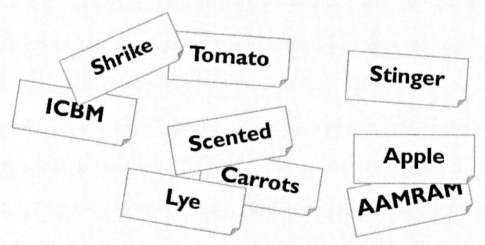

Figure 4-2. A sample set of cards from the MultiMEGA SharePoint project

Card sorting does *not* supply you directly with your navigational hierarchy: What it gives you is clues into the mental models of your users. Imagine if a participant from MultiMEGA sorted by geography instead of lines of business (which makes sense for that user, because they are responsible for accounting tax codes in each jurisdiction). This user knows that our ICBM and AAMRAM missiles are made in the United States, but the Shrike and our lines of scented soaps are made in Great Britain. This user would have a very different set of initial buckets on an open sort.

It's not possible to have this type of sort drive your navigational architecture. For one thing, you don't ask your participants to create multilevel hierarchies. For another, card sorts can go wrong, with participants sorting the concepts according to the familiar existing pattern of the current intranet. A user who sorted these concepts by division may create a sort like the one shown in Figure 4-3.

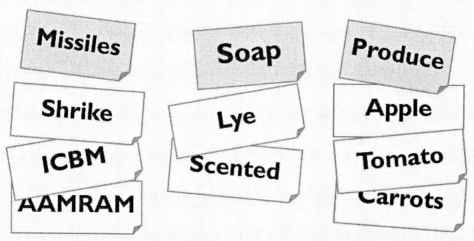

Figure 4-3. An open sort in which the users grouped by Missiles, Soap, and Produce

You will find that different groups or individuals can come up with completely different mental models of how the concepts should be grouped. Your goal as an IA is to understand how your users group the concepts and how you can take advantage of their mental models to build a site architecture that makes sense to them and that helps them to find the content they are looking for. Very importantly, it gives you clues to metadata you will need to use that will allow people to find or view information in a way that makes sense for them and that helps them get their work done more efficiently. Feeling out the point of view or mental models of your users can help to guide you in the building of the IA, producing a site that makes sense to the broadest collection of users.

After you have done a few open card sorts to get an idea of what the overall concept groupings look like, you can then run some closed card sorts to see how consistently people can figure out which category to use for a wide variety of concepts and to test the categories for validity. If you find that most concepts are put in the same place by a majority of the people, you have a pretty consistent model that works for most people. However, if a particular concept is distributed among a number of categories, or if the participants ask you to allow them to make duplicate cards so they can be slotted into more than one category, you know that you have a more slippery concept and you may have to create links to it from multiple locations. For example, MultiMEGA is dedicated to workforce diversity. Many people doing card sorts put the Diversity card into the Our Values group, but others put it into the Human Resources bucket. Some people being tested even asked if they could put it in both locations. These differences are clues that, if used properly, can improve the overall findability of the content. In a blow up of a section of a navigational mind map, presented in Figure 4-4, we solved it by making Our Values the "home" of Diversity, but we put links to it in the Employee Center (the place where most human resource content is located on our site).

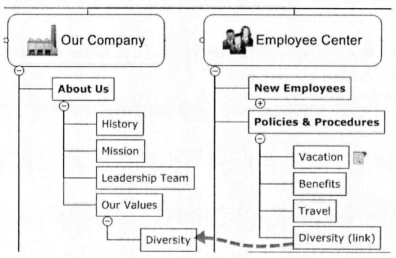

Figure 4-4. Diversity is findable in both locations: one is its home and one is a link.

People often wonder how many subjects they need to use in a card sort exercise in order to get a valid result. Jakob Nielsen of the Nielsen Norman Group (a noted usability consulting firm

http://www.nngroup.com/) reports on a detailed statistical analysis that shows that 15 is a number that

gives a statistically valid result (http://bit.ly/cardsortsize). However, we are usually not using the card sort results as a direct driver for the IA, but more as a way of exposing the mental models of our users, so even this number of participants may not be necessary for your project, depending on its size and budget.

Once you conduct a number of card sort workshops, you will want to analyze the results. A handy tool for this is a spreadsheet created by Donna Spencer that can be used to analyze the card sort data. This spreadsheet highlights concepts that are consistently placed in buckets and also those that are inconsistent. You can obtain the latest version of this spreadsheet and Donna's book at

http://bit.ly/cardsortcalculator.

At MultiMEGA, we wanted to give the Library and Research department a catchier name, so we tried Infoseeking and Intelligence. Our card sort experiments showed that this would have been a major failure; some people understood what this group did, but many didn't and they were not able to consistently figure out how to sort terms such as Periodical Subscriptions and Market Research.

In-Person vs. Online Card Sorting

Card sorting can be done either at in-person workshops or online. Both have their advantages and disadvantages. An in-person workshop allows you to have direct interaction with the participants in the card sorting exercise. The most valuable element you get from an in-person card sort is the insight you gain from the participants around the decisions they made and why. A disadvantage of an in-person workshop is that you can only run the workshop with a manageable number of participants, and each card sort requires a considerable amount of time and effort.

With an online card sort, you have the advantage of being able to run the card sorting exercise using as many personas as you wish. Once you have defined the content that the users need to sort through, you can essentially run an unlimited number of users through the online card sort. In addition, tools like Optimal Workshop's OptimalSort (http://www.optimalworkshop.com/optimalsort.htm) online web-based card sorting tool provides additional information and statistics that can be extremely informative when trying to create your categories. In Figure 4-5, you can see an example of an exercise that we ran on different aspects of educating people about IA and governance.

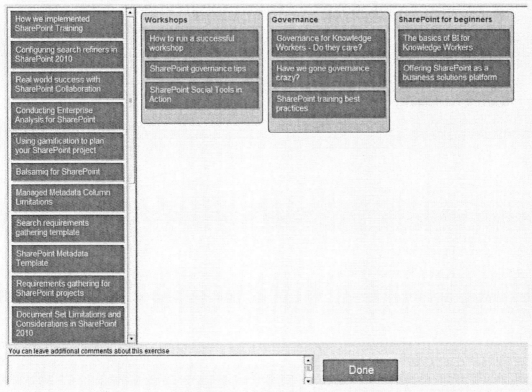

Figure 4-5. OptimalSort in action

The disadvantage of using an online card sort tool is that it skips direct interaction with users. Frequently you'll find that the conversations during the card sorting exercise can be just as valuable as the final results. Through interaction with participants, you may have many serendipitous moments that you can then use in your search implementation.

Card Sorting Summary

Card sorting is a useful, though not definitive, tool that helps the IA get a handle on how the people who will be using SharePoint understand the concepts they work with on a day-to-day basis. If you make use of this tool, you will often be surprised by how differently people can view the same concepts or how people categorize things. Learning this will help you build SharePoint solutions that come closer to meeting the needs of a broad spectrum of users.

Building the Navigation Map

In an ideal scenario, you will complete your card sorting exercises before you start planning your navigation. However, reality often gets in the way of the ideal. The first reality is that you will probably need to start the process of thinking through the top-level navigation before you finish the card sorting process. The second reality is that there are usually strong political forces that will dictate a lot of what happens on the top navigation.

There is some comfort when you feel you are being rushed, however: As much as every company feels it is unique and that it needs to build a "homegrown" solution, the reality is that there is a huge overlap between companies. While there can be a lot of differences in how product is delivered between an oil-drilling company and a law firm, the fact is that they both have news, communications from leadership, a company history and values, human resources and accounting departments, teams and projects, and so forth.

Almost every corporate intranet that I have worked on has most of the basic elements shown in Figure 4-6.

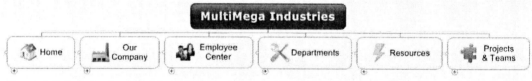

Figure 4-6. A navigation map showing the top-level sections of the MultiMEGA portal

---

▓ **Note** "Home" is really the top level of the navigation and not properly parallel to the other sections of the site, but I find that most people have an intuitive understanding of these top-level items as being the main navigation in which Home is the first item (even if you don't actually have a Home label on the navigation bar).

Many organizations have additional items such as Brands, Products, Reporting, Strategies, and many others. Sometimes Departments becomes Divisions. Also, the names can change quite a bit: Our Company can be About Us, or the Employee Center could be My Job. I don't mean to dismiss the very real differences between companies, but by the very nature of being a company, there are a lot of similarities. Note that these overlapping similarities all go out the window for special purpose sites. For example, an intranet site dedicated to managing sales and marketing materials across a global corporation will have a very different mandate, and none of the top menu choices shown here may apply.

The examples presented so far have been focused on corporate intranets. That is, they are inward facing. This means that the users of the site are the employees of the company, and they all have similarities in that they have a specific kind of relationship with the company (they are employees). Of course, if you are working on a team that is building a public-facing web site, whether it is an information site about a company or an e-commerce site that sells products online, you always have to consider your audience and their personas. The design you create has to be tailored to the needs of the people you are serving.

Functional vs. Organization Chart

In the introduction to this chapter I mentioned that we would not be building the structure of our site according the organization chart. In Figure 4-6 you can see, in the MultiMEGA navigational model, that there is very little that would have to change if the company were reorganized. The Employee Center (EC) is an example. The EC holds information about benefits, health and wellness, compensation plans, employee performance, and so forth. A majority of the content in the EC belongs to the Human Resources (HR) department. However, just because they dominate this area doesn't mean that all the information found here comes directly from HR. For example, in MultiMEGA's How-To section, there are instructions and forms for requisitioning a cell phone or a laptop computer, which is owned by IT.

The Resources area of the site (often called Tools and Resources) is a place where commonly requested material from across the organization can be found. It often contains things like letterhead and logo files, links to the travel booking system, emergency procedures, facilities information, branch office links and addresses, and other types of frequently required content. Remember, we don't allow information to be duplicated, but we do allow multiple ways to find the same content.

▧ **Example** There is often an interesting battle between the "corporate brand police" and people who are just trying to get their jobs done. The owners of the corporate brand (usually marketing and communications) want to protect the corporate brand from incorrect or risky use, and they are right to do so because the corporate brand is a valuable company asset. In order to maintain this control, they want all requests for use of logos and other brand images to come through them. On the other side of the equation are people who are trying to just write a letter or a proposal, author a slide deck, or finalize a contract. They will often do what it takes to get their jobs done, such as doing Internet searches for company images and downloading grainy or pixilated images. The trade-off is between marketing and communications becoming a bottleneck for getting work done or leaving the high-quality brand images out in the open in a shared location for any staff member to use (at least ensuring that they are using high-quality and up-to-date files). Every company deals with this issue a little differently.

As much as possible, we are trying to design a site that makes it easy for employees to find the crucial information they need as quickly and efficiently as possible. However, within every company there is still a fairly well-known and well-understood corporate hierarchy known commonly as "departments." This departmental organization cannot be eliminated from the structure of the portal without leaving many people lost because they can't find content according to a structure that they know exists and that they are familiar with.

The way to deal with these departmental sites depends a lot on the organization and its size. In a larger organization, or perhaps in the larger departments, it may be necessary to create two views of the department, depending on the various audiences that may visit the site. There is an external view, which is the default view for anyone coming to the site from any other department in the company. They will see a blurb about the department (what they do, what their mission is) and who the head of that department is. There may be departmental news and calendars and contact information, in case you need to contact anyone within the department. There also may be easy-to-locate forms and instructions for dealing with that department or requesting something from them.

There is another view of the department as well: The internal view, whose audience is the employees who work within that department. This view may incorporate some of the same elements as the external view, but it would typically have more useful day-to-day content that people within the site need to know to do their jobs efficiently. For example, there may be alerts that point out safety issues and the calendar may be more detailed, with specific departmental events that are too fine grained for a general audience. The internal home page may have employee recognition elements and discussion forums on problem solving.

In many environments, these two very different views are both available to all employees, but the one seen by default depends on your departmental membership.

There are other ways to split the departments, but before I can get into that, I want to show you a high-level model that resonates most strongly with my customers and really helps them to get a clear picture of where certain content belongs.

Above-the-Line and Below-the-Line Models

There is a model that has been used for SharePoint governance for a number of years now. I am not sure if the originator is Joel Oleson or Microsoft (or maybe it was Joel Oleson while he was working at Microsoft). The diagram in Figure 4-7 was used to illustrate how governance should be applied to SharePoint intranet solutions.

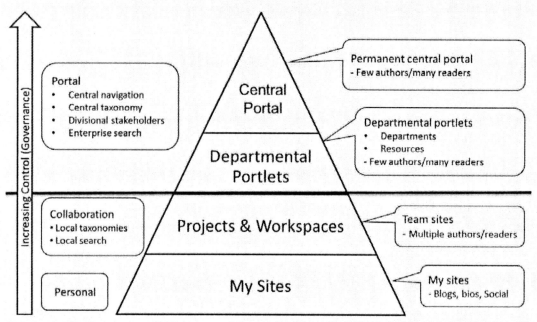

Figure 4-7. The classic pyramid of governance

The Central Portal is the area of the site where the home page is, and the news and communications from the leadership, the Employee Center, and all the other information that is communicated out from the owners of the portal to the company as a whole lives here. There is a lot of control, with a relatively small number of authors and contributors who have been trained on how to use the tools. There is a process here: Getting content published requires approval (sometimes multiple layers of approval), translation (if this is a multilingual site), and careful vetting of images to ensure good visual consistency and to reduce risk and liability (for posting inappropriate content, for example).

The next layer, Departmental Portlets, is where various departments and functions have their content. This can also be centrally controlled or there may be a number of fairly high-level teams (who have also been trained in SharePoint web-content management) who are responsible for the content in these sections. These areas are constrained by similar processes and controls as in the Central Portal.

The Projects and Workspaces area represents collaboration sites that often don't implement the SharePoint publishing infrastructure. They are sites for projects (having a definite lifecycle) or for teams that are homogeneous (from a particular group) or cross-functional. These sites are designed for document management and other collaborative tools, such as discussion forums and wikis. They need to be managed by people trained in how to use them effectively, but there is much less control (compared to the Central Portal), so that team members can configure them to work best for the task at hand. The main feature of these workspaces is that rather than a few authors writing for many readers, this is meant to be a shared space where there are lots of creators and consumers of content.

Finally, My Sites are individual sites controlled by each user. This is where each employee (if this feature is enabled) can store private documents or share documents with specific people. It is also the place that keeps the users' profiles, so that they can publish their headshot, a bio, and what skills they have or projects they have worked on. Some areas of My Sites are quite tightly constrained, and others allow the user quite a bit of freedom.

On the pyramid diagram is an arrow, rising up the left side. Originally, this denoted an increasing level of governance as you moved up the pyramid. As it turns out, governance is more complex than just saying it is loose at the bottom and tight at the top of the pyramid, but that's a discussion we'll get to later in Chapter 10. There we will learn what governance is and what it means. For the purpose of this discussion, we are talking about processes and rules that ensure that only high-quality content gets exposed to the organization as a whole.

What I have found to be most useful about this diagram is the heavy black line that crosses through the middle of the pyramid. When talking to stakeholders, I describe the difference between communication sites (above the line) and collaboration sites (below the line). In the communication sites, the content is created by a relatively small number of people for consumption by a relatively large number of people. The content is carefully written and checked before publication, and it is the place where a lot of thought needs to be given to make material easy to find by a broad spectrum of users.

When my project stakeholders understand this model (which they grasp pretty quickly), it helps them to think about where a particular type of content belongs and who would have control over it.

There is another distinction that often (but not always) separates the content above the line from that below: publishing versus nonpublishing (or collaboration) infrastructure in SharePoint. The content that appears above the line is almost always built using web-content management (WCM) tools and concepts. This is content that is made of text, images, and graphics, where the content is created and managed by people who are specifically trained in how to create these types of pages. There is often a workflow around getting the pages approved and published, and the pages are not usually very interactive. There is a lot of enforced consistency (through the use of templates and style limitations) so that all of the content has a consistent look and feel.

An extremely useful post was written by Marcy Kellar on her blog that shows the key issues you need to consider when working on publishing (WCM) areas versus collaboration areas in SharePoint

(http://bit.ly/WCMvsCollab). In it she makes clear the distinctions between publishing and collaboration with her "Cheat Sheet," which is reproduced (with permission from Marcy) in Table 4-1.

Table 4-1. *The Marcy Kellar publishing versus collaboration "Cheat Sheet"*

	Publishing	Non-Publishing
Purpose:	Communication	Document Management
	Entertainment	Project Management
	Marketing	Collaboration
		Data Entry
		Business Intelligence
Scope:	Internal (Intranet)	Internal (Intranet)
	Extranet	Extranet
	Public Facing	
Users:	Few Contributors (Authors)	Many Contributors
	Many Readers	
Page Types:	Publishing Pages (from Page Layout)	Content Pages
		Web Part Pages
		Wiki Pages
Site Templates:	Publishing Site with Workflow	Team Site
	Publishing Site	Meeting Sites (All)
	Enterprise Wiki Site	Document Center
		Group Work Site
		Records Center
		Blog (arguably belongs here)
Example Content:	Landing Pages	Large Lists
	News Articles	Interactive BI
	Wiki Pages*	Project Data
	Blog Posts**	Gantt Charts
		Shared Calendars
Special Requirements:	Highly Customized	Lots of Space
	Content Query Web Parts	User Autonomy
	Public Facing	Organic Growth
	Hidden Left Nav on Some Pages	

	Publishing	Non-Publishing
Keywords	Marketing	File-share
	Content Schedule	Documents
	Content Rollups	Custom Site Template
	Marketing Copy	Projects
	Content Sliders	
	Controlled Content	
	Branding that is "Sexy," "Wows," or "Pops"	

*SharePoint 2010

**SharePoint does not categorize blogs as web content and the blog site template does not fall under the Publishing Site Picker tab. In my opinion, it SHOULD fall under publishing.*

Returning now to the pyramid, I have recently modified the pyramid diagram to take into account the concept of departmental sites that have an outward facing side and an inward facing side (Figure 4-8).

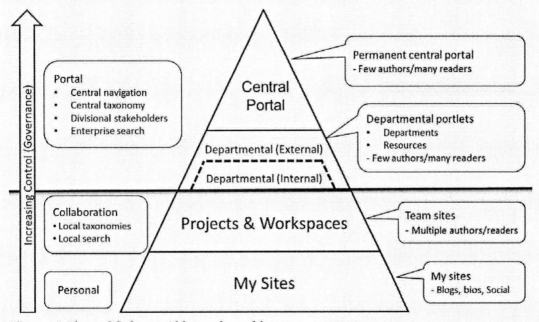

Figure 4-8. The modified pyramid for two faces of departments

The reason for including the dashed line this way is to indicate that while the departmental sites have been split, they are both still "above the line," in the sense that they are tightly controlled and make use of the publishing infrastructure (WCM) to display their content.

However, there is another way to construct this. Some departmental sites may have an external view, especially if they have a story to tell to the rest of the organization. However, many or most of the departments don't have a wide audience within the company, or due to constraints on resources, they are going to be more autonomous and self-governed. For this reason, these sites are created below the line, near the Projects and Workspaces area, as collaboration sites (Figure 4-9), even if they do have parts that are shared more widely with the company.

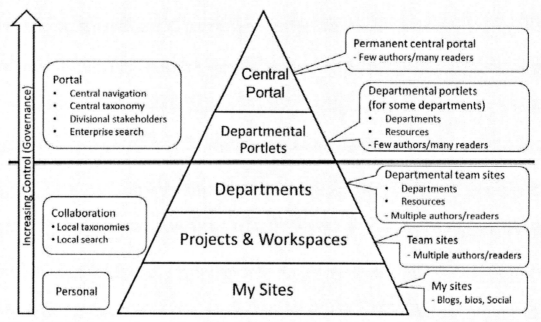

Figure 4-9. Putting departments below the line, with only a few portlets above the line

These different models do make a big difference, because they may impact how you navigate to these sites, how they are managed, and how their content is created and updated. The choices to be made are based on complexity and resources. But care is needed. The owner of the portal may believe that by simply passing on responsibility for the departmental sites to the department owners (via a below-the-line model) there will be enough governance and training given to ensure that the sites are built and managed properly so that the users of the content can find what they need to work effectively.

Helping your stakeholders understand the different capabilities of SharePoint (collaboration versus publishing) and how these can be applied to the structure of your site will help them determine where new sites and content should be added, how that content should be governed and managed, and how your users will find what they are looking for when they use the site.

Mind Mapping for Navigation

In Chapter 2, I explained how mind mapping really changed my life as a consultant, and we discussed mind mapping software. One of the earliest tasks that I used MindManager software for was building navigational maps. The process of building these maps interactively, in front of the stakeholders I was working with, really gave me my first lessons in shared understanding. Many people have preconceived notions of what the navigation of the site should look like, and it can be very hard to convince them otherwise. Allowing them to see the effects of their choices in real time can help them understand the reasoning for alternatives you or other stakeholders are presenting.

Here is an example of how this interactivity can help. In Figure 4-10 you can see the map that I was using when I was working with a team to define the sub-elements of the Employee Center category. One of the questions that popped up was why Tuition Reimbursement was under the category Career Development.

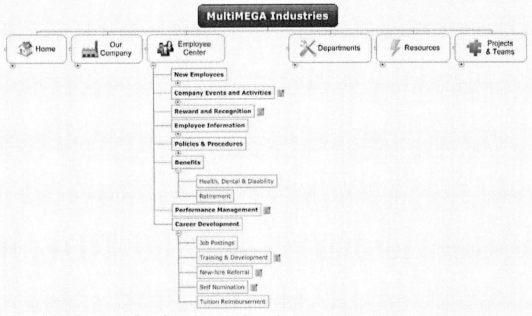

Figure 4-10. The expanded Employee Center in the navigation map

Someone on the team said: "That is clearly a benefit, so move it to Benefits." So I dragged Tuition Reimbursement from under Career Development and dropped it under Benefits. You can see the result on the map in Figure 4-11.

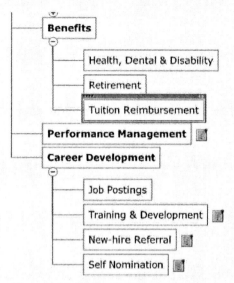

Figure 4-11. Tuition Reimbursement has been dragged and dropped under Benefits

But the head of human resources said: "No, it has to live under Career Development!", so I moved it back, but I offered: "How about we move it, and link to it from the benefits page?" In Figure 4-12, you can see how I satisfied this argument, helping the team choose the final location for the concept, but making sure that people could find it from either spot.

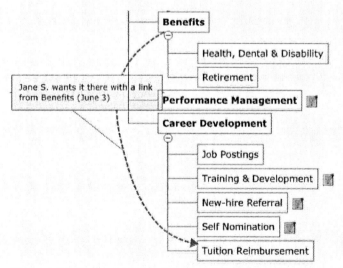

Figure 4-12. The resulting location for Tuition Reimbursement with a link and a label showing why it is there

This change satisfied the structural desires of the manager, but also served as a mental model to the other stakeholders, and certainly many other employees, who may be looking for information about tuition reimbursement.

▓ **Note**   One of the most important principles I try to follow when designing an IA is to make sure that content is not duplicated. There should only be one copy of any document. The obvious reason for this is that when it comes to updating or even deleting a document, it can be very hard to make sure you have synchronized your changes and that every copy is either up to date or deleted. However, not duplicating content doesn't mean that you can't have multiple links to that content. That way it can be found by people who have different mental models of where that document should be found.

A key thought to keep in mind when working interactively with teams like this is that shared understanding does not have to imply complete agreement. When the team members working on this project leave the room, it's not necessary that they all agree with the choices made. However, they should all understand what choices were made and why they were made. For this reason, I often annotate the map (as you saw with the call-out box on the connecting line in Figure 4-12). Fortunately, MindManager makes it easy to hide these call-outs, so the map doesn't get too cluttered, yet they remain accessible for capturing the decision-making process. I am then able to create PDF versions of the map and e-mail them to the workshop participants so they are waiting in their inboxes before they get back to their desks.

As you build out the model of the navigation of the site, it is crucial that you have the key decision makers in the room. If they are not there, the maps will get modified between meetings—or worse, the decision makers will want to make changes when they finally see the site at a time when making changes costs the most.

As I described in Chapter 1, building this navigational map is a bit of a dance with the stakeholders. You will have some people who are adamant about particular structures or layouts—sometimes in ways that will create a hard-to-use or inflexible site. You need to be able to show them how the navigation will really feel and work by navigating the map on the screen, moving items around and showing the impact. Usually, you will be able to make a breakthrough and arrive at a model that enhances usability and meets the users' needs. However, if you can't, we'll talk about usability testing in the next chapter.

Summary

When you design a SharePoint solution, you are building a structure for the organization of information. There is no value to that organization if your users can't find what they're looking for. The navigation is something that is difficult to change after the site is live, so an investment has to be made in ensuring that it is going to work well.

In this chapter, we looked at card sorting as a method for discovering the concepts, groupings, and mental models of the people who will become the eventual users of the intranet site. This relatively simple and practical approach will give you a treasure trove of useful information.

Once you get down to laying out the site navigation, the use of mind mapping as an interactive tool will give you a shared understanding of the options and possible choices in a highly efficient way of working with your stakeholders. I have found this tool to be the best and quickest way to get to signoff via a process that can be easily understood through graphical maps that have been shared for feedback and adjustment prior to going live.

CHAPTER 5

Wireframing for SharePoint

You can't do sketches enough. Sketch everything and keep your curiosity fresh.

John Singer Sargent

When working with a team of people to design a SharePoint site, there is often a desire to get a graphic artist to make a full-fidelity composition of what it will look like when it's finished. By full fidelity I mean a perfect simulation of a finished page (or pages), usually made in Adobe Photoshop. This is always a difficult thing to do properly because the details of what the site is meant to do and how it is meant to work have not yet been defined. When we ask the designer to do this, he or she will have to make assumptions and take wild guesses about how the site will work.

Creating these types of comps too soon leads people to start focusing on things like fonts and colors and pictures at much too early a stage in the project. Stakeholders can tend to take the designer's best guess about how the site *could* work and make those into features of how the site *will* work, which is sometimes not in the best interests of the functionality of the final site.

What we want our stakeholders to do instead is focus on functionality. We want to create pages that are internally consistent and also consistent with other pages across the site. We want to understand how users will make sense of the site, and we want to be able to test those ideas and make changes if necessary. When the site is already a comp in Photoshop, changes are difficult, time consuming, and expensive to make, so we are reluctant to make them.

This chapter will look at various ways to do wireframing and then look at a detailed example of creating wireframes with a popular wireframing tool.

Definitions The terms I use in this chapter are used differently by different people. Just to be clear, here is what I mean: A *wireframe* is a sketch (not necessarily on paper) of a page, with little regard to exact pixel dimensions, colors, images, or fonts. Sometimes I will use the word *mockup* interchangeably with wireframe. When I say *comp* I mean a realistic rendering of what the page will look like when it is done. It uses the images, colors, and fonts that will potentially be used in the real site when it is finished. (Comp is short for composition or comprehensive layout.)

Issues with Wireframing

To accomplish our functional design goals, we want to work not with comps but with wireframes, which are just the bare skeletons of the page. They have nothing to do with font, color, and image; they are about layout and function. Up until a couple of years ago, I always had a problem with wireframing, which was mostly due to the tools I had access to. At the low end was Microsoft Word or PowerPoint. I hated creating wireframes like the one shown in Figure 5-1.

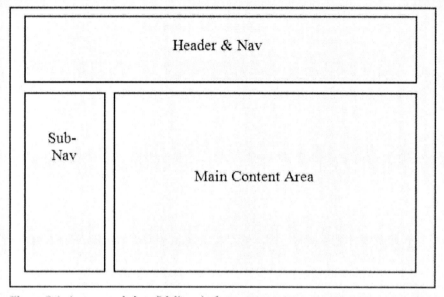

Figure 5-1. An extremely low-fidelity wireframe

To me, this seemed like a waste of time. It was too blocky, with not enough detail to carry any real, useful explanatory power.

At the other end of the spectrum for me was Microsoft Visio. Visio is a program that I love to hate. It is so powerful and capable, but I have never invested the time that I need to really learn it well. I know that sounds silly, but I only use it from time to time, and there never seems to be time to learn its nuances. The result is that every time I have to use Visio, I end up doing a lot of swearing because it never seems to do what I want it to do when I want it to do it.

Now, just because I have trouble with Visio doesn't mean that everyone does. I have seen lots of great Visio wireframes, the most spectacular of which are done by Erik Swenson (you can see these on

his blog: http://erikswenson.blogspot.com and in his book: http://amzn.to/esbranding). Erik creates very high-fidelity Visio diagrams that show exact pixel placement of every element. Figure 5-2 shows a screenshot from Erik Swenson's excellent branding blog of a Visio wireframe.

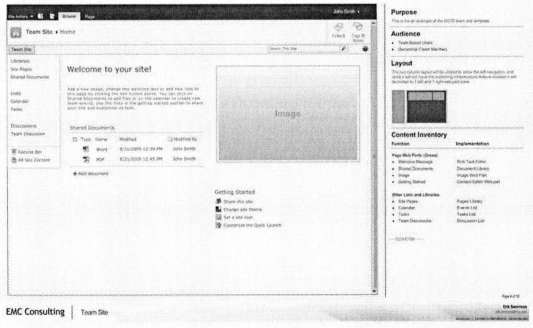

Figure 5-2. A very high-fidelity Visio wireframe. It looks like SharePoint, but it's not.

If you are as experienced and adept as Erik is at Visio and you have taken the time (as Erik has) to build a library of preconstructed components, you may be able to create similar, extremely high-fidelity wireframes. However, I am not that adept, and I also don't feel that I can be as efficient with the client if I were to try to get to this level.

Now, to be fair, even Erik doesn't build every wireframe to this level of detail. Figure 5-3 shows a more schematic Visio wireframe that he has built.

Figure 5-3. A more schematic Visio wireframe

As you can see, this looks a bit less like an actual operating web page, but for me, even this would require a huge time investment to get just right. And, here's the kicker: If the client says: "Can we just try moving that component lower down and move the links into the center area?" My response would be "NOOOOOoooooo!!" because I have invested so much time and energy to make this look good.

So the question I was asking myself a few years ago was: How can I do better than the blocky nature of Word and PowerPoint, yet not get bogged down in Visio hell? The answer I found is a tool called Balsamiq.

Wireframing with Balsamiq Mockups

Balsamiq is a wireframing tool that is a perfect fit for its purpose and, unlike a few other tools I have tried in the intervening years, is super quick and easy to learn to use. You can try it for free or buy it for $79 (at

the time of this printing) at http://www.balsamiq.com. It runs on all platforms (Adobe Air is a prerequisite, which is installed for free as part of the initial setup).

■ **Note** I just love the *story* of Balsamiq. I have been following the product and its creator from just after it was first released in 2008. The product was conceived by Peldi Guilizzoni as a "micro-ISV"; a one-person startup. Peldi has blogged about his entire journey from a one-man-band coder/marketer/support team/CEO into a company that has netted $9 million in sales over its first three years. He now has a staff (or a family, as he likes to call it) of about a dozen people spread around the world. If you have any interest in entrepreneurship done right, you'll love to read Peldi's story (http://www.balsamiq.com/company).

Figure 5-4 shows a sample wireframe made using Balsamiq. As you can see, it has a cartoonish look to it, with a kind of a comic-book font style (no, it's not Comic Sans, but it's close).

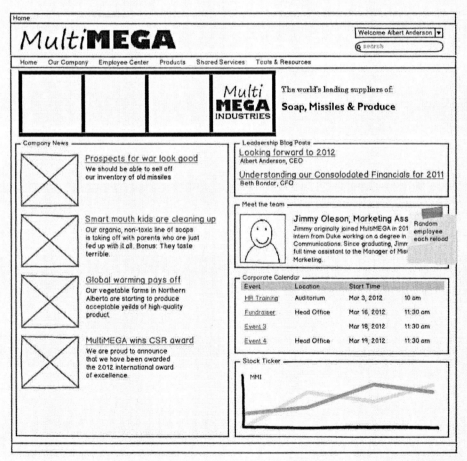

Figure 5-4. A wireframe of the MultiMEGA home page made with Balsamiq

This cartoon style has advantages and disadvantages. One disadvantage is that a client may look at a wireframe like this and say "I can't show that cartoon to my stakeholders!" I believe that this disadvantage can be mitigated with proper expectation setting: When you work with a client, you need to tell them that the wireframes you are producing are purposefully cartoon-like. The reason is that you want to be clear that the wireframe is not meant to represent the final look and feel of the site. The reason you use a cartoonish font is too implicitly state that whatever font we end up using, it won't be this one.

The goal of a low-fidelity wireframe such as this is to focus on the elements that really matter at this stage in the process: How will the page be split up? What is the function of each area? How will navigation work on the home page compared to subpages? These questions need to be answered before you can focus on fonts, pixels, colors, and shapes. At least, that's the ideal-world scenario.

Reality creeps in (again): Your stakeholders often have trouble visualizing what the final site will look like when looking at these wireframes. Even when you explain that the site won't ultimately look like this, they are nervous. They know that while they are taking a series of calculated steps that will bring them to the final result, they may not feel comfortable showing these wireframes to their superiors during status update meetings. They are afraid they will be asked questions they can't answer. So, as much as it pains me to say it, you often need to produce a comp of the site to use as a "taste" of what the future site will look like. So, while I would argue that you should try hard to avoid committing to a design too early in the process, sometimes it is unavoidable and you have to get your graphic designers to create the comp of the final home page.

░ **Tip**   Sometimes you can avoid having to go through the steps of solidifying a design too early by showing the client an example of another site you've built for another division or another organization that gives them a feel for what the finished product can look like. If you have explicit permission from your previous customer to do so, this can be a great solution: You show them the wireframes for the site and then the final site as it turned out. Note: If your stakeholders need to present progress to upper management, this won't work, and you will have to produce something that gives a taste of what the current project's final site will look like.

Using Balsamiq

The Balsamiq interface is quite simple and straightforward to learn to use. There is a collection of grouping buttons that show you subelements of the user interface components available for you to use. In Figure 5-5, the Text button has been selected, showing just the text-related items in the UI Library. You can see that there are items for Breadcrumbs, Icons, Links, and many other elements.

To use any element, you can either just drag it from the UI Library onto the screen to the position where you want it to appear, or start typing its name into the Quick Add box at the top left of the screen.

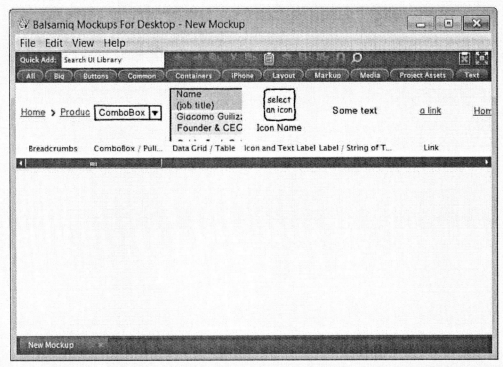

Figure 5-5. The Balsamiq interface

In this section we will walk through a series of steps to build a small mockup.

Dragging from the Toolbar to the Screen

When you drag an element onto the screen, it is automatically opened with a window into which you can enter string content. In this case I have dragged the ComboBox from the UI Interface onto the drawing canvas. As soon as I drop the component, a text window opens into which I can type the text content for that component (Figure 5-6).

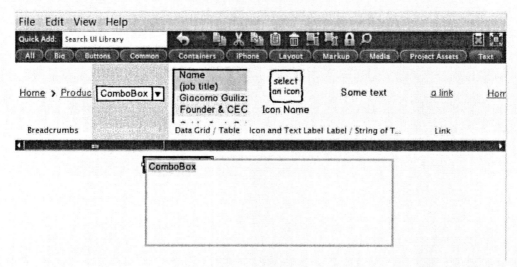

Figure 5-6. Dragging and dropping a UI component onto the canvas

Adding Your Own Content to a Text Box

As you type, your values will replace the initial default text (Figure 5-7). You can enter as many rows as you need, pressing Enter to separate the rows.

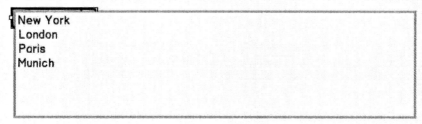

Figure 5-7. Entering values for the ComboBox component

Then, clicking outside of the box finishes the placement process (Figure 5-8).

Figure 5-8. The final ComboBox after clicking outside it

Working with the Properties of an Object

When the item you have added is selected, a floating property box appears. You can drag this box to any location you wish, so that it doesn't obscure anything you want to work with (Figure 5-9).

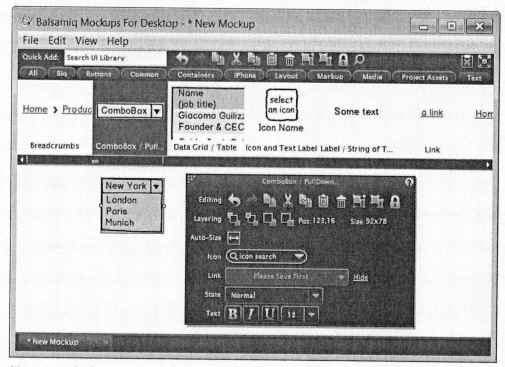

Figure 5-9. The floating property box appear when you select an item

Using these settings (Figure 5-10), you can do things like set the state of the item, it's depth position (in front of or behind other items), and text features (size, weight, etc.).

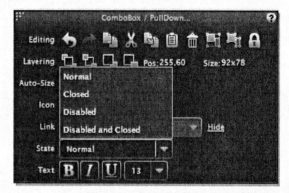

Figure 5-10. Setting the state of the ComboBox

Sizing Containers

This interface makes it very easy to get the objects looking just how you want them. If we choose from the Containers area and drop a window onto the screen (Figure 5-11), we can select its size as we drag the handles (little boxes around the edges). While dragging, the box shows you its pixel dimensions. When you release the drag handle, the box showing the dimensions will disappear.

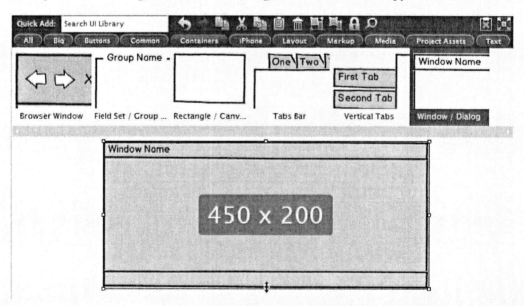

Figure 5-11. Sizing a container

I work with people who use this to set the exact dimensions they intend to use for the final design; however, I usually do not. I usually ignore the dimensions because it is the high-level layout that I am interested in, and the exact sizes of boxes and fonts will be set later.

Working with Multiple Objects

1. We can see that box that I just added has obscured our ComboBox, so I will use the Layering area of the floating menu to send it to behind the previously created object (highlighted in Figure 5-12). Clicking the Send to back icon will move the new window so that it is behind all other objects on the screen. The floating menu helps you by showing you a tool tip for each icon as you mouse-over it. It also shows the keyboard shortcut you can use instead of clicking with the mouse.

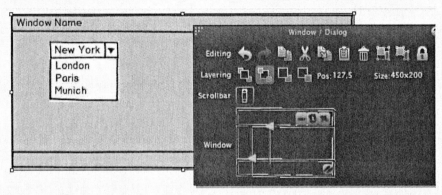

Figure 5-12. Moving an object to appear behind another one

2. Now we see the window is behind the ComboBox. From now on in my design session, I want to make sure that the window does not move around (if I were to accidentally click it to move it). So I will click the padlock item called Lock in Place (Figure 5-13), which will prevent it from moving.

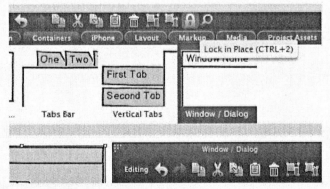

Figure 5-13. Locking an object so that it can't be modified by clicking the Padlock icon (shown with blue background)

3. If I ever want to move that window, I can unlock it by right-clicking it and selecting Unlock Window from the context menu that pops up (Figure 5-14).

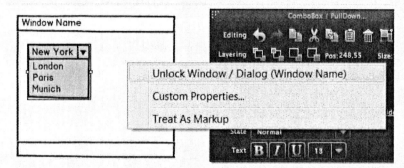

Figure 5-14. Unlocking an item that has been previously locked

Making good use of locking and unlocking will save you countless headaches as it is easy to mistakenly move the wrong object, which slows you down as you try to keep everything properly aligned.

Aligning Objects

Aligning objects as you add them to your design is very easily done, as automatic alignment guides appear when dragging and sizing objects. Add a button to the design and you can see the blue center-line and gray right-alignment guide as you resize the button (Figure 5-15).

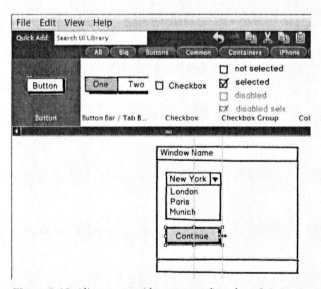

Figure 5-15. Alignment guides appear when dragging components

I was happy to see these autoalignment guides added to Balsamiq. It just makes it so much faster to get everything looking just right. Especially because of the hand-drawn look of the boxes, it can be tricky to make sure they are perfectly aligned.

Linking Mockups to Simulate Behavior

One of the most interesting things you can do with this tool is to link multiple mockups together so you can test usability of the interface. To do this:

1. First, save your current design.

2. Once this is done, each object allows you to link it to another, preexisting page you have already built, which is saved into the same folder where you have saved the current page. In Figure 5-16 you can see that the Continue button has been selected, as that is where you want to link from when clicked. The Link item in the floating toolbar can now be switched from No Link to any other saved mockup.

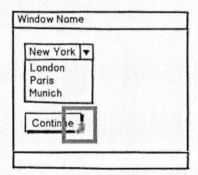
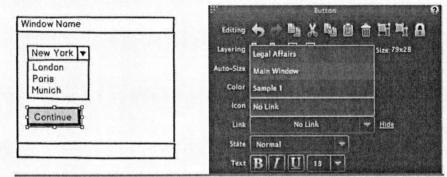

Figure 5-16. Linking the Continue button to another saved page

3. Once linked, the object has a little arrow attached to it, indicating that it is a link (Figure 5-17).

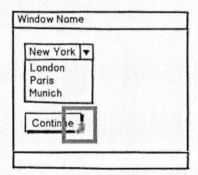

Figure 5-17. Link indicator arrow

4. When you want to test the user interface, you can ask to see the mockup as a "Full Screen Presentation," as shown in Figure 5-18. When you do so, you get a clean screen with your mockup displayed and a large arrow you can use to point at various objects.

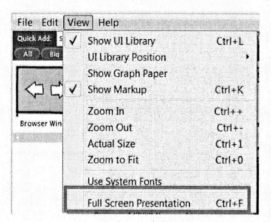

Figure 5-18. How to show a full-screen presentation

5. When you mouse-over a link, the pointer turns into a hand, and below the hand it shows you what the destination screen will be when you click the link (Figure 5-19).

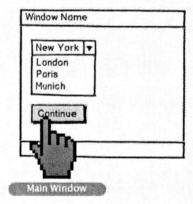

Figure 5-19. Clicking an active link in a linked mockup

The full-screen view with active links makes it very easy to demonstrate the design to your stakeholders. It allows you to get a feel for the flow of the site. You can show your stakeholders what the process of using the site will feel like to a user.

Sharing Your Mockups

If your clients have a copy of Balsamiq, you can send them the files and they can experiment with different ideas themselves. If they don't have a copy of the tool, you can create a PDF from your files. If the file has internal links, they will be linked to one another in the PDF. This will allow your clients to walk through the site navigation even if they don't have Balsamiq.

Another alternative for sharing is to purchase a subscription to MyBalsamiq (Figure 5-20).

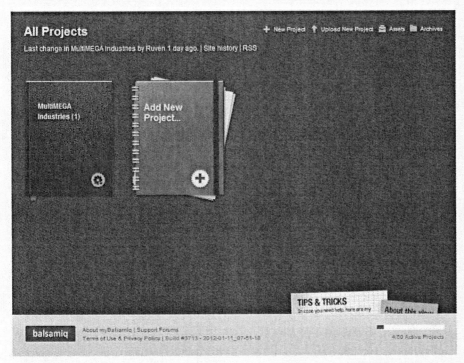

Figure 5-20. The MyBalsamiq.com home screen, showing my projects

MyBalsamiq is a service that allows you to upload your wireframes to a site where you can share the mockups with your stakeholders and edit them interactively right on the site.

Using Symbols

Another feature of Balsamiq that makes building the wireframes easy is the concept of *symbols*. These are reusable components that have a shared central copy. For example, you could create a basic page that includes the logo and the top navigation for your project. Now, every page you create can use that symbol. If you decided to change your top navigation, you only need to edit the symbol to fix every page.

To create reusable symbols for your project, do the following:

1. Select all the elements on the screen by clicking the mouse and dragging the selection box over all the elements.

2. Use the Grouping icon on the floating menu to group them, then name the group and click Convert To Symbol (Figure 5-21).

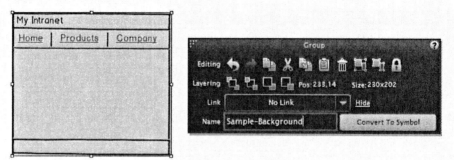

Figure 5-21. *Creating a symbol*

3. You will now be able to see the grouped item in the Assets area of the UI Library. You can then use the symbol as if it were one of the built-in elements and build your UI on top of it. In this example, I have used the symbol to drag an object representing a page onto the screen (Figure 2-22).

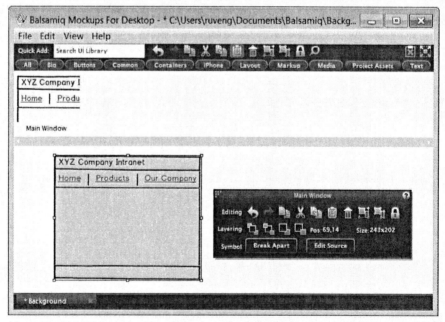

Figure 5-22. *Adding a symbol to the canvas*

Now that you are using the symbol, if something changes, only the master copy of the symbol needs to be modified and all the objects built from it will automatically be updated. For example, if you rename one of the main menu items, all the pages that use that symbol will automatically change as well. This is a very important, time-saving feature to have when you are creating a lot of wireframes for a project.

Markup Elements

Balsamiq supports a number of markup elements that make it easy to turn the wireframe into an annotated document (Figure 5-23). Menu options allow you to show or hide the markup. This can be helpful during a live demonstration.

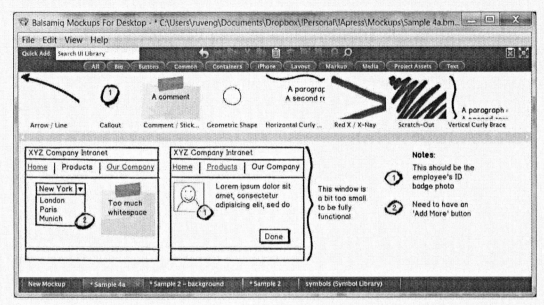

Figure 5-23. Illustrating some markup elements

This concludes our walk-through of Balsamiq. I have continued to be impressed with it as a well-priced, very functional tool. It is also well supported, and there are new features added or enhancements made all the time. I recommend it as a tool that hits a perfect sweet-spot of ease of use and power.

From Wireframe to SharePoint

In Figure 5-24, you can see the SharePoint site that was constructed from the wireframe in Figure 5-4. I am most definitely not a graphic artist, and I haven't implemented anything beyond out-of-the-box SharePoint, but you can see quite a good connection between the original wireframe and the resulting SharePoint site.

Figure 5-24. The final MultiMEGA site built from the wireframe design

It is usually not the case that you would go directly from the wireframe to the SharePoint site, because there are a number of things to be worked out that are not covered by the wireframe, things such as fonts and font sizes, colors, and images. These items are the purview of the graphic artist, who will create the comp (as described at the start of this chapter). It is the comp that needs to get sign-off first, before the site gets built, as it defines the style guide (the document that defines all the style elements) for the site as a whole.

Impression Testing

Impression testing is a technique for verifying the usability of the pages you create that tracks how users click your wireframes when asked to perform a task such as "How would you find the news archive?" or "Find the salary and benefits policies."

Impression testing is a fantastic tool that you can use to discover whether your assumptions during solution design are accurate. Impression testing allows you to find out how accurate your assumptions are as users are performing tasks using the wireframes. Online impression testing tools also provide some great visual analysis that you can use to improve or refine your solution.

A special type of report called a *heat map* uses colors to show where users clicked on the wireframes or images you assigned to each task. This way, you can see exactly where users are clicking for each particular task or if they are having trouble locating the information in the task. See Figure 5-25 for an example of what this can look like. (Note: The figure is a simulation taken from a real example.)

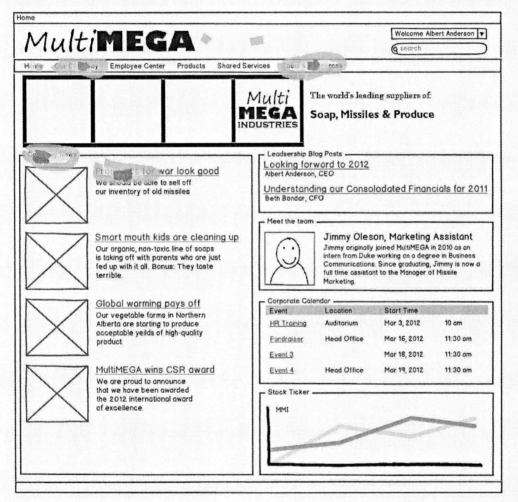

Figure 5-25. Example (simulated) heat map from the task we previously tested

Although impression testing can be done in a face-to-face meeting, a far better way is to use online impression testing tools such as the Optimal Workshop's Chalkmark online screenshot testing software

(http://www.optimalworkshop.com/chalkmark.htm).

To set up an impression test, you first need a number of tasks you would like to test. A good rule of thumb is to identify five to ten of the users' most likely performed tasks.

You also need a comp or a wireframe of your solution. If you have already implemented your solution in SharePoint, you can simply take a screenshot and use this. However the great thing about impression testing is that you can also use a wireframe that you have developed as a proof of concept before implementing this in SharePoint. By using impression testing before implementation you can quickly resolve any issues before you implement, saving you both time and rework effort. The same applies if you are adding new functionality after the site is live and you would like to test it before making a change.

Now that you have your tasks, wireframes, and screenshots ready to go, you simply create an impression test in Chalkmark. You can then send out the URL to selected users within your organization and ask them to be participants. It's best to run this with a number of different participants. Since this is online, you can run it with as many participants as you like. The more information you gather, the more statistically significant your results will be.

Analyzing Impression Testing Results

After all of your participants have completed the impression tests, you can view the results through Chalkmark. By far the most valuable information you will get from impression testing is the heat map.

The heat map will show you where users clicked on a particular area on your wireframe or image for the task that you have defined. It's a great way to see if your IA makes sense to users. Impression testing is a great way to ensure that users understand your design and can actually use it for the purpose intended.

Summary

Low-cost tools that help you rapidly build and try page layouts and then work with your users and stakeholders to verify they will do the job they were designed to do have been a tremendous boon to IAs. Working with your stakeholders to achieve a shared understanding of what will and won't work and fitting that in with what is desired from a design or aesthetic can sometimes be tricky. For most intranets, the function is the most important thing: People will be using this every day, and it has to do the job. But how it looks matters a lot to people as well, and that desire sometimes forces compromises. Testing the designs with actual end users before implementation will highlight the places where your users are having problems and allow you to adjust before the design is finalized.

This chapter has walked you through the basics (and there is not a lot more than the basics) of Balsamiq as a rapid wireframing and lightweight prototyping tool, and then looked at how impression testing can show you the real-world results of your designs and whether your users will be able to achieve the goals you have set for your SharePoint deployment.

CHAPTER 6

Complexity, Wickedness, and Dialogue Mapping

"Something wicked this way comes."

—Ray Bradbury

I had been using mind mapping techniques for more than a year when I first met Paul Culmsee at the Best Practices Conference in San Diego. Paul showed me a whole new world of mapping that took what I had been doing to an entirely new level. He led me into the world of "wicked problems and dialogue mapping," which he had learned from Jeff Conklin. This chapter will give you an introduction to the material I learned from Jeff and Paul, but I am going to limit it to illustrating one specific aspect of a SharePoint project: scoping.

This chapter is a little bit different from the others in this book: My goal throughout has been to give you techniques and tools that are fairly easy to learn and put into practice right away. This chapter covers a technique you can't pick up overnight. You will need to read the source material carefully and practice it diligently, or even take some training, before you will become proficient. However, I still think it is worth covering this approach in some detail, because it is one of the most important things you can learn if you want to move past the "best practices" approach and start to effectively tackle real-world problems.

What Are Wicked Problems?

It basically comes down to this: There are problems that are tame, and there are problems that are wicked. Here is an example of a tame problem: How can we create a mission to land a man on the moon? As it turns out, this is an exceedingly complicated problem, but the goal can be summed up succinctly: Fly a man to the moon and bring him back to earth alive.

Here is an example of a wicked problem: How can we reduce poverty in your city? The thing that makes this problem wicked is that even getting agreement on the goal would be a nightmare. How do we measure poverty? Reduce it by how much? What approaches will definitely work? What approaches will definitely not work?

I will summarize the definition of wicked problems, but I highly recommend that you read Jeff Conklin's book *Dialogue Mapping* and Paul Culmsee and Kailash Awati's *Heretic's Guide to Best Practices* for deep drill-downs into these issues.

Let's look at the major characteristics of wicked problems in the context of a SharePoint project.

1. You don't really understand the problem until after you've developed the solution.

When you approach the implementation of a SharePoint project for your customer, you don't really have a full understanding of the issues, problems, politics, operations, personalities, and a host of other things about that organization, team, or department. You may be well into the design or even build a solution before you hear that they have another, stand-alone system that will need to be integrated. Or, there may be a secret merger in the works that gets announced just before you go live.

The very act of developing the solution exposes more (and more and more) of the problem that you had no chance of knowing about before you started. The result is you either have to push many issues off as being "out of scope," thus diminishing the value of what you deliver, or you have to expand the scope and either get more resources (time/money) or your project goes over budget and is late. None of these options is very appealing.

2. You don't know when you've accomplished your goal.

If you haven't clearly articulated concrete goals for the project, you never know whether you're finished. If your goal is to "use SharePoint to increase collaboration in the enterprise" or "enhance communication," how are you going to know whether you have done this? Some of your stakeholders may have a detailed mental model of what this looks like in their minds, but that may not match the model of a different stakeholder, and many others may not have given it any detailed thought at all.

In an earlier chapter, I talked about project success being driven by shared commitment to a goal, and that to get to shared commitment you need to have shared understanding. If your stakeholders have different or undefined ideas of what success looks like, you have no hope of succeeding.

3. Solutions are not right or wrong, they are just better or worse.

There is no objective "right solution" to any problem. The reasons for success or failure can be hard to point to: Maybe you had a great solution, but it was poorly communicated. Communication planning for SharePoint projects is crucially important: People don't like change, even if it's to improve a system. You have to tell them it's coming, why it's coming, and why they'll be better off once it is in place. Maybe the solution was really well communicated but usability was weak. It is very possible that some people will say the solution was good, but others may disagree. It is fundamental with wicked problems that there may be no initial agreement on what the real problem is and what success would look like.

4. Every wicked problem is unique.

Although there are types of projects (e.g., corporate intranet, public-facing web site) that have grouped sets of similarities, there are enough differences between organizations, teams, and projects that make each problem different enough to add wicked levels of complexity.

This point contradicts a point I make elsewhere in the book: There can be a lot of similarity and overlap between SharePoint projects. However, I am going to let this contradiction stand because while the projects are similar from a *technical* point of view, the culture and personalities involved in a project can be quite different. It is this social complexity that explains the unique aspects of each project.

5. Every solution to a wicked problem is a one-shot operation.

If you are building a solution that requires a lot of planning, design, and engineering, it is too time consuming and expensive to build it multiple times. You have to get it right on the first pass. The killer is that the first wicked problem issue states that you don't understand the problem until after you've built the solution. As Conklin says in *Dialogue Mapping*, "this is the 'Catch 22' of wicked problems": You are stuck in a paradox of needing to build it to know what's required, but not having the time or money to build it multiple times.

6. Social complexity.

There is another factor that acts along with problem wickedness to derail the solution you want to build. You are working with groups of people who are not all clones of one another. They have their own ideas, their own mental models, and their own personal goals and desires. When you couple this with a wicked problem, one that does not lend itself to obvious or provably correct answers, there is bound to be conflict and fragmentation. This can be particularly painful on SharePoint projects because the solution will touch so many people in so many areas, with a social complexity that can rival the United Nations!

The goal is to apply the technique of dialogue mapping to drive from fragmentation to coherence through shared commitment and shared understanding.

Dialogue Mapping

The technique of dialogue mapping is not a silver bullet that solves the issues of wicked problems and social complexity. What it does do is make meetings (the place where much of the project planning work takes place) much more effective. If you've ever been to meetings where you feel that the same stuff keeps getting rehashed or where forceful people take over the proceedings, preventing new ideas from surfacing, then you will appreciate what dialogue mapping can do.

Before I learned dialogue mapping, I had had a lot of practice using mind mapping techniques to facilitate meetings. In doing so, I had already discovered two of the three ingredients that Conklin identifies (Figure 6-1): facilitation/mapping and shared display. The third ingredient I had not yet learned was IBIS notation.

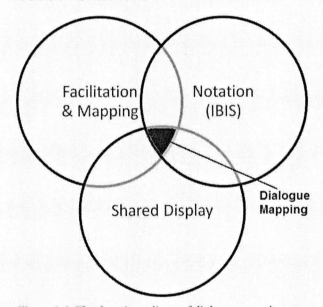

Figure 6-1. The three ingredients of dialogue mapping

IBIS Notation

Issue-Based Information System (IBIS) notation (Figure 6-2) is deceptively simple.

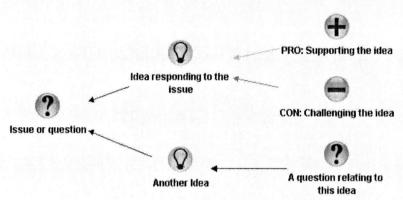

Figure 6-2. The IBIS notation

As you can see, IBIS notation has only four primary symbols and a small set of rules. In this map you can see the basic elements: There are questions, which are responded to with ideas. Ideas can have PROs or CONs, which support or challenge the idea. Any idea or PRO or CON can be responded to with another question.

The wonderful thing about the simplicity of this notation is that even though it can take some practice to become fluent in its use, it is immediately understood by the participants at a meeting. You don't even need to explain yourself when you set up the projector and start mapping a meeting. The participants start to see what is going on right away.

■ **Note** IBIS maps can be created on paper or using different types of software. The most commonly used software for IBIS is called Compendium. This software can be downloaded for free from the Compendium Institute (http://compendium.open.ac.uk/institute/). I recommend that you start by downloading the Compendium software and follow along with the instructional material in Conklin's book.

In the first example above, I used the Compendium software to create the map to give you an example of how Compendium looks. As we discussed in Chapter 2, I am a fan of MindManager, so I also use it to create IBIS maps. There are slight differences in how the maps appear. In Figure 6-3, I have re-created the same illustrative map using MindManager to show you the similarities and differences. The key difference for me is the ability to use the MindManager collapsing capability that allows me to hide sections of the map by clicking the minus links. The disadvantage to using MindManager over Compendium is that Compendium makes it just a bit easier to add the nodes with the right icons attached.

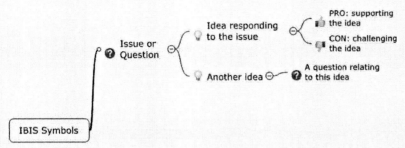

Figure 6-3. The sample IBIS map rendered in MindManager

Now that we understand the basic node types, let's look at an example mapping session.

1. We are asking the question: How can our site be more "social"? We begin by asking our initial question. IBIS maps always start with a question, but not just any question; you want to start with an open-ended question that can't just be answered with "yes" or "no."

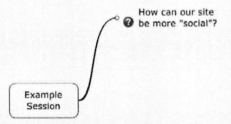

2. Someone has the idea: Let's implement My Sites. We add this idea, and attach the "idea" icon to it.

3. We immediately get a quick PRO and two CONs. Note that we try to order them so the PROs are on top of the CONs. Just like the use of icons, these little touches help with the readability of the map.

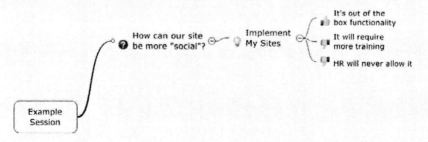

4. We start to explore the CON that human resources would never allow it, asking "Why not?" (Short questions such as "Why not?" or "How so?" can act as connectors that keep the map following the IBIS rules—you must avoid the temptation to directly connect the ideas to the PROs and CONs.) We get a couple of responses.

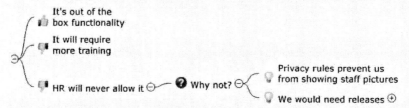

5. We can now carry this further, exploring the privacy issues, and asking how much effort it would take to get releases. Notice in the image below that "We could make this an "opt-in" shown as a CON. Don't get confused. While it seems that this is a PRO toward using My Sites, it is a CON against the argument that "Privacy rules prevent us from showing staff pictures." The argument is always in reference to the node that precedes it, not the original argument.

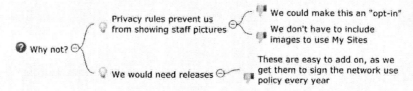

We now have quite quickly and efficiently captured the thought process and argumentation of this important discussion (Figure 6-4).

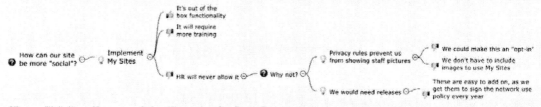

Figure 6-4. How the map of the discussion looks so far

I'd like to explain a few things about why this mapping process is so incredibly useful. This map does a couple of really powerful things for us: It captures and assists with the thought process that the team is working through. And it makes arguments visible, so they don't need to be rehashed. We've all been in meetings where there is a type of person who may slam down his or her fist and ask "Why are we discussing My Sites? I've already told you that HR will never allow it!" When this happens, you can point to the relevant section of the map and ask: "Are there more reasons that we haven't listed yet?" It then becomes clear to the fist-banger that just yelling about something that's already in the map doesn't serve any purpose. This is a tremendous time saver and allows the team to move on from proclamations that things simply "won't work." They get to explore the alternatives and make a decision based on that exploration.

Another valuable benefit is that later, in three months, when someone asks "Why didn't we do X?" we can refer to the map that shows not just the decision, but the argumentation that led to the decision. This can be a huge savings because without the argumentation, and under pressure, someone may say "I don't know why we said 'no' to My Sites, let's put them in." There may have been some really important thinking that went into a tough decision six months earlier, but no one remembers what that was. Now, a spur of the moment reversal opens up the whole can of worms that was previously discussed. If you had the map to refer to, you could quickly remind everyone about the issues and discussion that led to the previous decision. The bottom line is that the map captures not just the choices made but why they were made.

Dialogue Mapping for Scoping

One of the toughest problems I face when meeting a new client is getting onto the same page with them about the scope of the project. I often have not met the client until the kick-off meeting, and all decisions that were made up to that point were dealt with by others. I'm not criticizing the presales team: They have usually done a great job, but they are not project implementers, and so it is crucial that the implementation team and the client align their visions of the solution to be developed.

The way I use dialogue mapping for this task is to prepare a map with some of the key questions that need to be well understood if we are to have a chance at success. In Figure 6-5 you can see the original map.

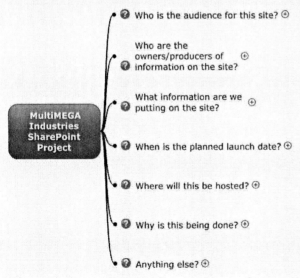

Figure 6-5. The starting point for a scoping exercise

119

We then work through the map with the client team, building out and exploring the answers to each question and adding new ones as they are raised. Let's investigate each of these in turn.

Looking at the Audience

In Figure 6-6 you can see the process we went through to understand who the audience is (a very quick answer) and who the owners and producers of content on the site are (an answer that had to be explored more deeply).

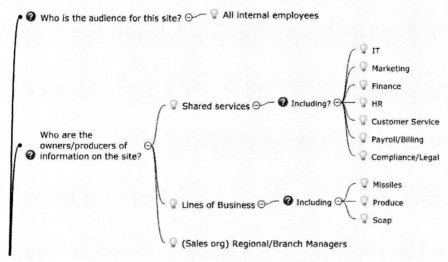

Figure 6-6. Building out the scope map, looking at the audience and owners

Looking into the Content Owners and Authors

After working through this section, we can see the various departments and teams we will have to work with when we define the content owners.

We then started to explore the type of information they wanted to see on the site and saw details emerge, which resulted in Figure 6-7.

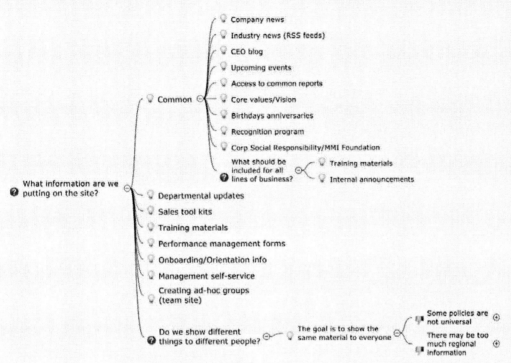

Figure 6-7. Content analysis

Understanding the "Why" for This Project

When we explored the "why" of this project (Figure 6-8), we learned of their goals to bring the newly merged units together with one vision. One thing that is important to understand is that we were not moving toward solution building, and the actual final specification, defining what would be built, was different in some respects from what was said during this session. However, without this map, we would not have been able to create a specification document that would meet the vision of the key stakeholders.

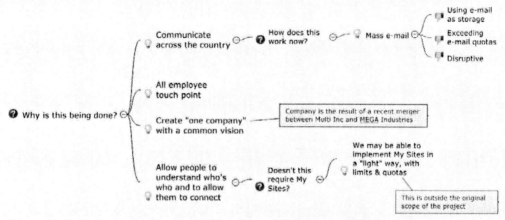

Figure 6-8. Exploring the motivations for building this site

Final Elements

During the discussion, the question of workflows and data entry forms came up. We added those under "Future Capability" (Figure 6-9). But then another very important issue arose: multilingual requirements. Anyone who has ever worked on multilingual sites knows that it creates a huge amount of complexity in many areas. Site design and structure become much more complicated. Even worse, the management of the site going forward has many more complexities as well. You can see from this map, that there was a tough dilemma to be solved. It became clear that this decision would need input from others within the company, because the decision had serious costs and legal implications.

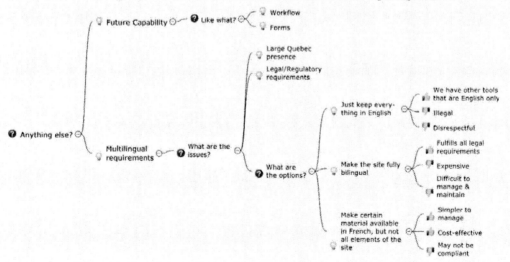

Figure 6-9. Additional areas of interest

I hope these examples of mapping have shown you the power of the tool. The other great thing about this approach is that clients love it. They are always impressed by how clearly this approach captures their thought processes, and it gives them confidence that our team knows what we are doing and that we are likely to deliver a solution that really will solve their problems.

Another View of Complexity

Dave Snowden (http://www.cognitive-edge.com/blogs/dave/) has also built a model for discussing complexity called the Cynefin (pronounced kin-evan) Framework (Figure 6-10). His model has a lot of great ideas in it, and a lot of thought and research has been put into this approach, but I want to discuss just a couple of the key elements for our purposes.

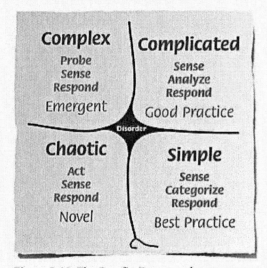

Figure 6-10. The Cynefin Framework

The Simple Domain

A lot of books you will read or sessions you will attend at conferences will bill themselves as presenting "best practices." This often warrants a derisive laugh from experienced SharePointers because they know few situations lend themselves to simple "cookbook" best practices.

In the Cynefin model, only those tasks where the cause-and-effect relationship is fully understood by all can be dealt with as a best practice. Best practices are repeatable and obviously so. For example, you know that a certain percentage of your users are color-blind, so it is a best practice to not make an important operation dependent on distinguishing between those two colors.

The Complicated Domain

The next level is one where the relation between causes and effects can be understood, but it requires expertise and experience in order to be able to do the proper analysis and come up with the right response. Note: In this case (as with the simple domain) there *is* a right answer. It's just harder to get to.

An example here would be "Should we use one site collection or multiple site collections for our site?" This is an issue that does not have a cookie-cutter answer (though some would like it to be). There are a number of considerations, pro and con, that need to be thought through. Some options will add complexity, and others will limit the growth of your site. You need to have a thorough understanding of what the issues are in order to make a correct choice.

Snowden defines "Good Practice" as choosing one of several possible answers, but choosing the right one is not rote, you have to figure it out based on analysis.

The Complex Domain

In the complex domain, no matter how experienced or expert you are, you just can't predict what will happen. You have to attempt low-risk activities and see what the response looks like. Based on the responses, you can either stop that activity or increase it, all the time watching for the reaction. As you proceed in this domain, you find approaches that work in your unique environment but may not work in other environments. Snowden calls this "emergent practice." A SharePoint example may concern deciding how much freedom to give site owners in team sites. In one organization, a certain level of limitation may be tolerated, but in another, too many limits could kill adoption and no one will use the new system.

The Chaotic Domain

There is no cause and effect in the chaotic domain. As a result, you can't make any predictions, you just have to do *something* and then be ready to very quickly deal with what happens as a result. You may have heard the term *analysis paralysis*. I think this is what happens when you desperately try to take something from the complex/chaotic domain and analyze it hard enough to move it into the complicated domain (which is impossible).

SharePoint is a technically complicated platform. It takes truly expert knowledge to be able to follow good practices. But when you are dealing with the social and political complexity of issues like "Who owns this content?" and "How much freedom should we give our users?," you find yourself on the left side of the Cynefin diagram. You have to make decisions and monitor the results closely, always being ready to respond to both successes and failures, continually adjusting as you steer (shakily) toward your destination.

Summary

This chapter looked at wicked problems, SharePoint project scoping, and a taxonomy of complexity (Cynefin).

I only touched briefly on both wicked problems and the Cynefin framework. These are very rich and detailed approaches to understanding problems: Their proponents have spent years analyzing and refining them. I hope you will take the time to investigate these further, but the point I wanted to make here is that if you can recognize the type of problem you are working with, you can avoid common pitfalls, such as trying to apply hard and fast best practices. Some of the biggest issues we have in SharePoint projects are the ones that need to be dealt with first:

- What are we really trying to do?

- Who are the real influencers and decision makers?

- Do we understand the goals of all the stakeholders?

- Do all the stakeholders agree with one another on the goals?

The use of visual tools, and especially the IBIS system of issue and dialogue mapping, can help you to get to the bottom of these questions early in the project. An added benefit is that the maps you build work well to document the thought processes that led to the final decisions. I cannot overemphasize the importance of this. After all, how will you know whether the project has a chance at success if the people who will be judging that success have different mental pictures of what success looks like? Because of SharePoint's all-encompassing nature, its own complexity, and the fact that most stakeholders don't really have a strong idea of what SharePoint does or how it works, these approaches are crucial to success in your SharePoint projects.

The next two chapters are concerned with a really interesting and powerful aspect of SharePoint: Dealing with business processes, understanding how to document and analyze them, and understanding how to think about SharePoint as a business-process enabler that can make a measurable difference for your SharePoint customers.

CHAPTER 7

Business Process Mapping

If you can't describe what you are doing as a process, you don't know what you're doing.

—W. Edwards Deming

A lot of what we have been talking about so far is concerns mapping the information for a web site. We have mapped the navigational structure and we have mapped the content structure. What we have not done at all is map (or 'model') any type of *flow*. Information is not static, it doesn't just sit there. Information has to be created, it may change over time, it may move (change locations), and it may be archived or deleted at some point. In order to understand everything about our data, not just where the information lives or how it is structured, we need to be able to map the data flow as well. Fortunately, there is a well-established body of knowledge on how to map these flows called business process modeling (BPM).

Note BPM goes beyond just mapping, it can be expressed as a "language" that lets you simulate, or even execute, business processes, hence the title business process modeling. I will just be sticking to mapping processes in this chapter.

BPM is not just about document flows; it is used to model all kinds of business processes, from hiring, to purchasing, to complaints management. There is a whole discipline devoted to BPM, and there is a formal notation standard that governs the creation of these models called Business Process Modeling Notation (BPMN), which uses specific shapes and connectors to capture an accurate representation of a business process. In fact, these models can be so complete and accurate that BPMN can be used as a kind of programming language that process automation systems can execute to carry out a process. There are many types of tools that enable the creation of BPMs, and many can validate the notation to ensure that it specifies a process that is able to run.

This chapter is not about rigorous and formal process mapping. That is a subject for another book (and many have been written), and I can assure you that I am not an expert in the subject. However, if we want to understand how to apply SharePoint to solve our customers business problems, we need to understand how the information and documents support the process flow; we can do that by taking advantage of tools to capture this flow in a graphical form and share it with our stakeholders.

You may at first find it odd that there are two chapters on business processes in this book, but the importance of this subject cannot be understated, and the two chapters have different purposes: In this chapter we discuss the tools for capturing and documenting business processes and also discuss simple workflow implementation. In Chapter 8, the emphasis is on understanding business needs, identifying potential processes that need to be improved, and then measuring the return on investment (ROI) of the processes you automate.

SharePoint and Workflow

I once heard someone say "SharePoint is like a flashlight that illuminates every bad process within a company." This is true, because when you are working on a project that involves document organization (or reorganization), you become aware of the process issues that go along with document management.

During your discovery sessions, you'll hear a lot about things "falling through the cracks" or other process failures. The problem is that many SharePoint projects reveal a paradox: Our clients want to become more streamlined, automated, and *better* at what they do, so they hope (they hope *really hard*) that SharePoint will do this for them. But I have found that when most organizations sign up for a SharePoint project, they generally think they are signing up for an information organization project, not a business process reengineering project. They don't allocate a budget to do the hard work involved in tearing apart an existing process, understanding how it works, and then designing a robust solution. They certainly don't expect their SharePoint team to be spending a lot of time working on this.

Now, this is not always the case. In Chapter 8 you will see how business process projects can work. And not only do they work; they also have a much easier to measure ROI then straight portal or collaboration projects. But to make this work, your stakeholders have to know going in that your focus will be on process modeling and workflow building.

If you are lucky enough to be asked to solve a business process, you may find that you have jumped out of the frying pan and into the fire! You will be asked to create a logical, functional workflow for a process that is in all likelihood chaotic: It cannot be automated (yet), because it probably cannot even be coherently described. Now, that last sentence may seem provocatively over the top, but it is often true: The operations of many businesses run in a very ad hoc way. The outcome you can expect for any particular process depends very much on who is doing the work. Despite what the internal operations manual says (if there even is one), the way that individuals get things done usually depends on personal relationships between coworkers who know the right department and the right person to call. In many organizations, nothing can really get done until you absorb this specialized inside knowledge. The fact that this hard-won inside knowledge may be seen as job security by some people makes your job all that much more difficult.

Workflow is sometimes looked at as the silver bullet that will allow a company to solve its worst problems, like wanting to "never be late with delivery again." The problem is that you can't automate a process that is not perfectly understood and defined. As soon as something happens that doesn't fit the automated workflow, you have to break out of the automated flow and start taking manual steps. When you do that, you can no longer trust the workflow; your reports can't give you the true state of your operation. And once the system is no longer trusted, everything breaks down. This is one reason why I usually shy away from automated workflow in the early stages of a SharePoint project. As I stated in Chapter 1, my three rules for SharePoint are: simplicity, simplicity, simplicity. For example, let's look at a simple kind of process management can be the tracking of the status of a collection of proposals.

The Very Simple Approach

When I start to work with SharePoint process, I tend to start really small: I set up a drop-down that captures the current state of a document. For example, imagine a proposal library where each document had a cover page that had checkboxes with the following labels as shown in the Status drop-down in Figure 7-1.

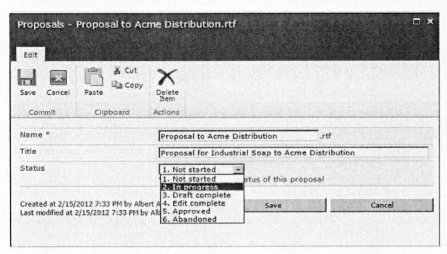

Figure 7-1. Using a Status drop-down to track progress

Now you have an easy way of tracking your proposals just by creating a custom view (Figure 7-2). In this view I have grouped the proposals by Status, allowing you to track the state of all outstanding items. Even something as simple as this can go a long way to solve the "falling through the cracks" issues that many companies face.

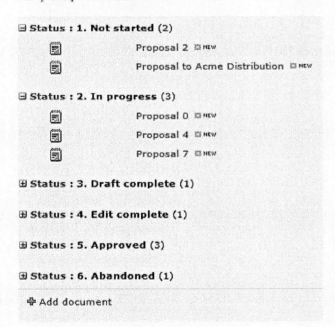

Figure 7-2. The Proposals Library grouped by Status with two of the groups expanded

▓ **Tip** You may have noticed that I have numbered my status columns. For example: "1. Not started." The reason I do this is because the groups themselves would normally appear in alphabetical order (ascending or, optionally, descending), which doesn't work well in this case as I want to see them in the sequence order that makes sense for my purposes.

The way to set the view to group the results like this can be a bit hard to spot if you are new to SharePoint. You have to scroll down near the bottom of the screen when you edit the view and expand the Group By option, as shown in Figure 7-3. Then you can select which field to group by (you can group by a second level as well, but I am only using one here). You then can choose whether to show the groups expanded or collapsed by default—I usually choose Collapsed.

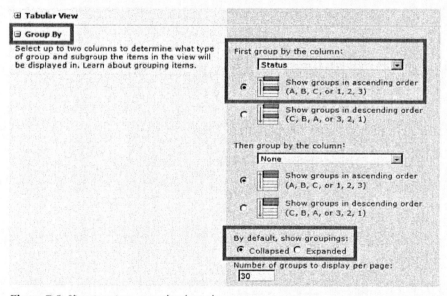

Figure 7-3. How to set up grouping in a view

When you combine grouping like this with version tracking, you can go back to any proposal and see who changed the status, when it was changed, and what it was changed to. If your list or library has versioning turned on, you can use the item drop-down to view the history of that item. When you ask to see the history, you will get a pop-up window that looks like the one in Figure 7-4.

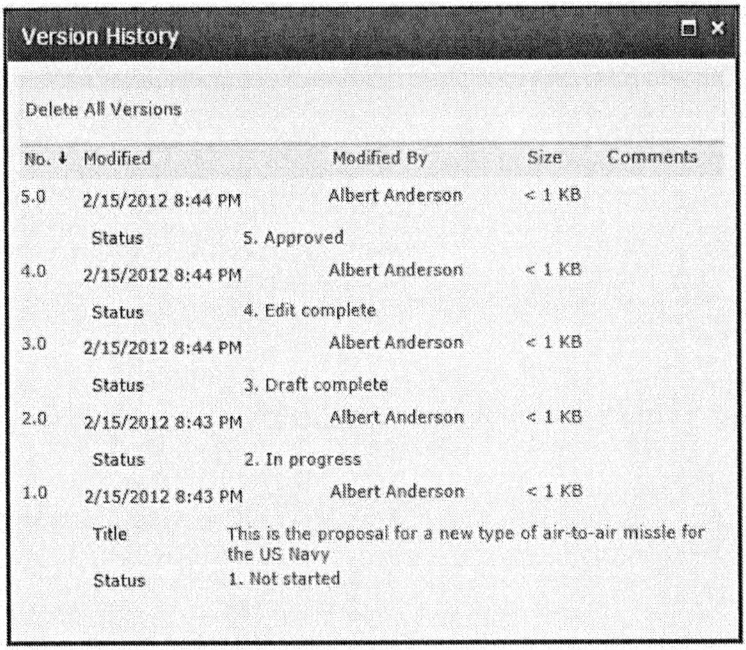

Figure 7-4. Document history showing status changes

What I have just shown you is a very simple approach to managing documents as they flow through their lifecycle. This is not a fully robust system, however. I haven't looked at the problem of a document sitting in a particular state for a long time or of someone skipping steps and going right from "In progress" to "Approved." There is also nothing to enforce the rule that only a manager can mark the document as approved. However, once you create this type of extremely simple solution, you will quickly find which elements work well and which ones require more power or alternative approaches.

In the next section, we turn our attention to some tools for capturing and documenting business processes.

Tools for Process Mapping

There are a number of vendors who make sophisticated tools for mapping and managing complex process flows within SharePoint. The high-end vendors include Global360 and K2. They create tools that can interface between SharePoint and other outside systems. Nintex makes a tool that runs inside SharePoint and integrates very well with it. Nintex is also the single most popular SharePoint add on (according to a presentation I saw by Gartner at the 2011 Microsoft SharePoint Conference). All of these tools include graphical editors that are used to capture and create workflows. Those tools are beyond the scope of this book; the tools from Global360 and K2 are incredibly powerful and complex, but if you need that level of power, they are essential. Nintex is much less complex, but within SharePoint it is very powerful. It also has a graphical way of capturing workflows and implementing them. In this section, we will look at two tools that are great for capturing and mapping the business processes with your stakeholders, but they do not implement the workflow. In many cases, you may implement manual workflows or simple SharePoint workflow automation to streamline a process.

▓ **Note** In SharePoint 2010, there is a graphical version of the workflow designer that uses Visio to both create and track SharePoint workflows. I am not covering that here because it is about *implementation* of the workflow, and it is too limiting when you are trying to capture and document processes with your stakeholders.

As a SharePoint IA, I know that I can't know everything, so in my work I don't implement any automated workflows. I am lucky to have a talented pool of colleagues who have used the SharePoint built-in workflows and also Nintex and K2, and we have used the appropriate tool for each project. Let's take a look at how to capture workflows with a graphical tool.

Mapping with BizAgi

BizAgi (www.bizagi.com) is a British company that has been making process automation tools for over 20 years. Their name stands for Business Agility, and they sell a sophisticated business process modeling suite. The reason that I started to use BizAgi were twofold: I hated using Visio for business process mapping, and its modeling tool is available as a free download.

The other great thing about BizAgi is that its web site has tons of free tutorials and videos on BPMN and how to do modeling with BizAgi. After I used it for a bit, I found it to have some really powerful features, which I will demonstrate in this chapter.

Defining the Problem

We are going to model an expense approval process using BizAgi Process Modeler. For this example, we're going to do a very simple process: An employee (we'll call that person the "submitter") fills out a business expense form and submits it. If the amount of the expense is $50 or less, it goes directly to the Accounting Department for payment. The Accounting Department then issues an approval notice. If the expense is more than $50, it must go to the submitter's manager, who can approve or reject the expense. If rejected, a decline notice is sent out. If accepted, the form is routed to accounting for payment. Clearly there is a lot more to this process in real life than what I have stated here, but this will serve well for our illustration.

Getting Started with BizAgi

When you open BizAgi, you will see the working screen as in Figure 7-5.

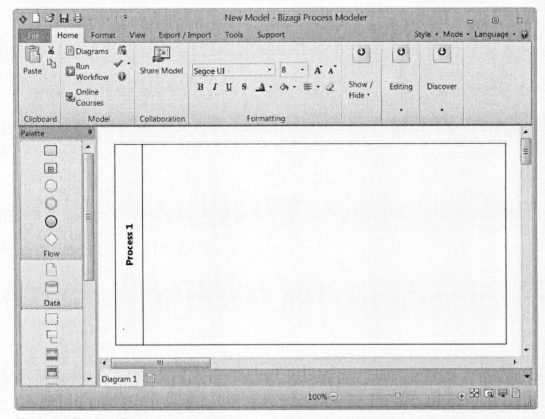

Figure 7-5. The BizAgi startup screen

You will notice a toolbox of items (called a palette) on the left, a working area in the center, and the ribbon across the top. The first think we are going to do is change the name of this process to "Expense Approval" by double-clicking the word Process 1 in the diagram area.

Business process diagrams are often called "swimlane diagrams" because we use horizontal lanes (reminiscent of a swimming pool) to depict the various participants in the process.

Adding Swimlanes

In Figure 7-6, I have scrolled down in the palette to the Swimlanes area (highlighted) and dragged three swimlanes into the process area. I double-clicked inside each swimlane to enter the names of the three players in our process: Submitter, Manager, and Accounting.

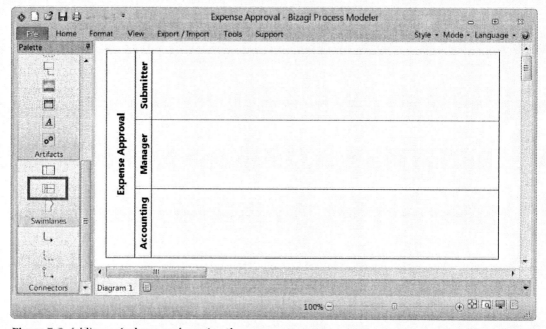

Figure 7-6. Adding swimlanes and naming them

Starting to Add Documentation for the Diagram

One of the really great features of BizAgi is how thoroughly you can document your process just using the tool. In Figure 7-7, you can see that I have right-clicked the process name and chosen Properties. I was then able to write up details of this process. Later, when you see this process exported to Microsoft Word, you'll be able to see all this written material included.

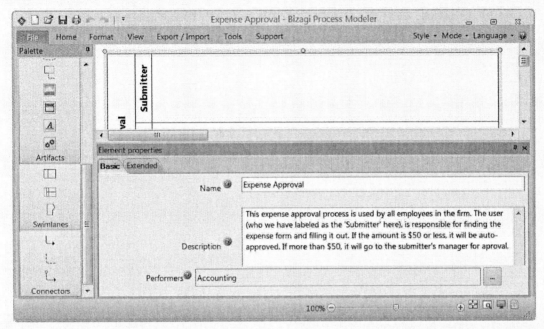

Figure 7-7. Documenting the workflow

This is one place that BizAgi really shines. I have seen it used (in a non-SharePoint situation) to document a very complex process. The behind-the-scenes note taking was a major benefit in that scenario.

Starting the Workflow

In Figure 7-8, you can see how the screen looks as I drag the Start action onto the surface. The magic of BizAgi is the cloud of icons surrounding the center icon. What they do is allow you to add the next element without having drag it from the palette or drawing a connector. All I have to do is click the next item in the process and it automatically gets added right away.

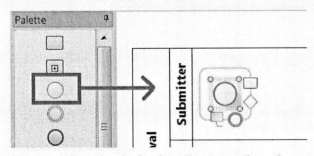

Figure 7-8. Dragging the first item (Start) onto the surface

On the left side of Figure 7-9, you can see what happens when I click the Task icon: It creates a task box that overlaps my current position. As soon as I drag it over to the right side (of Figure 7-9), you see that it is there at the ready, with the next set of icons ready for action.

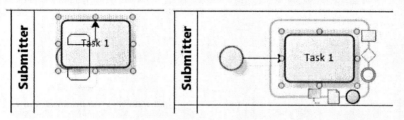

Figure 7-9. Clicking the Task icon and then dragging it into place

As soon as it is positioned correctly, BizAgi gives you alignment cues by flashing nearby items when the one you are moving lines up perfectly with them.

Adding More Items

For the remainder of the diagram, we follow the exact same steps, using the icons that radiate from each item to continue to the next one. If we miss a line, or make an error, we can just delete the item on the page and drag a new one on, adding additional lines as required. You can see the finished diagram in Figure 7-10.

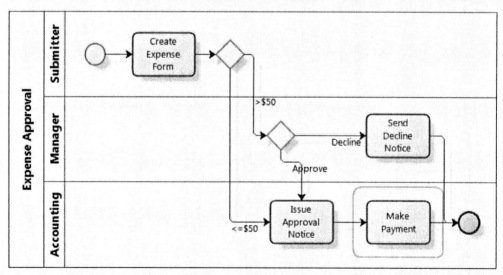

Figure 7-10. Completing the addition of items for this workflow

The features of the BizAgi tool make it very quick and easy to create great looking diagrams like the examples shown. The combination of alignment and sizing tools and easy to select Next item icons are examples of a really smart user-interface design.

Validating the Workflow

BizAgi has great tools to help validate the workflow diagram, both to check that the diagram is put together properly and also to validate the correct use of BPMN. I'm personally not a real stickler for notational correctness, but it is valuable to have the diagram automatically checked. In Figure 7-11 we can see what happens when we click the Validate button in the ribbon: A window opens showing the errors.

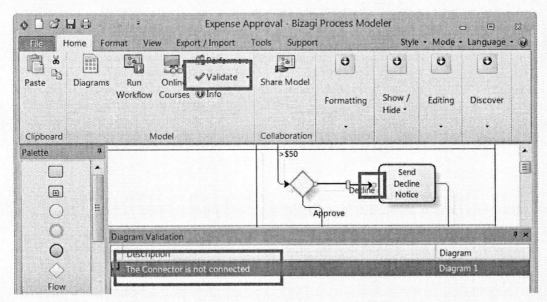

Figure 7-11. Validating the diagram

Clicking the error selects the item in error and moves it to the center of the screen. If you are building complex workflows, it is worth using the validation tool to ensure you haven't left anything in a state that doesn't make sense.

Exporting as a Document

BizAgi's document export capabilities are very strong. In Figure 7-12 you can see the many options to choose from. I have highlighted Microsoft Word and also SharePoint options. With the SharePoint export option, BizAgi uploads your diagrams to SharePoint and allows you to browse them there and read the documentation attached to each element.

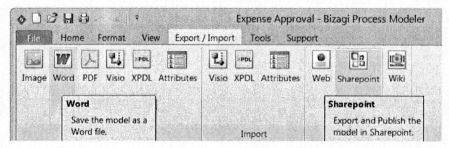

Figure 7-12. Choosing export options (showing Word and SharePoint)

When you export to Microsoft Word, you get to select which items from the diagram you want to export (this can be very fine grained) and then which Word template you'd like to use; two come with the product, but you can define your own.

As you can see in Figure 7-13, the result is a really nicely formed document that shows the diagram and then a well-structured layout of all its elements.

1   DIAGRAM 1

Version: 1.0

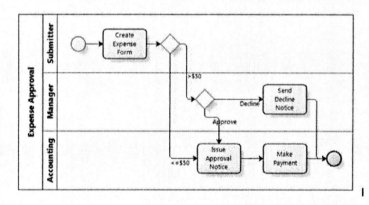

1.1   EXPENSE APPROVAL

Description

This expense approval process is used by all employees in the firm. The user (who we have labeled as the 'Submitter' here), is responsible for finding the expense form and filling it out. If the amount is $50 or less, it will be auto-approved. If more than $50, it will go to the submitter's manager for approval.

1.1.1 PROCESS ELEMENTS

1.1.1.1 ☐ Create Expense Form

Description

The user uses the "Expense Form List Item" in the expenses list to create the item and kick-off the workflow

Figure 7-13. Page 1 of the Microsoft Word export result

I have found BizAgi to be a really powerful, easy to use diagramming tool. Their web site is full of training content, including many videos, and the product is free for you to use. It's just a really great solution.

Producing a SharePoint Workflow

This chapter is about documenting processes and workflows, not building them. However, I did want to show you one possible way you could build out this workflow using SharePoint Designer (SPD), in case you have not yet seen how that looks. In Figure 7-14, you can see what the SPD design surface looks like when building out a workflow.

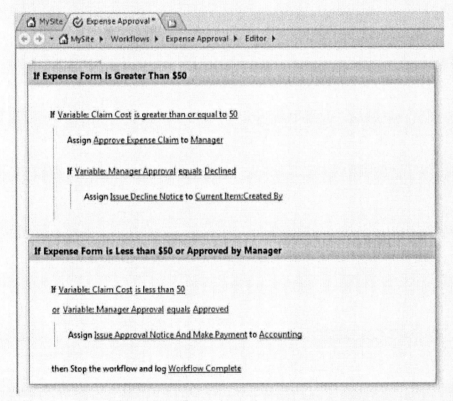

Figure 7-14. A workflow built in SharePoint Designer

The SPD tool has improved greatly since SharePoint 2007, making it much easier to use and adding powerful functionality. However, don't let that fool you. Building out workflows that *work* and that are robust and flexible is not easy. You either need to build up your skills with lots of practice or delegate that task to someone who knows what he or she is doing. It is particularly difficult to troubleshoot complex workflows.

Mapping with Visio

A couple of times in this book you have heard me criticize Visio. I don't want you to get the wrong idea: Visio is powerful, useful, and, for many of us, part of our normal desktop suite. The problem I have with Visio is exactly its benefit: Because it is so powerful, it can be tricky to use properly for advanced functions, especially if you don't invest in learning how to use it really well.

I have to confess that I have not invested a lot of time in learning to use Visio really well; I may have been spoiled by built-for-purpose tools like Balsamiq and BizAgi. But, not too long ago, I decided to fire up Visio to try building a swimlane diagram. It turns out that Visio 2010 has become much easier to use for this task. In the next three images I am very briefly going to show you a couple of the features of Visio 2010 and how they apply to the creation of swimlane diagrams.

In Figure 7-15, you can see how I drag a new swimlane onto the drawing surface and it automatically knows where to fit. When I release the swimlane, it will pop perfectly into place.

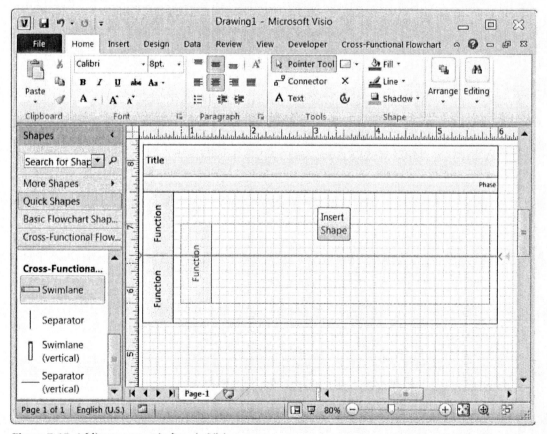

Figure 7-15. Adding a new swimlane in Visio

What really surprised me though about they way Visio works now is that it has the same pop-up capability that BizAgi has. On the left side of Figure 7-16 you can see what happens after I drag a shape onto the drawing surface: A floating selection window opens, and as I mouse-over each shape icon, a temporary shape appears. When I click, the new shape is finalized and the connector is automatically drawn (as you can see on the right size of Figure 7-16).

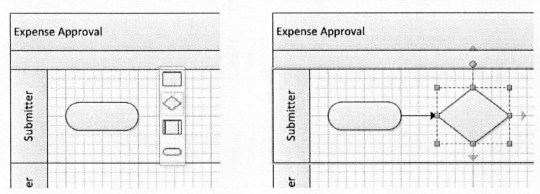

Figure 7-16. Adding shapes to Visio swimlane diagrams

Another clever innovation that saves time when adding an item between two existing shapes is that instead of removing the connector, making room, and then dragging in the new shape and adding the connectors back in, you can just drag the new shape on top of the existing ones. In Figure 7-17 you can see the two connector dots light up, showing you where the new shape will be added. When you release the mouse, the shape is automatically added, with the connectors are properly placed and the old shapes moved apart to make room.

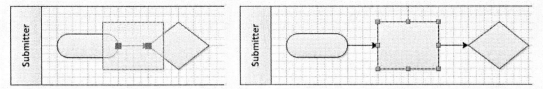

Figure 7-17. Inserting shapes into a Visio swimlane diagram

In other parts of the book I have talked about getting to a shared understanding by working interactively with the client. In the past, I never would have done this with Visio, because I was not practiced enough to do it smoothly. But now, the new features of Visio 2010 make this a real possibility.

■ **Note** The diagrams that I have shown above were made with the professional version of Visio 2010. The premium version includes BPMN stencils that follow the formal BPMN 1.2 standard. So it is possible to create compliant diagrams with that version of Visio. In addition, the Visio BPMN shapes have slots for documentation, and there is a validation engine that will validate your Visio BPMN diagrams.

Visio has really made great strides in ease of use and specialized templates for process mapping. It is definitely a viable tool for this and, if it is a part of your desktop suite, you should definitely try it. However, if you don't have access to Visio or you consider the cost too high, BizAgi will serve you very well.

Summary

Whether it is a business process, such as hiring a new employee or dealing with expenses, or a document workflow process, such as approving a press release for publication or responding to a request for proposal, you need to be able to capture and analyze these processes to be able to get an understanding of the business issues your stakeholders face on a day-to-day basis. No matter how well you design a taxonomy and a collection of document repositories, you know that there has to be process—even if it's a badly designed one—that's going to govern how those documents are going to get into the system, how they will be processed through the system, and how they will be migrated out, archived, deleted, or moved to another system.

This chapter discussed how to very simply create some workflows that can radically improve business processes without implementing a lot of automation. We then looked at tools for documenting workflows from BizAgi and Microsoft Word.

We looked at practical, usable, and (in BizAgi's case) inexpensive tools that you can learn quite quickly and apply to your projects. I hope you will practice using these tools and learn a bit about BPM so you can help your stakeholders to describe and document their processes and then help them to streamline and automate them.

CHAPTER 8

The Art of Creating Business Process Solutions

By Sarah Haase

To get through the hardest journey we need take only one step at a time, but we must keep on stepping.

—Chinese Proverb

This chapter takes a slightly different point of view from the previous chapters. As I explained in Chapter 1, the tools and techniques contained in this book apply to you whether you are a member of an outside consulting firm brought in to complete a specific project, a contractor brought in to take on a specific role for a predetermined time, or an internal employee working on SharePoint in the organization you work for. However, in most of the explanation and examples, I have been writing from the point of view of an outside consultant, because that is my job.

This chapter, written by Sarah Haase, gives you the point of view of an internal employee. Sarah works at a large organization where she deals with different internal teams and departments over a period of years. She therefore has a different viewpoint on how she has to show value for her work and how she has to deal with the various groups within her organization. I think this is an interesting and valuable perspective to add to this book, as it no doubt applies to many of you.

It is interesting to note that even though Sarah is an employee of the organization, she acts very much like a consultant: She calls the teams that she works for her "customers," and she has to justify her work to them, showing them that she is providing value. In many organizations, departments have the option to use internal resources on a project or to hire external consultants. The internal service providers have to provide value if they want to continue to be hired by other teams.

The other thing about this chapter that is a bit different is that Sarah is taking a very process-oriented point of view, one that has measurable present states and measurable future states that provide for calculable return on investment (ROI). This approach is valuable no matter which role you are in—inside employee or outsider—and Sarah has managed to hone this to a fine art.

There are some elements of this chapter that repeat and reinforce the outcome planning and business analysis that was covered in earlier chapters, but here these are tilted toward discovering process improvements that can be implemented in SharePoint.

A Process Approach

Processes, like road signs, should be clear and direct. They should evoke a series of concise responses to effect a specific, desired outcome.

The problem is, humans are organic. In an effort to meet business objectives, work more efficiently, and manage our time well, we load up our processes with too many steps and too many desired outcomes. Unable to stand under this mammoth weight, our processes devolve quickly. They morph into a convoluted string of manual tasks that everyone performs but no one understands. In the end, we hate the very processes we hoped would save us. But the underlying need for the processes doesn't disappear. So, inevitably, the cycle starts again. We abandon the overgrown processes we have come to hate, clarify our business needs, and voila! A new process emerges.

Sound familiar? This is proof you are not alone! Process pain and mismanagement are epidemic. They exist in all industries, in all organizations, and with a wide variety of toolsets. To prove the point, let's look back at our road sign analogy. Figure 8-1 shows a road sign that works.

Figure 8-1. A clear, easy-to-understand road sign

When you approach a STOP sign, you know what the process is:

1. Bring your vehicle to a complete stop.
2. Wait for traffic to clear.
3. Proceed.

Are you ever confused by these steps? No. Do you ever think you should add additional steps to this process? Maybe get out and check your tire pressure or check to see if your brake lights are working? No. The purpose of this sign is clear, and there is no value in adding additional steps to the process. Now take a look at Figure 8-2.

Figure 8-2. Say what?

Are you confused? You're not the only one. What are we supposed to do after seeing this sign? What's our process? It looks like we should be sitting, but what comes next? Are we going to be impaled by a rectangle? Or are we supposed to prop our stump of a leg on something? I have no idea.

Now relate this back to the processes in your organization. Could you create a clear diagram to illustrate the need for each of these processes? Do you have a clear process flow that outlines key stakeholders, key steps, and end goals? All too often our processes are nebulous. They don't have a clear start and end. And if we tried to diagram out the steps within the process, we'd end up with a diagram that looks like the example in Figure 8-3. Good luck, indeed!

Figure 8-3. The land of confusion

So we know that some of our processes are broken and that SharePoint 2010 provides key functionality we can use to improve them. By structuring our content in SharePoint lists, mapping out workflows, and pushing data to our users on a just-in-time basis, we can streamline our work processes and automate manual tasks. But before we start evolving our processes, we need to explore some universal truths.

Universal Truths

I've worked with end users in many organizations. And while companies (and their employees) vary wildly, there are underlying similarities in how they all work. I call these similarities *universal truths*. Understanding these truths will help you relate to your users and build successful business process solutions. So before you go anywhere or improve anything, take a look.

1. *Businesses shouldn't be run via spreadsheets stored on shared drives.* And yet, most of them are. If you did nothing but convert large, unwieldy spreadsheets into structured SharePoint lists that included query-based list views and out-of-the-box or custom SharePoint Designer workflows, you would be a raging success. Why? Because spreadsheets never live alone. As people find new requirements and new data they need to store, they'll add more spreadsheets to the mix, requiring data to be copied and pasted from one spreadsheet to another. The time spent creating, maintaining, organizing, and copying data between these spreadsheets is time lost.

2. *Users (even well-intentioned ones) will generally take the path of least resistance.* They will create myriad files and store them in file repositories. After all, this is what they are used to doing. Our job is to educate and provide users with other options.

3. *Users will be interested in functionality that can improve their lives.* But most of the time they don't have the time to investigate this functionality on their own. They need information architects and designers to paint the vision. Often I throw out 15 ideas for each individual idea my business users choose to implement. There's nothing wrong with a 15:1 ratio. The key is to keep offering ideas that will maximize user opportunities. Even if they don't implement your ideas right away, they will likely circle back to consider some of the ideas again later.

4. *If information architecture is optional, most users will opt out.* Many users are unfamiliar with information architects, but that doesn't mean they don't need them. Information architects drive a higher return on your SharePoint investment, as illustrated in Figure 8-4. Why? *Because information architects understand content and can tie that content to key SharePoint features.* Information architects help turn your content into structured data that can be routed via workflows, displayed in key performance indicators (KPIs), and leveraged in pie charts. But how do you get users to buy into the information architecture process? You need a carrot-and-stick strategy. Information architecture services should not just be recommended, they should be *required* for all projects that result in a new SharePoint site being created. If you can offer SharePoint planning services free of charge and have a good reputation for delivering top-notch solutions, you have all the "carrots" you need. If you can require team members to work with you in order to have a SharePoint site or site collection created, you have your "stick." If this model doesn't work in your organization, you'll need to improvise. Just remember to include both the carrot and the stick.

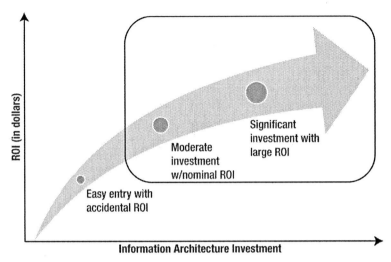

Figure 8-4. The benefit of adding information architecture

5.   *SharePoint markets itself . . . once you deliver your first couple of wins.* I've
     managed several corporate knowledge bases, and they all have one thing in
     common. Regardless of the technology they're built on, the amount we
     invested in them, or the number of cool features they have, all these
     knowledge bases were giant, sucking holes of need. No matter how long I
     evangelized their use, they would never spawn a cult following. They would
     always require care, feeding, and emotional propping. SharePoint is just the
     opposite. If you build SharePoint solutions that automate business processes
     and save time and energy, people will come—in droves.

6.   *Your SharePoint solution isn't complete until you've measured its effectiveness.*
     This is an astonishingly common "miss." People build great SharePoint
     solutions—solutions that save their companies hundreds of thousands of
     dollars per year—and fail to quantify their success. Your job does not end
     when a new SharePoint site is launched. Your job ends when you have
     measured the site's effectiveness.

These universal truths aren't complex. They merely reflect the basic instincts of most business users. But
understanding these universal truths gives you an edge—an edge your counterparts don't have. These
truths are the keys for obtaining buy-in, effecting real change management, and learning how to
quantify your results. By incorporating these truths into your business process strategy, you will
fundamentally shift how your business users view their tools. And SharePoint will spread like wildfire.

But before we dive too far into roadmap and prescriptive process modeling solutions, let's examine
the broader field of process engineering.

Process Engineering Methodologies

Process engineering (or process systems engineering) focuses on the design, analysis, control, and
optimization of processes. Although process engineering is a fairly new concept (born out of the
chemical engineering field in the early 1960s), it has quickly grown in popularity. Its concepts have been

applied to nearly every field and industry, from technology and manufacturing to biomedical research and financial services.

Process engineering is focused on driving efficiency and simplicity, but there are many different methodologies for achieving these outcomes. These methodologies are prescriptive, providing criteria and litmus tests you can use to analyze and optimize your current processes with SharePoint. Let's examine a few of the most popular process engineering methodologies.

Six Sigma

Probably the most widely recognized of all business management strategies, Six Sigma strives to increase quality by minimizing variability and eliminating defects. Initially conceived and implemented by Motorola in the 1970s, Six Sigma has grown beyond a manufacturing model to serve as a methodology for evaluating business processes.

Within the Six Sigma methodology, all business process steps are evaluated through a rigorous five-stage evaluation process called DMAIC (Define, Measure, Analyze, Improve, and Control). The DMAIC phases strive to:

- *Define* the problem or the opportunity.

- *Measure* the current process, collecting all relevant data.

- *Analyze* the current process and isolate the underlying cause for poor performance.

- *Improve* the current process by eradicating the causes of poor performance.

- *Control* the new processes to prevent against process erosion.

The goal is to reduce variability in process steps, thereby lowering the number of standard deviations you are from the mean.

The best measure of Six Sigma's success is its overwhelming popularity. With Six Sigma certification programs scattered across the globe and many companies adopting white belt, green belt, and black belt certification processes, Six Sigma has quickly morphed into the gold standard for process engineering. To learn more about how Six Sigma is being implemented in corporations across the country, pick up a copy of *The Six Sigma Way: How GE, Motorola, and Other Top Companies Are Honing Their Performance* by Peter S. Pande et al.

Business Process Modeling

Business process modeling (BPM) is a broader discipline that focuses on representing processes visually so they can be analyzed and improved. The process of identifying and depicting routine business processes (along with their exceptions, options, and alternatives) provides key benefits for business and IT teams. It highlights inefficiencies and redundancies, enables teams to better understand complex work streams, and provides a common visual language for documenting and sharing processes across departments.

BPM techniques have evolved significantly over the past 50 years as generalized flow charts have evolved into block diagrams, Gantt charts, PERT (program evaluation and review technique), and diagrams. Today's BPM experts use case diagrams, activity diagrams, event-driven process chains, Unified Modeling Language (UML) diagrams, and Business Process Modeling Notation (BPMN) to model business processes. To learn more about BPM and how it can be used to analyze and improve your organization's work processes, pick up a copy of Michael Havey's book *Essential Business Process Modeling*.

Capability Maturity Model Integration

It may be a mouthful, but Capability Maturity Model Integration (CMMI) is one of the leading process improvement methodologies in existence today. Patented by the Software Engineering Institute of Carnegie Mellon University, CMMI focuses on identifying process strengths and weaknesses. The goal is to incorporate process improvements so weaknesses can be reworked into areas of strength.

CMMI champions the adoption of process best practices. These best practices range in subject areas from causal analysis and risk management to requirements management, disaster recovery, availability management, data collection, supplier management, and project management. Best practices are grouped into formal CMMI models, including:

- CMMI for acquisition
- CMMI for development
- CMMI for services
- People CMM

Organizations can be appraised to determine how they compare to the CMMI model best practices. After being appraised, the organization will receive a level rating that indicates their current location on the evolutionary process scale. CMMI models have a scale that ranges from Maturity Level 1 (Initial) to Maturity Level 5 (Optimizing). For more information on CMMI, visit http://www.sei.cmu.edu/cmmi/.

▓ **Note** Sadalit Van Buren has built a SharePoint maturity model that standardizes the evaluation and ranking of organizational SharePoint health. You can use the model to holistically evaluate your current SharePoint implementation and define benchmarks for future improvements. Although this model is less comprehensive and complex than CMMI, it does provide a SharePoint-specific measurement methodology. To learn more about the SharePoint maturity model, visit www.sharepointmaturity.com.

Business Process Reengineering

A close cousin to BPM, business process reengineering (BPR) focuses on streamlining workflows and business processes by finding and eliminating inefficiencies. By ensuring that each process step is clear, concise, and adds elemental value, companies are able to cut operational costs, improve customer service, and become more competitive.

Although BPR is not a new concept, it has surged in popularity alongside collaboration and social technologies like SharePoint. Never before have business users had ready access to collaborative toolsets to track and automate work processes. Instead of being reliant on IT for all their systematic process solutions, SharePoint business users now have the ability to redefine their work. The features are all there—from out-of-the-box document library workflows to list view web parts, KPIs, data view web parts, and SharePoint Designer custom workflows. The only obstacle is ensuring that business users understand how these features can make a difference in their day-to-day lives.

Before you begin tying SharePoint features to business processes, however, you need to step back and evaluate the current flow of content in your organization.

The Forgotten Layer of Content Management

Many organizations have a content management system (CMS) in place to warehouse their business-critical content. These systems offer a deep capability set, including the ability to create and store content, provision access based on user groups or roles, track and report on compliance with state and federal regulations, tag content with metadata for easy retrieval, and reduce duplication of effort by enabling content reuse. The type of content stored in a CMS varies by industry, but may include case files for law firms, documentation for software firms, digital image assets for photography studios, and UPC/SKU content for retailers. The CMS can vary as well—from purchased solutions like Documentum, SharePoint, Vignette, and OpenText to home-grown tools built for a specific organization's needs.

Although the a CMS serves a critical function, it cannot stretch to house and govern all the data generated by business users. Think of all the e-mails that users create and send on a daily basis. Add in all the data stored in Excel spreadsheets on shared drives and you have a huge mass of unstructured content.

Why do users create all this unstructured content? Because they have underlying business process needs that are not being fulfilled. Remember, business users are responsible for keeping the wheels of motion turning. They have to keep data flowing, but they often don't have the time, inclination, or expertise to design complex solutions. So they use e-mail, Microsoft Excel, and other tools to fill the gaps. I often refer to these gap measures as the poor man's workflow. They are critical to business success but are not regulated or optimized. They are the forgotten layer of content management.

So how do we bring these temporary processes and unstructured content into the light? How do we standardize them, moving from hidden manual workflows to automated, streamlined business processes? This is our focus—the art of creating business process solutions.

Through the remainder of this chapter, I'll outline all the key strategies you'll need to create your own business process solutions. I will help you evaluate your landscape, define your benchmarks, and find the right "first project." I will examine the development lifecycle stages, provide a methodology for storyboarding your solutions, and recommend a formula for calculating your ROI.

But how do we know this is the "right" strategy? How do we know it will make a difference in your organization?

1. *This strategy was built "in the trenches."* It has been implemented successfully in many types of organizations and has saved companies hundreds of thousands of dollars.

2. *It fulfills unmet needs.* Most business users are in process pain. They spend too much of their time managing e-mail and moving data from one location to another. They know their processes are inefficient and would love to find a better, faster, smarter way to work. But they're so busy they don't have time to figure out how to make that happen. This is where you come in. If you have the time (and SharePoint expertise) to automate their processes, they will buy in. And they'll bring their counterparts along for the ride.

3. *It relieves the "soul crushing, spirit destroying" work.* Manual workflow processes are, well, manual. They require an intelligent human to be present, clicking away. Some users don't mind a bit of this "clicky" work, as it provides a commercial break from other, more taxing, duties. But since these workflows tend to grow over time with an ever-increasing number of requirements and manual steps, they quickly become an albatross—weighing on the psyche of your business users. Get rid of them and your users will love you.

4. *It drives user adoption.* Are you struggling to get users up and running on SharePoint? If you use SharePoint to automate manual tasks, eliminating the "soul crushing, spirit destroying" work that your users hate, they will buy in. No marketing campaigns or gimmicks needed.

5. *It relieves change management challenges.* It did not take much effort to get people to embrace color television. Yes there were technology challenges, concerns about the number of shows being broadcast in color, and the need for people to upgrade their hardware, but color television fundamentally sold itself. There was no need to create change management strategies for driving color television adoption. The same can be said for driving business process optimization with SharePoint. If you choose your first SharePoint project carefully and build the right set of SharePoint followers; SharePoint will not require a large change management effort. On the contrary, you will be deluged with ongoing SharePoint requests.

Get This Bus Moving!

It's time. We've set the stage, talked about universal truths, reviewed common process management disciplines, learned about the forgotten layer of content management, and bought into the need for creating business process solutions. Now it's time to build your process roadmap. This roadmap will be your "couch-to-success" plan. It will help you evaluate your organization, refine your goals, define benchmarks, select and implement the all-important first project, and calculate its return on investment. And it doesn't matter what point you're starting from. You can start as a SharePoint administrator, an IT business owner, or a business end user who is looking to make a difference in your organization. All you need is a vision for where you want to go.

▓ **Note** You may remember an earlier discussion of roadmaps in Chapter 1. While Chapter 1 provided a roadmap for a holistic SharePoint implementation, this chapter provides a narrower roadmap focused on finding (and implementing) SharePoint process solutions.

As you journey through the roadmap, look for project examples from MultiMEGA Industries (our created company for our examples). As the world's leading supplier of soap, missiles, and produce, MultiMEGA has some key opportunities to shorten routine business processes and save time and money. Are you ready? Let's get started.

Step 1: Evaluate the Landscape and Define Your Role

You can't reach your destination if you don't know what it is. So before you jump in and find a business process you want to improve, you need to define your current organizational landscape and see what the business needs are. Ask yourself (and others) some key questions, including:

- What do we value?
- How do we work? (In other words, how formal are we?)
- What matters to management?
- What does "good" look like?
- How do we talk about our successes and failures?

You want to find and analyze a picture of success at your organization. Find a recent project, sale, or initiative that *worked*. It could have generated a buzz, created key opportunities for growth, or merely spurred some lively discussion and debate. Once you find this example, dissect it to find out what made it so successful. Was it the quality of the idea, the person who championed it, or the approach that person took?

Now look for the ideas that never took off. Pay particular attention to the great ideas that never gained any traction. Backtrack and try to figure out what was missing. Was the idea too complex? Did it require too much of an upfront investment? Or was it too hard to understand?

Once you have a current picture of success and failure, evaluate the political landscape at your organization. Is your leadership team looking to invest in people with new ideas? If they are, find what is needed to get the ball rolling so you can build your stairway to success. If the political landscape is bleak, don't get discouraged. Take the time to find examples of success and backtrack. Chances are, someone in your organization has changed the game and achieved success. Go talk with those people and figure out how they did it. Their success can rub off on you.

Once you've laid the groundwork and documented your current organizational landscape, it's time to outline your vision for the future. This is the point where you pick your focus and define your role. SharePoint offers a plentiful supply of focus areas, including:

- Process optimization

- Information architecture

- Community development (a.k.a. building a SharePoint community within your organization)

- Project management

- Change management

- Knowledge management

- Content lifecycle management

- Records management

- Enterprise content management

Consider your talents and interests and choose a path that inspires you. Maybe you want to allocate a percentage of your time to automate your team's manual processes. Or maybe you're looking to drive SharePoint user adoption within your organization. Once you have some ideas, commit them to paper. If you're not sure where to start, consider drafting a personal mission statement. Here's the mission statement I created for myself back in 2006:

> *Use technology to automate manual tasks and save money.*

Don't worry about formalizing or perfecting your mission statement right now. The goal is to get some ideas down on paper. You can refine your mission statement as you build the rest of your roadmap.

Step 2: Gap Analysis

Once you know where your organization is and where you want to go, it's time to do a gap analysis. At a fundamental level, you need to decide what key job roles are required for your vision of success. Assuming you are building a business process solution, some of the critical roles may include:

- IT manager

- Business owner
- Information architect
- Business analyst
- Usability analyst
- Graphic designer
- Developer
- Quality analyst
- Technical writer

Obviously you can't fill all these roles yourself. If you are looking to design or build a department dedicated to business process reengineering, however, you may want to look at adding these roles to your organizational structure. If you are an individual contributor, you may need to wear multiple hats (at least until you build your personal brand and land your first couple of project wins).

Depending on your situation and vision for success, this gap analysis may be fairly simple or quite extensive. Either way, you need to make sure you complete four key tasks:

1. Identify the experience level and skill set you will need to fulfill your vision.

2. Perform a self-assessment, listing the experience, skills, and other qualifications that lend themselves to this new function.

3. Determine what tools, funding, and leadership support you will need.

4. Determine what tool or professional training you need.

▓ **Example** MultiMEGA Industries has a dedicated collaboration team focused on deploying, supporting, and evangelizing SharePoint's use in the organization. As a member of this team, you've had the opportunity to meet with SharePoint business users across the organization and have seen inefficient work streams that can be improved by structuring content in SharePoint lists and implementing workflows. You believe you can best serve MultiMEGA by focusing on business process optimization with SharePoint. To prepare for this new role, you've drafted a mission statement, performed a gap analysis, and determined that you need additional training on information architecture, building wireframes, and using SharePoint Designer to build custom workflows. You've worked with your collaboration team manager to achieve buy-in and are pursuing training options.

Step 3: Build Your Foundation

So you've chosen your focus area and closed the experience and training gap. Now you need to obtain approvals and buy-in from management. Depending on your environment, organizational culture, and current function or role, it could take weeks, months, or even years to obtain this buy-in and support. If you face significant challenges achieving the buy-in necessary for your long-term vision, you may need to iterate through this roadmap several times—each time focusing on implementing a smaller goal. If you want to become the SharePoint business owner for your organization but are in a business end-user role today, you may not be able to jump directly into the role of your dreams. You may need to start off with a midrange goal like becoming the SharePoint lead for your department. Once you have achieved this goal, you can iterate through the roadmap again, focusing on the next logical step in your evolution.

After you have the leadership buy-in you need, you'll need to start addressing other key foundational elements. These elements may include:

- Driving user adoption.

- Funding your model and vision. Will you be funded via a capital request, via a departmental budget, or via a bill back charge to the business teams you work with?

- Coordinating with other organizational teams that are already in the SharePoint space.

- Developing a security model (including permission schemes and standard operating procedures).

- Clarifying roles and responsibilities for business users, business owners, site owners, site collection administrators, and farm administrators.

- Creating an end-user support model, including standardization of support levels and support level agreements (SLAs).

- Coordinating farm administration and support.

- Performing broad-based program management—including SharePoint road mapping, upgrade plans, outsourcing models, and so forth.

- Devising a SharePoint governance model.

Each of these areas requires a great deal of time and consideration—more than I can provide guidance on within the scope of this chapter. While Chapter 10 does provide guidance on driving user adoption and governance, you will need to evaluate your organization's financial climate (complete with financial systems and policies) to determine the best way to fund your project. You will also need to partner with your IT department to define elements such as security, support, administration, and upgrades.

Step 4: Define Benchmarks

You've defined your vision, filled in technical or experiential gaps, and built your foundation. Now you need to define your benchmarks for success. These benchmarks serve as goals and toll gates for your journey. They will help you define what success looks like and give you a series of checkpoints on the path to achieving your vision. Think of these benchmarks as mile markers on your own yellow brick road. Line them up in order of effort, skill, and difficulty so you can achieve some quick successes right away. These quick successes will fuel your passion—spurring you on to tackle the remaining challenges.

Your benchmarks should be specific and relevant to your long-term vision. All too often people define "generalized" benchmarks chock full of industry buzzwords, feel-good sentiments, and great word-smithing. These benchmarks make for great sound bites, but they are totally ineffective. They fail to inspire, motivate, and drive others to buy into your vision. Take a look at these examples:

- I want to reduce duplication of content.

- I want to reduce the time it takes to complete business processes.

- I want to use wikis to promote information sharing.

How do you measure against these benchmarks? They are passive, subjective, and unspecific—failing to provide any quantitative data you can compare against. How do you show that you've reduced duplication of content if you didn't take the time to quantitatively measure how much content was duplicated before you started? To be effective, your benchmarks should be clear, direct, action oriented, and specify a "from" and a "to" point. Here are some updated benchmarks that meet these criteria:

- I will eliminate 15GB in duplicated storage within the next six months.

- I will reduce the length of our office supply procurement process by 15 percent.

- I will grow our wiki to contain 200+ articles written by 10+ authors within the next six months.

Defining your benchmarks as action statements exudes confidence. Adding quantitative measurements of success ensures that you have taken your baseline measurements and have a relevant measure of your efforts. Adding in a timeframe ensures the benchmark stays relevant. If your journey is interrupted for any reason (organization shifts, time off of work, etc.), you'll want to revisit your benchmarks, validate their authenticity, and refine their timeframe.

Once your benchmarks are set, you will want to commit them to paper and share them with others around you. Post them around your cubicle or paint them on your office wall. These are your new rules to live by. You should be able to recite them to others in the elevator, dream about them at night, and keep a running tally in your head of the progress you are making on them.

▓ **Example** As the new SharePoint process solution architect for MultiMEGA industries, you have defined a series of benchmark goals. Within your first 12 months, you will:

1. Find, build, and deploy a minimum of six SharePoint process solutions.

2. Work with MultiMEGA's finance department to build, certify, and document a methodology for quantifying your return on investment.

3. Generate more than $125,000 in annual ROI.

Step 5: Find the "Right" First Project

So how do you build excitement about your vision and about what SharePoint can do? Depending on your organization and situation, you may have some unique challenges. If you are building or leading a team, you need to ensure they buy into your vision and are equipped to succeed. If you are starting out alone and are building a SharePoint implementation from scratch, you will need to harness the "power of one" and drive adoption. If you are trying to reclaim a SharePoint implementation gone wrong, you will need to pioneer a renaissance movement.

Regardless of the specific challenges you face, you need to find your first SharePoint project. You need to choose carefully, however. This first project will be your inaugural step into the art of BPR. You need to deliver a solid solution that saves time and money and turns your first customer into your first follower. Why is a first follower important? Because your first follower is the person who will teach others how to follow you. Your first follower validates your vision and shows others how to jump on the bandwagon. If you invest in this first follower—delivering a SharePoint solution that meets that customer's needs perfectly—he or she will become your first champion. And a champion is what transforms you from a lone SharePoint nut into a SharePoint leader.

But how do you find this first customer? And how do you turn that person into your first champion? Figure 8-5 outlines the key to finding your first SharePoint project.

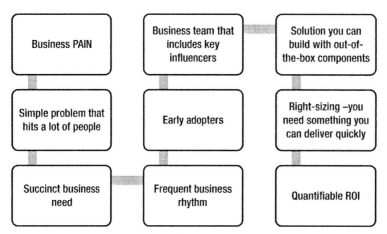

Figure 8-5. The key to finding the "right" first project

Let's break down some of these project selection guidelines. First, you need to find something that causes people *pain*. You're not looking for something that is mildly annoying. You're looking for the soul-crushing, spirit-destroying work that makes your users want to gnaw off their own arms. A two-hour, 104-step process for logging timesheets would be a great example of business pain.

You also need a succinct problem that hits a lot of people. Your purchasing system may be hellish, but if it doesn't impact a large number of people and can't be broken up into small logical chunks for optimization, it's not the right first project.

To maximize your efforts, you want to look for repeatable processes (processes that have a daily or weekly business rhythm). Optimizing frequent processes greatly amplifies your return on investment.

This inaugural project will be a partnership between you and a business owner or business team. Since you are hoping this first customer will become your first follower and your first champion, it is crucial you select the right customer. You want to work with innovators and early adopters. These are the people who cling to the bleeding edge, the people who are always the first to adopt new technology. They will be willing to go out on a limb, to take a chance and see where it leads.

But it isn't enough to just find the early adopters. You need your first customers to be key influencers and change agents as well. They need to inspire the masses to follow in their footsteps so you can build support for your vision.

So how do you find these key influencers? Look around your organization for the people everyone goes to when they have a question. Key influencers tend to be the informal help desk for their department. They are the ones who have all the contacts and know where to go to find more information. If you can find a project that pulls in early adopters *and* key influencers, you will be successful.

Once you find the right process that integrates with the right people, you need to make sure the solution can be built quickly and easily with out-of-the-box SharePoint features. You don't need the most elegant solution built with amazing customizations. You need a simple, reliable solution you can build within a couple of weeks. And let's not forget the all-important ROI. This first project will serve as a calling card—a testament to your business process automation vision. You cannot sell that vision if your solution doesn't have quantifiable benefits. As I'll discuss later in this chapter, these benefits can take multiple forms. They can include time savings, infrastructure cost savings, revenue generation, and so forth. The key is to ensure that your first project can be quantified.

Step 6: Dive In!

Now that you have your first project, you're ready to start mapping requirements. Since other chapters of this book thoroughly examine the requirements of the mapping process, this section will only provide a quick framework for storyboarding process solutions. This framework works for both external consultants and internal resources, but may need to be tweaked to meet your organization's specific needs.

BPR projects fall neatly into standard project lifecycle stages:

- Stage 1 (Initial request received)
- Stage 2 (Requirements mapping/storyboarding/process flow diagramming)
- Stage 3 (SharePoint development)
- Stage 4 (Iterative review)
- Stage 5 (Launch)
- Stage 6 (ROI calculation)

Most of these stages are self-evident. Stage 1 begins when a SharePoint request is received. These requests may be submitted through standardized forms or e-mails and can be requests for a new SharePoint site or enhancement requests for existing sites. Both "new" and "enhancement" requests follow the same process. First, you need to define who the business owner(s) is. This person or business is your customer—the people you are building solutions for. Ideally you will have a single business owner for each of your projects. If this isn't possible, set a hard limit at three business owners per project. (Having more than three business owners slows things down and increases project instability.)

Next, set up some time to meet with your business owner(s) so you can kick off your project. If you are in the same geographic area and have the luxury of setting up in-person meetings, do so. If you are in separate locations, set up a virtual meeting space. Here's a breakdown of the agenda for this initial meeting:

1. *Introduce your role and explain your SharePoint methodology.* Explain how you work, what service(s) you provide to your customers, and what process you'll be following to complete this project. Also let the business owner(s) know what is expected of him or her.

2. *Ask about the business owner's "vision" for the future.* This question is intentionally vague. It is intended to gather baseline feedback and won't be the final vision statement for your SharePoint design. Usually, users will respond with a vague statement like "I want a SharePoint site like Jane Doe has." There's nothing wrong with a broad answer. Just capture whatever the customer says and move on to the next agenda item.

3. *Ask about the need(s) the business owner is trying to solve.* In some cases, users will already have their scope defined. Most users get confused about this question, though. Don't worry about a lack of detail in their answer. Capture the response and move on.

4. *Get details on the business owner's current work process, including highlights, pain points, and bottlenecks.* Here's where the deluge starts. Many users have difficulty outlining a scope or vision for SharePoint, but most can wax poetic on pain points and bottlenecks in their current work processes. Encourage them to dive into the details and whiteboard their process. Along the way, capture:

    a. Key steps in the current process that can be automated using SharePoint.

b.   Key pain points and bottlenecks. These will turn into your solution's critical success factors.

c.   "Soul crushing" work that can be eliminated or automated. These are the wins that will act as change management agents. Eliminate work that everyone hates and you'll automatically build support for SharePoint.

d.   A rough percentage of time that can be shaved off the existing work process. (As you start working on simultaneous projects, you can use this estimate to prioritize your work and justify the procurement of additional resources.)

▓ **Example** As MultiMEGA's new SharePoint process solution architect, you are reviewing the quality control process for MultiMEGA's print production team. They follow a standard project rhythm—they build new print materials, conduct peer reviews, report and resolve issues, and release their final product. The problem is their issue-reporting process. Team members use multiple Excel spreadsheets to capture and track issues, causing delays with managing multiple documents. The team estimates they spend up to four hours per project syncing up spreadsheets. With an average completion rate of 200 projects per year, the team is losing up to 800 hours of productivity annually.

What if you moved this data to a single SharePoint issue tracking list so the team could report, assign, track, and close issues in one location? It would eliminate duplicate issue reporting and spreadsheet syncing, saving 800 hours of manual effort. Project managers could then create a dashboard with KPIs to track project analytics. And what if other teams could benefit from similar issue tracking functionality? You may be able to save this solution as a list template and reuse it!

---

5.   *Get a wish list of things the business owner dreams about.* Tell the business owner to think big and ask for the world on a stick. Don't worry about setting boundaries on the requests–just capture their answers. (At this point, most users have no idea what SharePoint can do, so their expectations shoot way too high or way too low. Don't sweat these details.)

6.   *Provide a demo of "similar" functionality that has already been launched.* At this point, you should have a fairly good idea of the pain points and potential SharePoint solutions that could be built. Now it's time to give the business owner(s) an idea of what SharePoint can do. Provide a 15-minute targeted demo of existing SharePoint sites and functions that most closely align with the needs of the business owner(s). If the customer needs a way to report and track work requests, demo issue tracking solutions that incorporate automated e-mail notifications and reporting. If the customer needs help with document storage and retrieval, demo a metadata-based tagging scheme that enables easy document uploading or tagging. The key is to demo live sites that mirror the new customer's needs. If you don't have any existing SharePoint sites that align with the business owner's needs, demo a sampling of other SharePoint solutions. If this is your first SharePoint project and you don't have anything to demo, start drawing out possible solutions on a whiteboard. The objective is to

"blow the lid off" the customer's expectations and get him or her "thinking big" about what SharePoint can do. You'll know you're hitting the right note when users start getting visibly excited and start tossing out additional ideas for how SharePoint can help optimize their business. Encourage them to brainstorm—the more ideas on the table the better!

7. *Connect the customer with business owners who are already on their way.* You are not objective. Clearly you are enthralled with SharePoint and have a vested interest in its success at your organization. In order to give your customers a fair (unbiased) view, recommend they touch base with other business owners who have already implemented SharePoint solutions. When these other business owners recommend SharePoint (and you), your customers will be doubly impressed.

8. *Revisit the goals and wish list.* Before you close out your meeting, revisit steps 3 and 5 to see what your customer's updated goals and wish list items are. By now, your customer should have a much broader list of features and functions he or she wants to explore. Capture as much of this information as you can. You'll have the chance to map these goals and wish list items into project implementation phases later.

Each of these eight steps is fluid. Depending on the size and scope of your project you may need to allocate two hours, four hours, or several full working days to get through all the steps. As the size of your projects expand, so too will the amount of design time that is needed. Be targeted about scheduling follow-up design meetings, however. The key is to take up as little of your business owner's time as possible. If you make the information architecture process too painful, users will opt out and you will lose a SharePoint deployment opportunity.

Once you have your design details gathered, it's time to design the SharePoint solution and solicit feedback. Tailor your design presentation to your audience. If your customer is informal and buys into your vision readily, you may be able to meet with the business owner and whiteboard your proposed solution. If your customer is more formal or requires executive sign-off, you will need to create wireframes (as discussed in Chapter 5).

Once your requirements are documented and you get management signoff, you are ready to build out the solution! When you have a beta version ready for testing, loop back with your customer to build a test and launch plan. Ideally you'll have an iterative review period that allows your customer to test the new solution with real business data. This will highlight weak spots and enable you to hone your design. Once the customer is satisfied, you are ready to launch.

A Study in ROI

As one of our universal truths states, your SharePoint solution isn't complete until you've measured its effectiveness. Regardless of whether you are an external consultant or an internal resource, there is always pressure to be cost conscious. By implementing cost-effective SharePoint solutions that provide clear, measurable ROI, you will be ahead of the curve. And taking the time to document and market your return on investment will impress your management team and build support for your future projects. But what is ROI and how do you quantify the ROI for your business process solution?

At its core, ROI is:

• A cool acronym,

• A method of quantifying benefits reaped,

• A way to "feel good" about an investment,

- A way to offset opportunity costs,

- A method for validating good decisions,

- A way to "spread the word" about your work,

- A way to attract new customers,

- A way to turn your current customers into SharePoint champions.

The reason for calculating ROI is straightforward—we want to validate our good decisions, feel good about our efforts, and let our management team know how smart we are. The hardest part is figuring out where to start. How do you know which qualitative and quantitative measurement techniques are right?

First, you need to take a step back and reaffirm your vision. If your vision is BPR, your ROI strategy must focus on quantifying the time and money you have saved.

Monetary ROI can take many forms, as illustrated in Figure 8-6.

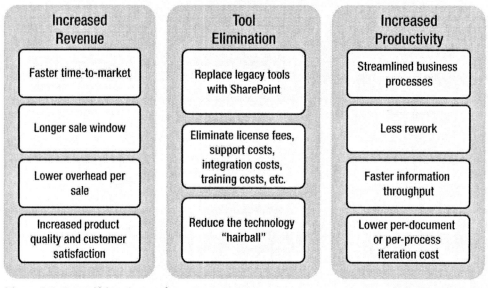

Figure 8-6. *Quantifying time and money*

Increasing process quality has a marked impact on overall product quality and customer satisfaction (with corresponding revenue increases). Streamlined business processes eliminate redundancies and shorten your time to market. In many industries, this condensed time to market results in a longer product lifespan, a longer sale window, and more revenue. Eliminating redundant tools can also generate significant cost savings, with opportunities to reduce or eliminate spending on license fees, support costs, integration costs, and so forth. By reducing the technology "hairball" your business users face every day, you will lower their per-process iteration cost, improve employee morale, and lower your overhead per sale.

Start your ROI calculations by reviewing the "Increased Revenue" and "Tool Elimination" columns in Figure 8-6. If you can quantify the impact you have had on your time to market, you should be able to review sales data and determine the corresponding revenue lift you are receiving. If you have been able to shorten the time it takes your employees to close a sale, you should be able to quantify your reductions in overhead cost per sale.

The next step is quantifying your productivity savings. Since most process optimizations result in "time" wins rather than direct "revenue" wins, productivity savings can be harder to quantify. Consider using a standardized formula (like the one shown in Figure 8-7) to calculate process costs.

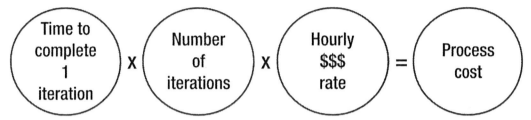

Figure 8-7. Base formula for calculating process cost

Note that this formula requires three key pieces of data:

1. The length of time it takes to complete one iteration of a process.

2. The number of process iterations completed in one year.

3. An hourly rate for a person's time in your organization.

Work with your business owner to find the time it takes to complete a process iteration and determine how many iterations occur annually. Ask your finance team for help in quantifying your company's hourly rate. Remember, you are looking for what an hour of time is worth in your company. This should include salary, benefits, licensing costs, hardware, and so forth. And don't worry about job grades—simply find an average dollar amount. You'll be applying this hourly rate consistently across all your process valuations.

Once you have all the data points, plug them into the formula shown in Figure 8-7 to determine your process cost. Note that you will be applying this formula twice—once to measure the cost of the team's original process and again to measure your new, improved process. The difference between the two process costs is your productivity savings.

A Practical Example

Earlier in this chapter we reviewed the quality control process for MultiMEGA's print production team. This team follows a standard project rhythm—they build new print materials, conduct peer reviews, report and resolve issues, and deliver the final product. The problem is their issue reporting. Team members use multiple Excel spreadsheets to capture and track issues, causing delays with managing multiple documents. The team estimates they spend up to four hours per project syncing up spreadsheets. With an average completion rate of 200 projects per year, the team is losing up to 800 hours of productivity annually.

We already have several of the data points needed for our process cost formula. We know that issue tracking takes four hours per project and that we have 200 projects (process iterations) per year. We talked with the finance team and they advised using an hourly rate of $45 for our valuation. This means our formula is: 4 × 200 × $45 = $36,000. So the current process cost is $36,000.

We thought we could improve this process by centralizing our data storage. We created a single SharePoint list the team could use to report, assign, track, and close issues. This eliminated duplicate issue reporting and spreadsheet syncing, saving the four hours that used to be spent on these tasks. Since the new process takes zero minutes to complete, our new process cost formula is: 0 × 200 × $45 = $0.00. With a previous process cost of $36,000 and a new process cost of $0.00, we have generated an ROI of $36,000.

Incorporating ROI Valuations into Your Project Timeline

We now know *how* to calculate ROI. But we have to hone in on *when* this ROI calculation should be done. Too often, SharePoint implementers try to calculate the return on their investment immediately after a project launches. The results are lackluster because the valuation is based on "assumed" benefits.

I recommend holding off on conducting your ROI valuation for three to six months after project launch. Waiting at least three months ensures that your process improvements have been implemented successfully and you have valid statistics on process iteration lengths, number of iterations, time savings, and so forth. If you wait any longer than six months, users may start forgetting the details of their previous process and have difficulty drawing comparisons.

It can be difficult to hit this three- to six-month target window, however—particularly if you are embedded in other projects. Here's a tip: When a project launches, schedule an ROI reminder on your calendar. You'll get an automated reminder when the three-month review window hits.

To kick off your ROI valuation, schedule a meeting with your business owner. Talk with him or her about the benefits the company has derived from the new process and work with the owner to identify potential revenue increases, productivity increases, and so forth. Make a detailed list of the new process's positives and negatives and work with your business owner to investigate and quantify as many data points as you can. Gather testimonials and user stories where possible. (These data can be used to show the morale wins for this solution.)

Once you have finished collecting your valuation data, it is time to build your first case study. Case studies are the "commercials" for your projects. They should highlight the business need(s), briefly explain the solution, and list the key benefits achieved (including real ROI dollars). Case studies must be concise and easy to understand but should include ancillary notes or appendixes that provide details on your ROI valuations. Figure 8-8 provides a case study for our print production example.

Case Study

- **Need**
  - Print production team used multiple Excel spreadsheets to submit, track and assign issues.
- **Solution**
  - Moved data online to SharePoint
  - Created a KPI dashboard to display project analytics
- **Benefits**
  - No more syncing of multiple spreadsheets
  - Everyone can add/view issues simultaneously
  - No more duplicate reporting of issues
  - Eliminates 4 hours of work per project
  - Total savings = $36,000/year

Figure 8-8. An example case study

Once your case study is built, you are ready to share your success. This is a collective win for your organization, so make sure you share the credit. Forward the case study on to your management team and to your business owner's management team, lauding the winning partnership you forged. If possible, present your case study in leadership meetings, team meetings, users group meetings, and so forth. Emphasize that your process savings are enabling teams to stop eating up time with manual tasks, thereby freeing up resources to focus on value-added work.

Moving on to the Next Project

Whether you are an external consultant or an internal resource, you need to evaluate where you will go and what you will do after your current project is completed. If you are an internal resource and want to focus on building SharePoint process solutions on an ongoing basis, you should start scouting new projects before your inaugural project is completed. Continue being picky about the projects you take, however. You want projects that reflect business pain, hit a large number of people, and involve a frequent business rhythm. You also need to ensure that the project is sized appropriately, can be built using mostly out-of-the-box components, and has quantifiable ROI.

It may take a few months (and a few projects) to build your business process reengineering brand, so be prepared to sell your vision and recruit business owners to work with you. As word spreads of your success, people will start soliciting your help. Prepare for the deluge! Standardize your process and determine how you will prioritize work.

Once you have a few projects completed, start compiling a cumulative ROI total for all your projects. This large ROI number will be an attention-grabber that you can use to justify more resources, more training, and so forth. As you expand your reach, keep these tips in mind:

- Don't avoid projects just because they might not have a large ROI valuation. Champions become champions through big *and* small wins.

- Create a case study for every project. These case studies are your keys to success.

- Create and memorize a two-minute, five-minute, and ten-minute elevator speech for each of your projects. You never know when you'll have the ability to tell your story.

- Document your process for valuing each project. As your ROI numbers grow, you will be asked to justify your facts and figures.

Summary

From the outset, it was clear that this was a "different" kind of chapter. Rather than being written from the perspective of an external consultant, this chapter focuses on how you—an internal resource—can change how your organization uses SharePoint.

You learned why and how processes devolve and how you (armed with an understanding of the universal truths) can change the way your business users work. You learned how process engineering methodologies like Six Sigma, Business Process Modeling, and CMMI have risen in popularity and discovered how you can identify the "forgotten layer of content management" in your organization. By targeting the business user's content—the content typically forgotten by enterprise-level content management systems—you can build business process solutions that spread like wildfire and make a difference in how your end users work with SharePoint.

Together we built a process roadmap strategy, a "couch-to-success" plan to help you evaluate your organization, build and refine your benchmarks and goals, select the all-important first project, map your project requirements, and implement your solution. We completed our journey by examining how and why ROI should be calculated and built a case study to summarize our inaugural project's success.

So where do we go from here? First, we need to acknowledge that processes are not inherently evil. But that doesn't mean they're implemented well. The key questions are: Will you be able to take what you've learned here and build more concrete processes? Or will your next new process suffer the same fate as its ancestors?

CHAPTER 9

Success with Search

By Michal Pisarek

If Edison had a needle to find in a haystack, he would proceed at once with the diligence of the bee to examine straw after straw until he found the object of his search. . . . I was a sorry witness of such doings, knowing that a little theory and calculation would have saved him ninety per cent of his labor.

—Nikola Tesla (1856–1943), *New York Times*, October 19, 1931

This chapter will look at various tools and techniques that the SharePoint information architect can leverage to create an effective search solution. Although the improvement of content findability is touted as an essential outcome of implementing SharePoint, and in some cases is the very reason for SharePoint to be implemented, search is often overlooked in the process of implementation for reasons ranging from being too difficult, to being too easy to simply turn on and get results, or it is left to the end of the project when time is running out.

The goal of this chapter is to make sure you understand why search can be difficult and to help you gain some knowledge of the various configuration options available (don't worry we aren't going to get too technical), how to effectively gather requirements for search, and how to provide a process you can use to help create a valuable and robust search solution. SharePoint search provides a veritable treasure trove of configuration options that can provide real value to an organization for relatively little effort. Scopes, custom results pages, refiners, and keywords can all be created without the need for an extensive development effort. However, before you can start tinkering with configuration, you need to understand your organization's vision for search and the outcomes you wish to achieve. Gathering requirements beyond the typical platitudes, such as we need a better search or more intuitive search experience, can be difficult. It is imperative for you to have tangible requirements or outcomes that can be implemented utilizing the many aspects that SharePoint search has to offer.

The Value of Search

There is no doubt that for many organizations the findability of content is one of the major issues they face. I have spent time looking into the importance of findability and putability (presented in Chapter 3), and here we will look deeper into how we can accomplish this within SharePoint. With the growth of content over the years, many organizations are beginning to feel the strain of the mountains of information they possess. A good search solution enables end users to find what they're looking for in addition to finding people and related content.

Because of the value that search can provide for an organization, it is surprising that many don't invest the time and effort needed to understand their search needs or desired outcomes. In many cases search is simply enabled and tested by having an administrator enter "test" as a keyword in the search box and then hope the correct results will appear, such as the screenshot shown in Figure 9-1.

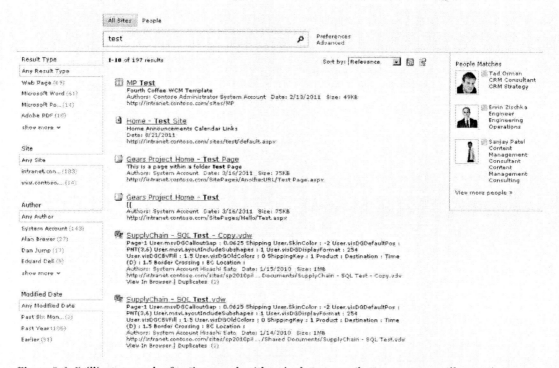

Figure 9-1. Brilliant example of testing search with a single test case that encompasses all scenarios

Let's be honest; search will be one of the most popular and utilized functions within the SharePoint platform. Even users who don't use the platform for their day-to-day activities will be drawn to the search capabilities that SharePoint offers. Power users of the new SharePoint intranet may only browse three or four articles per day, although they may have searched 30 to 50 times that day to find the information they are looking for.

Put simply, your search experience can make the difference between a good outcome with SharePoint and a great outcome. The key is to understand what makes a search experience great. Fortunately, SharePoint provides an amazing array of options for search to create your own search solutions utilizing your organization's content and presenting search in a way that makes sense to your end users. With a relatively small amount of out-of-the-box configuration, you can tailor your search solution to your organization. While you may need custom code in order to achieve what you want with other parts of the platform, in most cases the configuration options within search have the tools you need to satisfy your business requirements.

Why Search Can Be Difficult

Search can be difficult and time consuming to get right for your organization, yet on the other hand, it is also very easy to "turn on" and see results appear. A common myth is thinking that the default search capabilities in SharePoint are going to automatically work for your organization and provide you with the search results your end users expect. To provide your end users with valuable search results you first must spend time to understand your organization, and that is time consuming. Think of it as a journey, not a destination. As your users learn more about what they are searching for, you will in turn learn what a great search experience will look like for them.

Quite often search is one of the last requirements to make it into the solution scope. When your IT projects run over time or over budget, search is frequently a casualty. The assumption is that the out-of-the-box search will simply "work," and the rationale behind spending additional time on search requirements or fine tuning the existing search functionality will be outweighed by other features or enhancements. Since search is so easy to enable, why bother spending additional time on what can be seen as incremental improvements? Consider how many times a day you look for information and the frustration you feel when you don't find what you're looking for. Just improving your search results incrementally can have a significant impact.

Users have extremely high expectations around search due to everyday experiences with Bing or Google. These expectations extend from the consumer space into the enterprise world, and it can be difficult to create the same experience (Google and Bing have giant teams dedicated to search!). Low tolerance of failure around search can translate into dissatisfaction with other elements of the platform, potentially poisoning all of the other benefits and value that SharePoint provides.

This near magical experience of being able to search in the consumer space and find exactly what you need is difficult in the enterprise because of the unique context of every organization. The relevancy algorithms that Bing and Google use rely on links between pages that thousands or millions of people do as part the natural process of building web pages, writing blogs, and tweeting, in other words, using the Internet the way it was designed to be used. This doesn't work in the enterprise world, where searching is contextual in nature and rooted to a specific task, process, or event, which can be difficult for search engines to understand without adequate metadata.

In order for search to determine the context of content, a robust information architecture and sufficient categorization of content needs to occur. For many organizations this implies stricter governance around how content is structured, organized, and labeled. This can come as a shock to many end users, who may feel that including additional metadata to content is simply more work without providing them any instant or tangible value. In other words, they don't see what's in it for them.

Finally, search is simply a means to access the organizational content. However, there is one rule that is often overlooked—garbage content in, garbage content out. No matter how powerful the search capabilities in SharePoint are, if you do not understand the content in your organization or if most of it is of no value, then you will just have an easier way to find garbage.

Many people think that search is a panacea to the problem of bad content; unfortunately, it isn't. In many cases an organization can be better served by reviewing, understanding, and consolidating their content before implementing a robust search solution. However, the expectation is that search will magically find what end users need through the mountains of content that an organization possesses. Trying to convince stakeholders otherwise can be an uphill battle.

Prerequisites for Good Search

A good search experience stems from a solid foundation of other elements. You need to have a solid base in order to have search provide value. Search is interwoven and depends on many other elements that have to be considered; it cannot be viewed as a standalone piece of functionality that will work harmoniously with any and all content you have in your organization. There are key elements that must be considered, as presented in Figure 9-2. Let's look at these key elements in more detail.

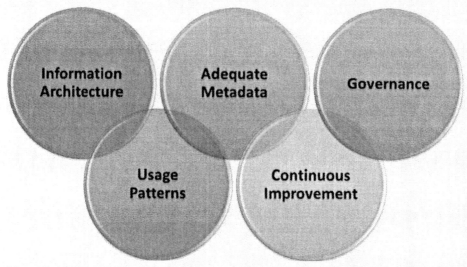

Figure 9-2. Good search stems from a good foundation of these elements

Information Architecture

Your SharePoint information architecture is going to help your users accurately determine the context of the content they are trying to find. Everything from site-naming conventions to where your enterprise search center is located and how users get access to search should be simple and intuitive. Ensuring that your content is named correctly, is stored in the correct location, and uses terminology that your users understand will ensure that when the correct search result appears they will instantly be able to recognize it.

Adequate Metadata

We have seen the importance of metadata in Chapter 3, but what about its importance in relation to search? Without adequate metadata you will not be able to provide the right context to both your end users and the SharePoint search engine for accurate search results. If search is viewed as a mechanism to easily query the metadata and attributes of content, you will begin to see the importance of correct categorization within the organization.

In many organizations the problem with their search implementation isn't search per se, it's because they don't have accurate and intuitive metadata on their content so that both the search engine and users can distinguish the correct context.

Usage Patterns

You need to understand what users are looking for, the context in which they're performing searches, and what their expectations are for the search results they will receive. By understanding these usage patterns, the correct configuration options can be determined. For example, imagine if you know that your users expect to see search results 5 minutes after content is created instead of the default 20 minutes. You can then set your incremental crawl times accordingly.

▓ **Note** Users often expect to be able to find content right away after adding it. It's important to explain that content does not appear until it has been crawled and that there are issues of system performance to be considered when adjusting the crawl frequency.

Not all users search the same way, even if they are searching for the same content. By understanding the usage patterns you'll be able to better target search results to users when they need it.

Governance

Governance is often overlooked when implementing search, but it should be part of any SharePoint governance plan. Your search governance plan should be composed of the roles and responsibilities around search, the roadmap for search, what content in the organization will be indexed, and how search will be leveraged to achieve business value. Business value is really a loaded term, but you need to know how you will make the best use of search. Will you spend time making experts easier to find or will you spend time ensuring that the most popular content is returned first in search results because you know your users know the content better than experts within your organization? Either way whatever you decide to do with search, you need to know what you are trying to do so that you can constantly drive toward these goals.

Continuous Improvement

As with other aspects of SharePoint, your search implementation should be continuously improving throughout its lifetime. With all the tools and tweaks that can be performed relatively easily, a continuous cycle of improvement can ensure you are at least moving in the right direction.

Your continuous improvement plan should have items such as how users suggest new configuration options like Best Bets or Keywords (which we will cover later), how often search should be reviewed, or the criteria for adding new sources of content. A simple example could be making sure you are looking at search reports monthly (which we will also cover later) to something more formal like sending out surveys periodically to get feedback on search.

Measuring the Effectiveness of Search

The question of measuring the effectiveness of search within an organization is one that can cause a heated debate. Most organizations have difficulty measuring the improvement that search provides because they are trying to measure vague requests, such as "I want a better search or a Google-like search experience."

For some organizations, measuring search can be so problematic that they simply don't bother to try to improve it at all. However, the adage says you only get what you measure, and this is particularly true for search. By providing a measurement you also have a tangible goal you are trying to achieve. This goal can then be the basis of any requirement-gathering activities or configuration that will be performed. Find the success metric that resonates with your organization and plan your efforts and investments toward that.

Trying to justify the effectiveness of search on an organizational-wide level, with a goal such as a 10 percent reduction in time to find content, can be both difficult and expensive. Instead try to measure the incremental improvements that search has made on specific use cases that have been identified, such as:

- The time spent to find the phone number and the department of any user within the organization has decreased by 50 percent.

- The time spent to locate the latest documents that were created by the current user has decreased by 40 percent.

- The time to find an expert within the organization based on a specific keyword has decreased by 75 percent.

- The time spent to find updated policies and procedures has decreased by 20 percent.

All of the above use cases can be easily measured before and after implementation. For instance, you can run 20 users through the above use cases to see how much time each currently takes (to set a baseline for your future measurements). Once your new search has been implemented, the same use cases can be ran again. You can then determine the tangible difference that search has made for the specific cases.

Typical Search Elements

Before we dive into how to start gathering requirements for search, let's review the typical elements the majority of search implementations in SharePoint possess. Most SharePoint search implementations consist of the out-of-the-box elements detailed below; however, with additional custom coding, anything is possible.

Rest assured that search is one of the most configurable areas within the SharePoint platform, and it can be leveraged in many different ways. We'll now look at some of the common elements of which you should be aware.

Search Scopes

Search scopes allow you to partition your search results into smaller segments based on particular attributes so results will only appear from that particular part of the index (Figure 9.3). It essentially allows users to filter search results before the query is executed. Scopes can be incredibly effective in search implementation if you understand how your organization groups different types of content together and its usage patterns.

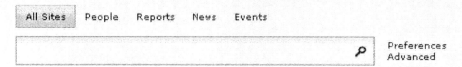

Figure 9-3. Search scopes in action

Search scopes can be modeled on many different business attributes. With the abundance of configuration options within SharePoint, you can mix and choose many attributes to create a search scope. Most commonly search scopes are based on content types, departments, authors, the location within the SharePoint site (such as this site or the site collection), the physical location of the content, or even time-based attributes (such as the date created or the date modified). Examples of typical search scopes would be physical location, content type, and whether it is time-based, task-based, or department-based. Let's look at these in more detail.

Physical Location

If an organization stores its content in multiple geographic locations, a search by location may be what makes the most sense for users when they are searching. Another way would be the logical location of the content, such as searching "file shares" for contents that are not stored within SharePoint.

Content Type

You can also model scopes after the type of content it represents. For example, a "policies and procedures" search scope can be very effective for some organizations. Other common examples could be a more generic search, like "news," "events," "documents," or "list items."

Time Based

Search scopes can also be based on dates. If your organization thinks of content in terms of yearly cycles, where the majority of the time users are looking for content created or modified in the last year, a time-based scope makes the most sense.

For instance you can create a search scope that only contains content that has been created in the past calendar year. Or you may have a number of time-based scopes such as "this year," "last year," or "two years and older." Time-based scopes work really well if you know that most of the time users are searching for content that has been recently created or if the business has many time-bound processes.

Task Based

Maybe your organization thinks of content in terms of tasks that users do, such as opening a new member account or processing a member termination. In this case you can model your search scopes on the tasks these users perform. When users are performing a task and looking for relevant content, they can simply choose the scope and type in a search term. Task-based scopes can be difficult to implement due to the wide range of possible content they may contain. Understand the tasks commonly performed by your end users and stakeholder groups and plan from there.

Department Based

If your organization thinks of content primarily in terms of departments, then it would make sense to model your search scopes on departmental boundaries. Of course in terms of breaking down the silo effect (where information is only visible or accessible to very narrowly defined sub-groups) this is not advised, but it is another option you can consider.

Search Refinements

Search refinements provide the user with the ability to filter search results after the query is executed. This experience is similar to those on eBay or Amazon where a number of filters are created depending on the result set that is returned. This is one of the new search improvements for SharePoint 2010 and has been one of the most well-received features from end users. Figure 9-4 shows how refiners make filtering results quick and easy.

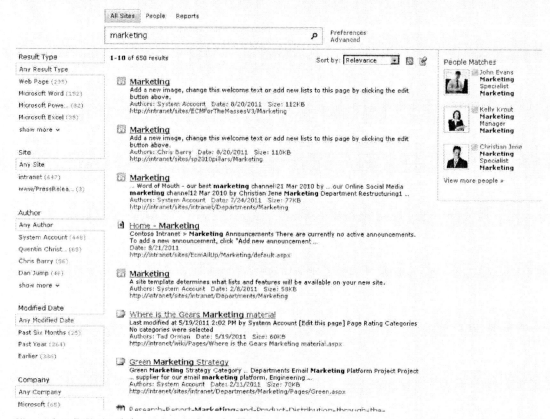

Figure 9-4. *Refiners (leftmost column) make filtering many results quick and easy.*

The ability to quickly and easily refine search results from thousands down to the exact result you need provides huge value to all users. In addition, the refinement panel is a treasure trove of configuration options that can be suited to any business process, task, or organization. We'll look at refiners again in the "People Search" section below.

Best Bets and Keywords

Best Bets" and Keywords allow an administrator to predefine a few key search results and have them prominently displayed at the top of the results list. These are great ways to steer users to common search results, to promote content, and to provide context for search if it's simply not possible for the search engine to distinguish the correct context. If you look at Figure 9-5, you can see an effective example of this.

All Sites	People	Reports

| holiday | 🔍 | Preferences
Advanced |

Result Type

Any Result Type

Adobe PDF (4)

XML Document (2)

Web Page (1)

Site

Any Site

intranet/sites (6)

www/Products (1)

Author

Any Author

System Account (5)

alixv (4)

Modified Date

Any Modified Date

Past Year (2)

Earlier (5)

Product

Any Product

Adventure Works ...

A. Datum Full Fr...

Adventure Works ...

1-5 of 7 results (2 duplicates)   Sort by: Relevance ▾ 🔲 📄

☆ **Vacation Request Form**
If you are looking for rhe vacation request form please click on the link above and follows the steps described.
http://intranet.contoso.com/HR/VacReqForm.aspx

▭ **X300 Full Frame**
X300 Full Frame Related Wikis Taking Pictures at Night: Datum Advanced Digital Camera X300 Exposure Light Timing: Datum Advanced Digital Camera X300 Product Datasheets © 2009 CONTOSO. All Rights Reserved Privacy Policy Sitemap Terms of Use Contact Contoso
Authors: System Account   Date: 12/17/2009   Size: 72KB
http://www/Products/CamerasAndCamcorders/Pages/X300-Full-Frame.aspx

▭ **Adventure Works 52" LCD HDTV X790W Television Sales Brochure**
Authors: System Account alixv   Date: 3/8/2010   Size: 43KB
http://intranet/sites/intranet/Tools/Market ... TV-X790W-Television-Sales-Brochure-UK110.pdf
Duplicates (2)

▭ **Adventure Works 52" LCD HDTV X790W Television Technical Brochure**
Authors: System Account alixv   Date: 3/8/2010   Size: 43KB
http://intranet/sites/intranet/Tools/Market ... 790W-Television-Technical-Brochure-UK210.pdf

▭ **Adventure Works 26" 720p LCD HDTV M140 Television Sales Brochure**
Authors: System Account alixv   Date: 3/8/2010   Size: 43KB
http://intranet/sites/intranet/Tools/Market ... DTV-M140-Television-Sales-Brochure-AS310.pdf

▭ **UserFileBrochures.xml**
... Corporate Promotions European **Holiday** Promotion Metadata TV and ... Corporate Promotions European **Holiday** Promotion Metadata TV and ... Corporate Promotions European **Holiday** Promotion Metadata TV and ...
Date: 2/11/2011
http://intranet/sites/intranet/content/UserFileBrochures.xml
Duplicates (2)

Figure 9-5. The result "vacation request form" Best Bet is displayed prominently as the first search result.

In this example, a user has typed in the search term "holiday," but the person was actually searching for the employee vacation request form. Since the search engine in SharePoint cannot read the minds of users (hopefully that is part of the next version), you can easily define the Best Bet to link the keyword "holiday" to the location of the employee vacation request form, making it appear magically to end users as seen in Figure 9-6. You could extend this by also including the "office holiday closure" calendar as a Best Bet for the search "holidays," if this is something your users are commonly looking for.

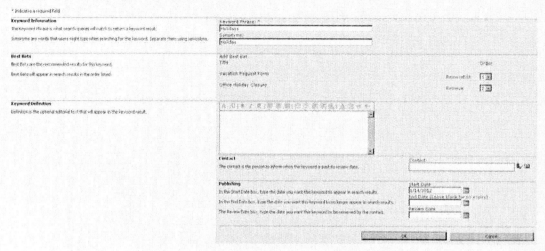

Figure 9-6. Defining a Keyword phrase with a number of Best Bets

Search Result Pages

The search results pages display (you guessed it) search results to users. Customizing search results pages is often overlooked; however, it can be a great way to ensure that users are seeing search results in a format that makes the most sense based on what they are searching for.

Displaying search results differently depending on the type of content that is been searched for can save users time and provide for a more compelling search experience. More often than not you do not want to see search results displayed the same way for every piece of content. For example, if you are searching for images, the title of the image may not be as important as a thumbnail preview.

Search results pages can also be a great way to encourage users to add the relevant metadata to content by surfacing this metadata directly into the results. This can frequently help with the adoption of categorization of content within the organization.

All the search results pages presented in this chapter are really just web part pages with search-specific web parts on them. You can create your own pages and insert whichever search components you need (as seen in Figure 9-7). Custom search results pages allow you to customize the search result's web parts on the page, including the actual search results, refinements, search boxes, or other web parts on the results page. You can also link a search results page to a particular search scope, providing even greater flexibility.

Figure 9-7. Search results page in edit view

People Search

In many organizations it's not what you know, but who you know that is important. The people search capabilities in SharePoint allow you to connect with and find people you work with.

The ability to find experts within an organization can frequently be more valuable than finding content. People search allows data from people profiles to be exposed through the SharePoint search engine. By leveraging user profile properties you can search for other users within the organization quickly and easily. In Figure 9-8 you can see a people search for the term "marketing" where a user has used one of the refiners in the leftmost column to filter the results to show just those marketing people who have listed marathons as one of their interests.

Figure 9-8. Well wouldn't you know it! Seems like there are three people in marketing that are interested in marathons.

People search is linked to the overall social capabilities of the SharePoint 2010 platform. Search results are highly influenced by the colleagues that users have added to their profiles. People search also provides a gateway to allow people to connect with other individuals within the organization. The connections these individuals make can be both social and professional and can have a tangible impact on the organization.

Search Suggestions

Search suggestions are preemptive Keywords that are shown to users when they are typing into a search query. They can be a great tool to steer users to common queries, help users save time by allowing them to select an existing search query, and provide an experience that is similar to the consumer search tools such as Bing or Google, as seen in Figure 9-9.

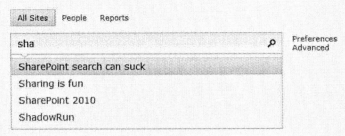

Figure 9-9. Suggestions appear as users type in the search box

Search Quick Wins

In any search implementation there are a number of simple configuration options that can be performed to maximize the value to your end users. Quick and easy search configuration options you might want to consider include document only search scope, define Best Bets and Keywords, search training, and defining scopes for your organization. Let's look at these in more depth.

Document Only Search Scope

In many organizations that implement SharePoint, users will be searching for documents far more often than any other type of content. You can quickly and easily create a document only search scope so the results that are returned are limited to physical documents with any file extension of your choosing.

Define Best Bets and Keywords

Defining Best Bets and Keywords is a great way to link predefined search results to common keywords. By associating specific terms with specific results, you can really improve the search experience for users by ensuring that common search terms are providing the correct results.

In order to determine which Best Bets and Keywords to implement, a simple survey can suffice. In your survey, simply ask users for the ten most common search keywords they use and the results they expect.

All SharePoint search implementations should have at least 25 Best Bets or Keywords that are linked to common queries before search is rolled out. Although 25 is not the number needed for all organizations, it is a rough rule of thumb that will ensure you are spending adequate effort on defining your Best Bets and Keywords. Additionally you should always be reviewing or updating your Best Bets and Keywords over the lifetime of your SharePoint search solution.

Search Training

One of the fundamental mistakes that many organizations make when implementing a search solution is assuming that end users do not need training to use SharePoint search (everyone knows how to use Google and Bing, right?). Most end users will need to go through training to ensure they understand what is being indexed, how to perform searches, and the best way to manipulate search results.

Training can be structured into various levels, such as beginner, intermediate, and advanced. However, all end users should go through some level of training regardless of their skill levels.

- Beginner training could involve locating where search is in SharePoint, how to do a simple keyword search, what type of content is being indexed, and how to navigate through search results.

- Intermediate search can focus effective use of scopes, how to filter results using the refinement panel, and adding colleagues from people search results.

- Advanced search can cover topics such as the search query syntax, federating search results with Windows 7, and using the advanced search capabilities.

Make sure there is some level of training for all users. There are a number of formats you can use depending on your organization. In my experience, a combination of in-person training supported by online reference materials works very well. Common elements such as scopes, refinements, and sorting may seem intuitive for you, but for many users these are foreign concepts that will require training.

Define Scopes for Your Organization

Each organization will have different scopes depending on how it functions. It makes no sense to have a time-based search scope if users organize and think about content in terms of departments.

After you determine the most valuable content and how the users group that content together (which I will cover later), you should create your scopes to mimic these patterns. Well-designed search scopes not only provide an indication on the type of content that is being searched, but they also improve search accuracy by limiting the total results to those items specified within the scope.

The process of defining scopes for your organization can be tricky, but a few simple scopes such as news items, events, policies and procedures, people, or other groupings that make sense your organization can provide tangible results.

Search Requirements Elicitation Process

There are many ways to gather requirements for search depending on your organization and your own personal skills and experience. The process I will describe here is a simple iterative process, by no means perfect, but provides a good starting point to ensure that you cover all of the bases needed so your search provides real value to end users.

▒ **Note** The requirements elicitation process has already been covered in Chapter 1, and the steps outlined here should be integrated into that overall process. However, if you are doing a purely search-related project, the information in this chapter will guide you through that stand-alone process.

As this is an iterative process, you can start from any step within the process and go from there. Thus it can be used in an existing search scenario or when you are creating a new search solution for your organization. Figure 9-10 shows the various stages I will cover in the next few sections.

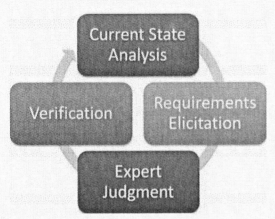

Figure 9-10. Simple search requirement elicitation process

While the diagram and process appear simple, each step can become fairly involved. We will explore each starting with current state analysis

Current State Analysis

Current state analysis concerns itself with understanding the current organizational context to help inform search decisions. You need to understand how your organization currently functions before you can start planning your search requirements gathering activities.

Think of the current state analysis phase as a prerequisite phase that will be used as a direct input into your future requirements gathering activities. The base level understanding you gain in the current state analysis phase will be invaluable in future phases. There are three simple activities and outcomes you want to achieve in this phase, as shown in Figure 9-11.

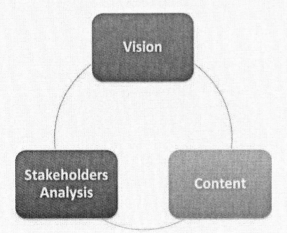

Figure 9-11. Current state analysis activities

1. *Vision*: Your vision for search will help drive and focus all future efforts for search.

2. *Content*: By understanding the content within your organization, you will be better able to focus on content of real value, while disregarding content that will provide no value to your organization.

3. *Stakeholder analysis*: In order to get a successful search solution, you need to understand who to ask and what role each person plays. Stakeholder analysis will provide you with this list of individuals.

Vision

The vision you have for search will guide you in what you are ultimately trying to achieve and help you identify the business value search will provide. You need to determine what the role of search will be within your organization beyond simply "finding stuff." Search can be leveraged in many ways, such as increased access to experts, innovation by exposing relevant content, increased compliance by surfacing correct content, or even custom-driven search applications.

Your vision should be closely linked to corporate objectives and business goals. This vision would then allow you, as the SharePoint information architect, to guide requirements-gathering activities. Beware though of having a search vision that contains common platitudes such as improved search, enhanced findability, or simply finding stuff. By having a tangible vision you will be able to structure your requirements-gathering activities and search implementation accordingly.

Of course, the difficult part is extracting the search vision from users.

The Cover Story Game

One technique I have used that works particularly well is the "Cover Story game" from the book *Gamestorming: A Playbook for Innovators, Rulebreakers and Changemakers"* by Dave Gray, Sunni Brown, and James Macanufo. The reason this works well is that this technique gives you enough structure to ensure that you get tangible examples without constraining users from being able to really explore the many possible end states that may be applicable for search in your organization.

The *Gamestorming* book describes the "Cover Story game" as follows:

> *Cover Story is a game about pure imagination. The purpose is to think expansively around an ideal future state for the organization; it's an exercise in visioning. The object of the game is to suspend all disbelief and envision a future state that is so stellar that it landed your organization on the cover of a well-known magazine. The players must pretend as though this future has already taken place and has been reported by the mainstream media. This game is worth playing because it not only encourages people to "think big," but also actually plants the seeds for a future that perhaps wasn't possible before the game was played. (p.87)*

In order to play the game you separate your users into groups of between four and six. Ensure that each group has markers and ask them to fill in the template shown in Figure 9-12, which is usually printed on a big poster and hung on a wall.

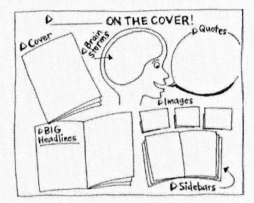

Figure 9-12. Post this on a wall or whiteboard to guide participants

Explain the object of the game is to define each category on the template:

- *Cover*: Tells the story of their big success with search
- *Headline*: The substance of the cover story
- *Sidebars*: Interesting facts about the story
- *Quotes*: Quotes from potential end users of the solution
- *Brainstorm*: Documenting initial ideas (this is important!)
- *Images*: Supporting the content with illustrations

At the end of the time period (usually an hour), have the groups present the cover story of their vision of search to the other groups. From the vision they have described, you can then determine exactly what the organization is trying to achieve.

For instance, if many of the cover stories revolve around finding experts within the organization, then it's an indicator that you should be concentrating your efforts around people search, user profiles, and a taxonomy needed to support this.

Content

In this section I will discuss the types of content that exist within the organization. The types of content identified and their value to the business and end users will inform search requirements-gathering activities. Put simply, you don't want to be wasting time and effort on content that provides minimal benefits. Another common misconception is that a great search experience can cover up bad content. This content analysis phase will determine the value of the content within the organization and also the state that the content is in. You will have a hard time creating a good search solution if the underlying content you have is substandard.

First, understand what content exists within the organization, and, just as importantly, there is a way your users think about that content. The best way to determine this is through a content audit. A content audit determines the sources of content, their use, their location, the owners of the content, when they are used, and where they reside.

There are multiple ways to perform a content audit. A simple and effective way is to give organizations a content analysis spreadsheet they can then fill out in their own time, such as the one presented in Figure 9-13.

Content Type	Location	Owner	Value	Usage
Contracts	File Share	Business Development	High	High usage
Customer Receipts	D: Drive for all content	None found	Low – only kept for compliance	Less than one access per month, only kept for compliance

Figure 9-13. Sample of a content analysis spreadsheet

Since a content audit can be time consuming, you need to ensure you have executive support for this so it is performed in an accurate and timely manner.

Users will go through their content and identify the type, location, owner, value, and how often the content is used. You can then use this information to target high-value content in your search implementation. It will also uncover any issues or hidden content that might have to be addressed before search is implemented.

Finally, a frequent by-product of the content audit is that it gets all users on the same page around how much content actually exists within the organization and whether it needs to be kept, tossed, added, or re-created.

Stakeholder Analysis

Stakeholder analysis seeks to understand who is involved in the implementation of the search solution. The better you understand who is involved in search, the less time you will waste having to navigate your way around the political landscape. You need to understand the stakeholders involved and also achieve a shared understanding between the stakeholders for ultimate search success.

The definition of a stakeholder includes anyone who cares about the project outcome (which could be many people), the things that influence them, and the environment they work in. This may include customers, sponsors, domain experts, end users, the project/implementation team, operational support, suppliers, and so forth. These people hold the source of your project requirements as well as the constraints and assumptions.

The first step in stakeholder analysis is to identify who they are. One of the best ways to understand the structure of an organization, the roles, and the people involved would be to look at the organizational model. You can ask for an organizational chart to evaluate the different functional areas (IT, human resources, finance, customer support, etc.), the reporting structure, and the different roles people may have in the company and the relationships among them. With this information you can target both the approach and the effort that may be needed to elicit the correct requirements.

For search, you can plan your requirements-gathering efforts based on the roles and people who would consume the end result (in this case, it would be the search experience and the search results). Search is often part of the stakeholder's (end user's) needs, so a natural stakeholder to focus on would be the end user. Observation techniques can be used to identify the types of information they look for on a day-to-day basis (this method is time consuming, but I find it captures the unstated requirements, or information needs, of which the end user isn't even aware). Another method is using surveys to understand information needs from a larger sample.

Some information you can capture for your stakeholders include:

- Name
- Title

- Role
- Location
- Special needs (in terms of their processes, information needs, expectations of performance, etc.)
- Authority levels
- Number of individuals in each role

In the end, current state analysis will allow you to understand the organization you are dealing with. Armed with that information, you can make better decisions in the other phases in the process!

Requirements Elicitation

The goal of requirements elicitation is to understand the needs of the organization and its users. In order to elicit requirements successfully, you really need to have a plan on how you tackle your requirements-gathering activities. In the previous phase, current state analysis, you determined the current state of the organization in terms of content. By understanding the stakeholders, the value of content, and the vision for search, you will have a head start into eliciting requirements from the correct people.

There are a number of requirements-elicitation techniques. Some of the common techniques are shown in Figure 9-14:

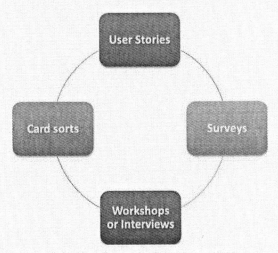

Figure 9-14. Requirements elicitation activities

You will see that some of these have been covered in earlier chapters, but they are no less useful for defining search requirements:

- User stories
- Surveys (ask them what works and doesn't work now, and what they'd like to see)
- Workshops or interviews (see Chapter 1 for more)
- Card sorts (see Chapter 4 for details)

Regardless of the technique, the first thing you need to determine is the information you are trying to illicit from your users (in other words, the purpose of your elicitation activity). The techniques listed above were chosen because they require a high level of interaction and collaboration from the participants. Many organizations may not be comfortable with this at first, but once this initial trepidation has passed, you will find that your participants will not only provide you with the information you need but they will also have fun doing so.

Functional Specification

The goal of the functional specification phase is to map the business or user requirements gathered to the functional specifications created for the implementation phase. This is when you take the requirements you have gathered and transform them into SharePoint configuration options for search.

Creating a good functional specification requires the following skills and inputs:

- *Business or user requirements*: Remember that ultimately you're trying to build a solution that will solve a business or user need while staying true to your search vision. You need to define the business problem you are trying to solve before you can create a functional specification to solve it. Don't make the mistake of jumping straight into the functional specification phase by confusing users with SharePoint specific terms. First, understand the business problem you are trying to solve, and then you can create a solution within SharePoint.

- *Technical SharePoint knowledge*: In many cases the SharePoint information architect will go down to a certain technical level of detail such as defining scopes as part of the functional specification. Keep in mind that it will be up to the person who creates or configures the solution to make sure that your functional needs are being met. It is far better to have detailed business or user requirements and then let the SharePoint architect craft a solution rather than you specifying the technical details that the solution should involve.

- *Assumptions and constraints*: By knowing your constraints in terms of time, budget, and scope, you can create a functional specification that is most feasible for implementation. For instance, if you have a limited budget, then creating a functional specification that will require considerable custom development would be a waste of time and money that the business is not willing to invest at this time.

We are not going to cover how to develop the functional specification here because this book would have to be two or three times bigger since the combination of both business skills and technical SharePoint knowledge is a vast topic. Some of the more technical elements you should consider would be your search topology, access accounts, Microsoft FAST Search versus SharePoint Enterprise Search, and the physical infrastructure needed to support your search environment.

However, the SharePoint information architect needs to understand the business and user needs in relation to search. There are many people who have amazing SharePoint technical skills and can perform the necessary configuration or development of custom code to satisfy these needs. Search is interesting because a lot can be achieved with simple out-of-the-box configuration. But before configuring anything, make sure you understand the business problem you are trying to solve.

Verification

The goal of the verification stage is to ensure that your search solution meets your business needs and vision. As part of your requirements gathering, you need to verify that what you collected and implemented is correct. Verification will ensure that your requirements are accurate and also help you identify new requirements in the process. There are a number of ways to verify and uncover new requirements, as shown in Figure 9-15.

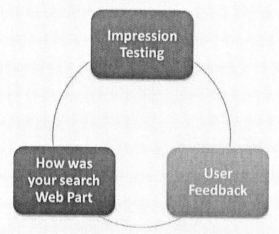

Figure 9-15. Impression testing activities

Verification is important since you want to be able to ensure that what you're creating is correct before you launch it out into the organization. Many SharePoint information architects make the mistake of not verifying the requirement until it is too late and the solution has already been launched. Remember, it is far more costly to try to correct a mistake that has already been implemented then to change a requirement before implementation begins.

Impression Testing

We covered impression testing in detail in Chapter 5, but as a reminder, impression testing lets you test your solution before spending a lot of time on development. It uses simple wireframes or screenshots and asks users to perform tasks as if they were looking at a real screen on a computer. When you see how users interact with your rough prototypes, you can find out very early if there are important design flaws. From a search perspective it's a great way to test whether custom scopes, refiners, and custom results pages are adding value to the end user's search experience.

User Feedback (Prior to Implementation)

The best way to find out what your users think about your solution is to simply ask them. Although this seems obvious, this question is not asked a lot, particularly in search. You want to ensure that your users can provide feedback *before* your search solution is implemented, but it is just as important *after* it has launched so that a continuous cycle of improvement can begin.

As discussed earlier in this chapter, users have an extremely low tolerance for failure with search due to their experience in the consumer search space. Frequently users can feel disempowered within an organization, particularly if they are searching for content and not getting the correct results. Users will simply give up and then your search solution is essentially a failure.

Before creating your search solution, make sure you're getting constant feedback from your users on all parts of the solution during the requirements elicitation phase. This can involve verifying scopes, ensuring that Best Bets make sense, and creating custom results pages that are going to provide value. By keeping an open dialogue with your users, you can not only verify that your assumptions and requirements are correct, but you will also open the lines of communication with end users, which will provide you with continual feedback for a better solution. Remember, collaboration is the name of the game, and even though you might hear things you don't want to, it will result in a better solution in the long run.

"How was your search?" Web Part (Post-Implementation)

After your search solution has been launched, you should ensure that there are ways for people to provide feedback on search. A common way to do this is to provide a way to rate search results and provide suggestions directly on search results pages using a "How was your search?" web part, which can be something as simple as an e-mail link, or it can be more complex, allowing users to rate search, add their feedback, and submit the results to an administrator.

Whichever approach you use, you will find that you'll receive invaluable feedback from users. Another by-product of this is that users will feel empowered because they have a direct influence on what is happening with search. Make sure that every piece of feedback that is sent to an administrator about search gets a personal response in return. The response should go back to the person who submitted the feedback and include details on whether it resulted in an improvement or change (e.g., a new Best Bet is added). The more open dialogue you can have with your end users, the more likely it is that your search solution is going to be a success.

Search Reporting

In SharePoint 2010, there are a number of fantastic search reporting tools available that can be used to both verify and uncover new requirements. Search reporting will provide you with hard data and statistics about how your search solution is performing. It is also a great way to measure the success of search by using common metrics such as ensuring that search queries with no results are kept to a minimum.

Search reporting is also extremely flexible in terms of adjusting the time period you want to query, scheduling alerts for reports, or even exporting the report data to a spreadsheet for further analysis. Some of the various search reports that are available are shown in Figure 9-16.

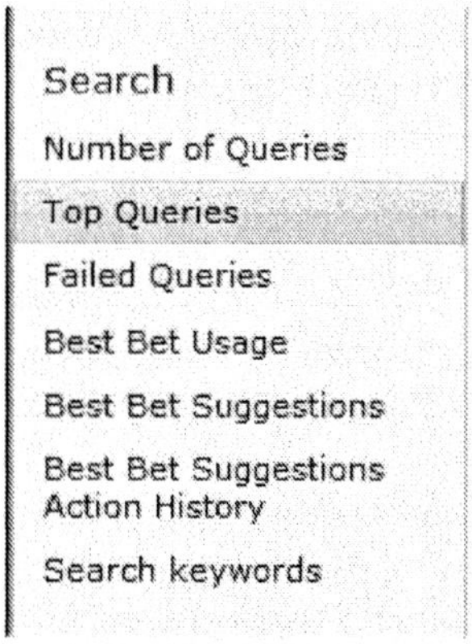

Search

Number of Queries

Top Queries

Failed Queries

Best Bet Usage

Best Bet Suggestions

Best Bet Suggestions
Action History

Search keywords

Figure 9-16. Various search reports available at the Site Collection level

There are an array of search reports available both from the end user side and from the administration side. From the administration perspective, there are reports such as crawl rate per type, overall query latency, crawl processing per activity, and others that can be used to improve and monitor search performance.

Of most interest to the SharePoint information architect are the site collection search reports that are available for each site collection that exists in your environment. It should be considered a crime not to use the SharePoint search reporting to improve your search implementation because there is a wealth of information that is generated automatically for you. Available reports include the number of queries executed, the top queries, suggested Best Bets and the Keywords used for searching. All these reports provide a wealth of information. Let's take a look at a few and how they can be leveraged to improve your search.

Number of Queries

The number of queries report shows you the total number of queries that users have entered over a particular timeframe. It lets you see how often your search solution is being used for a particular site collection or for a web application. You can see an example of this report in Figure 9-17.

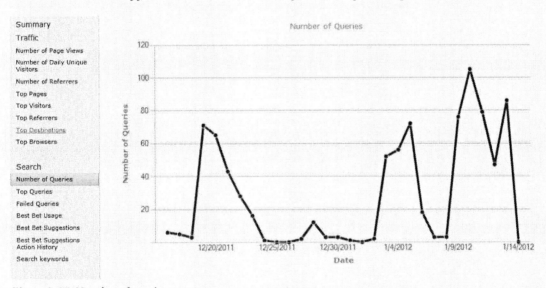

Figure 9-17. Number of queries report

It's a great tool to see how much usage search is getting, but it doesn't really tell you much about the quality of results that are being returned.

Best Bets Suggestions

This report recommends various URLs that are the most likely search results for a particular query based on the analysis of user patterns. You can choose to accept or reject the suggestions. If you accept them, the Best Bet and the corresponding URL is added to the search query list.

The combination of allowing users to suggest Best Bets and the ones that SharePoint suggests from this report can allow you to quickly and easily generate your Best Bets.

Top Queries

The top queries report shows you the search query text and the number of times the query was executed for your particular date range. This report is a great way to see the common queries your users are searching so you can gain insight into usage patterns. It also provides a way to target the top 10 or 20 queries to ensure you are providing the results for these queries that users expect to be presented with.

You can also use the top queries report to make sure you have Best Bets assigned for additional context to users in search results.

Failed Queries

The failed query report shows search queries that returned no search results or have zero click-through. This report can be used to identify search queries that are currently not providing the correct results or to improve the discoverability of content. You should ensure that you understand why failed queries are appearing in this report. For instance, maybe users are referring to a particular department by its previous name rather than the current one. In this case you could assign a Best Bet to the particular keyword that would direct the user to the correct location for the department.

Another way the failed queries report can be used is to measure the success of your search solution. A simple metric you can use to ensure you are constantly improving your search implementation is to make sure that the number of failed queries is reducing. It's a simple and easy metric to track, but it's also a great quantitative measurement.

Analyzing these search reports is relatively simple after search has been in use for a while, and they provide sufficient data for analysis. The real limiting factor here is time: Someone needs to be assigned to periodically review these reports and provide recommendations.

Summary

For the SharePoint information architect, search provides an interesting challenge. You need to understand the content your organization has, your vision for search, and your user or business needs to successfully implement a search solution. Add to this the exceedingly high expectations your users have from the consumer search space and this can potentially be a minefield.

However, by going through the process of understanding the current state of your organization, eliciting the most valuable business and user needs, translating these to functional specifications, and verifying that these are correct, you can create a great search solution.

This chapter has covered the various prerequisites for effective search, including consistent information architecture, adequate metadata, having a continuous improvement program in place, and ensuring that you are governing your search solution.

Delivering a great search solution (and keeping it great) requires some investment of time and effort. However, you can get a lot of value even with a minimal investment. Even doing a few of the steps outlined in this chapter can deliver a much better than usual search experience. If done correctly, search can be an area that is both fun and fulfilling to end users and can provide your organization with an incredible amount of value.

CHAPTER 10

Governance, Adoption, and Training

Mary, Mary quite contrary, how does your garden grow? With silver bells and cockleshells and pretty maids all in a row.

—Nursery Rhyme

The focus of the material we've covered in this book so far has been on how to design and build a SharePoint solution that meets the needs of your users and stakeholders. But what happens after that? You've created a great navigational structure, you've designed functional and usable pages, and you have created metadata that make your information easy to find. Do you just hand over the keys to your users and say "Done!"?

I hope your answer to that question is "No." Your beautiful site is like a garden, it will soon become overgrown with weeds, and all the carefully cultivated plants will die if they aren't taken care of. Tending your SharePoint garden is an ongoing task; you need to assign people to care for it and care about the outcome, and they need to be people who know what they are doing.

To stretch the gardening metaphor a little further (maybe too far?): You also can't just hand over shovels and seeds to people who are going to fill in some of the empty spots you have left for later expansion. The work they do has to fit in with the original plan so that the whole system will fulfill its purpose and so the garden will "make sense" to those who use it.

This chapter discusses three main elements that work together to ensure your SharePoint garden flourishes after delivery day: governance, adoption, and training. These three elements are deeply intertwined: Governance helps to drive adoption, as does training. The training function can be used to enforce the governance policies, leading to a better, more efficient environment, which is, in turn, more likely to be adopted.

Governance and Adoption

While thinking about SharePoint governance, remember (from our discussion in Chapter 4): There is a difference in approach between what I've labeled as above the line versus below the line. Above the line refers to the portal areas that contain content meant to be carefully controlled; it is consistent and reliable. It is content prepared by relatively few for consumption by relatively many. Below the line is where collaboration takes place, and it has to allow for less control and more freedom. This is where work-in-process happens, and there may be many private areas, or at least areas that few people visit except those on a particular team or on a particular project.

Part of what makes governance planning difficult is that it has to take both of these approaches into account. In the sections that follow, I will point out when I am talking specifically about above or below the line content.

The Rise of the SharePoint Governance Plan

When SharePoint started to take off as a product, Microsoft did a great job of convincing customers that SharePoint was a fast and easy way to tame the information flood.

▥ **Note** Microsoft doesn't announce too many details about the sales of SharePoint, but they did release an interesting statistic in 2011. For the previous five years, SharePoint has been selling at the rate of 20,000 licenses (users) *per day*.

The problem is that Microsoft may have done too good a job of selling the dream of SharePoint. It turns out that just installing SharePoint and flipping the "on" switch led to very messy results. It reached a point where there was a backlash around the implementation of SharePoint, because in many cases it just wasn't meeting expectations.

The first time I heard of the concept of SharePoint governance was in late 2006 when Joel Oleson started blogging about it. Joel was working for Microsoft at the time, and his early work lit a fire under the governance movement in the SharePoint world. Joel's perspective was that of an IT professional, and so his take on governance heavily emphasized that perspective. His posts talked about things like quotas, data retention policies, cost models, and managed deployment. But in addition to these, Joel did take a wider view, asking questions about branding, communications planning, and stakeholder and ownership. The first time I saw the famous Pyramid Diagram was on Joel's blog. (You can see the one Joel first shared at http://bit.ly/originalpyramid.) When I saw Joel speak about governance, I learned that his term for below the line was "Wild Wild West" because in most SharePoint sites, it was chaos down there. The work that Joel and others started led to a surge of activity around creating governance plans.

▥ **Example** We had a client once who asked us to come in and take a look at performance and governance issues with their SharePoint installation. It turned out they had over 8,000 team sites (including subsites) running on a server that was sitting under someone's desk. No one had any idea what the vast majority of the sites were for, who owned them, or whether they were still in use. It was interesting to note that there were far more sites than there were people with access to SharePoint!

Trying to Define Governance

If you search Bing for "SharePoint Governance," you'll get about 150,000 hits. Governance has become so universally discussed and debated that it is becoming a buzzword that means almost anything to anyone. I think that part of the reason governance has become overused to the point of meaninglessness is that it is a word that is viewed through so many different lenses. In the world of SharePoint deployment projects, consider these points of view:

- *If you are a project manager*: Governance applies to the process for managing the project and how decisions get made.

- *If you are a developer*: Governance applies to the coding practices and testing approaches.

- *If you are an IT administrator*: Governance applies to deployment processes, applying patches and backup policies, as well as deciding who gets new sites and what capabilities they will be allowed to use.

- *If you are a site owner*: Governance applies to how the pages look, what metadata need to be entered, what type of content can be added, how often content needs to be updated, and who is allowed to see some particular content.

Incorporating all of these points of view into one governance plan usually leads to a giant, monolithic document. It includes descriptions of how the governance committee should be constituted, what the rules should be for myriad settings, ownership, branding, new site requests, and so forth. I have to confess that I have written a number of these types of plans myself. The result is a lot of great work gets turned into shelf-ware: a document that sits in a binder and never gets referred to again.

Although I have only touched on a few of the issues that fall under typical definitions of governance for each of these roles, you can see how different they feel from each one another. This leads to endless debates about what a governance plan is: To one person, it describes the Service Level Agreement (SLA)the IT team has to follow for providing support. For others, it describes in detail what a user will be allowed to do on a collaboration site.

In the end, the governance plan often comes down to a giant rulebook. I don't mind if you call your rulebook a governance plan, it's just that I want you to think in wider terms than just the rules for your site.

■ **Note** In this chapter, I am not going to go through the nitty-gritty of creating a governance plan document. There are already great ones out there. I particularly recommend the "Governance Planning" chapter from the book *Essential SharePoint 2010* by Scott Jamison, Susan Hanley, and Mauro Cardarelli. I highly recommend purchasing the book, but the governance planning chapter is downloadable for free as a Microsoft whitepaper at http://bit.ly/espgovernance.

There are a few rebels in the world of SharePoint governance who've taken a non-rulebook approach to governance. One of them is Paul Culmsee (http://www.cleverworkarounds.com), who was the first person who showed me that the actual root of the word govern comes from the Greek for steer, and he introduced me to the concept of governance as steering.

When I attended Paul's SharePoint "Governance and Information Architecture Master Class," he tried to steer us (ha!) away from complex, highly detailed definitions of governance. He explained governance as a process you follow to move from an unhappy present state toward an aspirational future state (Figure 10-1). This definition brings governance out of "listing a set of rules" and onto a higher plane that focuses first on what you are really trying to accomplish and then asks you to explore how you will get there.

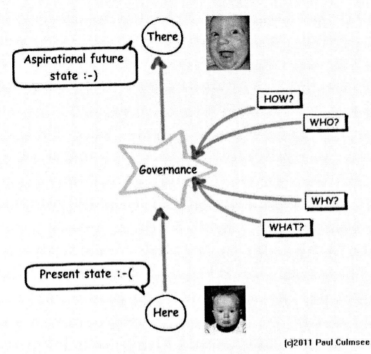

Figure 10-1. Paul Culmsee's seminal illustration that governance is the process that steers an organization to an aspirational future state.

The two big questions raised by this model are: "What exactly *is* our present state?" and "What exactly *is* our aspirational future state?" You can't just ask people these two questions and hope for an answer that you can use to determine the course of action to be taken. Getting the answers to these questions becomes a wicked problem (as discussed in Chapter 6). Getting to the bottom of them requires tools for digging out what these are and getting to a shared understanding of what they mean. You will find that often, even getting agreement on what the present state is can be a very contentious issue. It is Paul's experience that once your stakeholders have gone through the process of discovering and defining what the current and future states look like, the governance planning emerges from that as a mere formality—not meaning that it's not a lot of work, but there is no real controversy about what is in it.

There is a part of this governance planning thinking that I decided I wanted to investigate further by taking a step back, outside the world of SharePoint, by looking at a different definition of governance, one that comes from the public sector. The Governance Institute (http://iog.ca) comes very close to Paul's point of view when they say that "Good governance is not an end in itself, but rather a process and set of practices that enable organizations to meet their goals." They acknowledge that a simple definition of governance is difficult to capture, but their working definition is:

> *Governance determines who has power, who makes decisions, how other players make their voice heard and how account is rendered.* (http://iog.ca/en/about-us/governance/governance-definition)

I like the way this definition extends Paul's model by adding "how account is rendered." I once heard someone say that governance without enforcement is just suggestion. While I don't think that accountability and enforcement are synonyms, they drive toward a key concept that seems to be at the root of most governance planning failures: no follow-up, no enforcement, and no real accountability. Without these, the governance plan falls by the wayside and SharePoint fails to live up to its potential. Dux Raymond Sy (http://sp.meetdux.com/default.aspx), one of the most accomplished and popular speakers at SharePoint conferences, is famous for saying: "SharePoint doesn't suck. You suck." I think when he says this he is most commonly referring to either poor planning or poor governance.

Governance Hierarchy

The governance hierarchy diagram (shown in Figure 10-2) delineates the layers of responsibility and accountability for a SharePoint portal. It shows how the steering committee has strategic accountability for the use of SharePoint within the organization. The job of the *steering committee* includes:

- Establishing vision and strategy,
- Creating and managing the portal roadmap,
- Synchronizing the vision across business units,
- Acting as champions within individual business units as well as enterprise wide,
- Defining success factors and key performance indicators and measuring results,
- Procuring and allocating the intranet budget,
- Reviewing and tracking intranet project budgets,
- Providing operations team oversight.

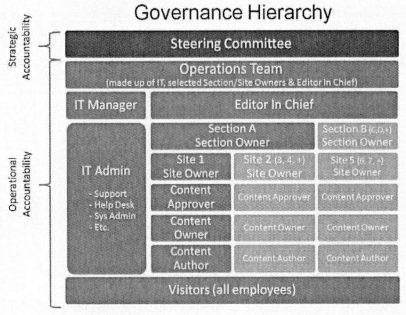

Figure 10-2. The SharePoint portal governance hierarchy

The *operations team* is a partnership between IT and business owners of the portal. Its job is to communicate and cooperate to ensure that the portal runs smoothly and efficiently. The team members have to work together to balance the needs of IT for control and manageability and the needs of the business for responsiveness, reliability, performance, and flexibility. The team as a group doesn't have specific roles and responsibilities; those are dictated by their individual roles further down in the hierarchy.

The *IT manager* is responsible for the physical infrastructure as well as operational aspects of the SharePoint service, including:

- Hardware service and upgrades,

- System assurance (uptime, performance, availability, security, disaster recovery, system updates and upgrades, monitoring),

- Development or procurement and subsequent deployment of new features,

- Help desk, second-level support,

- Training and coaching (Optional: In many organizations, this is owned by other groups),

- Key member of the operations team and the governance committee.

The *editor in chief* (sometimes called the portal owner) is the person responsible for the content that appears on the site. His or her responsibilities include:

- Approving overall content on the site, ensuring consistency of look, feel, tone, style (words and pictures), and overall site quality,

- Taking ownership of the home page, including approving content that appears there, ensuring it is fresh and accurate,

- Nurturing and supporting the internal SharePoint community,

- Leading communications efforts (letting the company know of new features or changes to the portal),

- Being a key member of the operations team and governance committee.

The *section owner* and *site owner* have the same responsibilities; it is just the scope of their role that differs. A section owner owns an entire top-level element of a site. If we look at Figure 10-3, "Our Company" is a section, and it would have a section owner. "Employee Center" would also have a section owner. A site owner may own the "About Us" site under "Our Company." These roles don't map one-to-one onto the map. For example, the editor in chief (who is already responsible for the home page) may be the section owner for Our Company and most of the sites contained within it, but there may be a separate site owner for the Corporate Social Responsibility site.

The responsibilities of these owners include:

- Maintaining quality for the content in this section or site,

- Ensuring that high-risk (confidential/inappropriate) material is not exposed on the portal,

- Ensuring that existing content is updated as required,

- Ensuring that content is removed from the site if it is out of date, expired, or otherwise no longer relevant (while adhering to the records management policy),

- Remaining aware of content in other areas to ensure consistency and to ensure that duplicate content does not exist elsewhere,

- Ensuring that published content adheres to style policies.

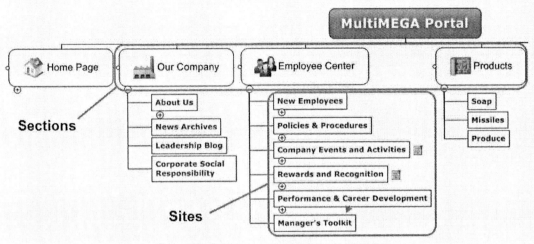

Figure 10-3. Sections and sites for MultiMEGA

The *content approver* role is not usually assigned to a separate person; the section owner may be the approver of content for the sites contained within that section. Or a site owner may be the approver for subsites. In some cases, where there are legal or other high-risk issues, there may be approvers assigned from the legal or other departments. The responsibilities of the approver include:

- Checking that content is factually correct,

- Providing oversight to ensure that high-risk (confidential/inappropriate) material is not exposed on the portal,

- Ensuring that content follows corporate policies for style and content,

- Being responsible for timely approval (not being a bottleneck),

- Ensuring that metadata has been properly entered,

- Ensuring content is posted to the correct location.

The *content owner* may be the same person as the site owner, or that person may just be responsible for a subset of content within a particular area of a site. You will start to notice that there are a lot of overlapping responsibilities at this level and the levels above and below. That is because at every level, people have an absolute responsibility to ensure the quality and impact (safety and risk) of the content on the site. As we move up the responsibility hierarchy, each level can catch issues missed by the layer below. A content owner's responsibilities include:

- Maintaining quality control for the content in this area or site,

- Ensuring that high-risk (confidential/inappropriate) material is not exposed on the portal,

- Ensuring that existing content is updated as required,

- Ensuring that content is removed from the site if it is out of date, expired, or otherwise no longer relevant (according to the records management policy),

- Remaining aware of content in other areas to ensure consistency and to ensure that duplicate content does not exist elsewhere,

195

- Ensuring that metadata are properly entered,
- Ensuring that published content adheres to style policies,

The next layer is where the actual work gets done: authoring. *Content authors* are responsible for:

- Creating content,
- Ensuring content adheres to corporate policies,
- Ensuring that high-risk (confidential/inappropriate) material is not exposed on the portal,
- Ensuring that appropriate metadata are properly and completely entered,
- Ensuring that the content is placed in the correct location within the site.

Finally, we get to the layer of those who have no hand in the creation, approval, or management of content: the readers. And yet, within an organization, you must put responsibility into the hands of readers to notice and point out material that is inaccurate, out of date, or that could put the organization at risk. You have to enable the readers to report issues by making it easy for them to do so. There should be a link on each page to report issues or at least to contact the page owner (every page must display who the owner of that page is). The captured information should automatically include the address of the page and where the problem was noticed, so it can be checked and corrected, if necessary, in a timely manner.

Now that we have looked at the theoretical structure of a governance hierarchy; but we also need to look at why governance remains an issue with many SharePoint installations. So let's look into what this often looks like in the real world.

SharePoint Governance and Adoption in the Real World

One of the hottest topics in the SharePoint world is the question of adoption. People who spend time and energy building SharePoint solutions for their companies want to understand why fewer people are using it than they expected, or if they are using it, why they're not taking advantage of the great features SharePoint offers.

I believe the single biggest cause of adoption failure is rooted in governance failure, not the failure to create a rulebook, but rather failure of leadership, accountability, and communication.

Let's look at each of those in turn.

Lack of Engagement by Senior Leaders

One of the strangest things about the failure of governance is that the governance plan itself often describes mechanisms that are intended to ensure that accountability exists; it describes in elaborate detail the composition and responsibilities of the governance committee, as I have just done above. But without the right level of engagement from the leadership, users don't get a robust system that they are encouraged or required to use. The lack of engagement by leadership leads to limitations of resources, and, as a result, adoption suffers. With lack of adoption comes even less perceived value by management, and the cycle spirals downward from there.

If we all know that we need strong leadership to get value from our often substantial investments, why does it so often go wrong? I have found that in the majority of cases (but certainly not all), senior management teams just do not believe that their SharePoint installation is strategic to their organization. They are not much interested in being part of a governance body ("I don't have time for more meetings!"), and they are not committed to ensuring that they model the appropriate use of SharePoint. When senior management does not want to devote time or energy to leading and championing the SharePoint implementation, then they will not be holding the people below them accountable for anything. And if no one is accountable, the rules in the rulebook quickly fall by the wayside. You can see the result in Figure 10-4.

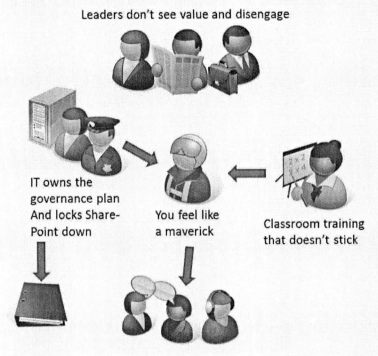

Leaders don't see value and disengage

IT owns the governance plan And locks Share-Point down

You feel like a maverick

Classroom training that doesn't stick

Others don't see value and adoption suffers

Figure 10-4. Too often, the real-world SharePoint scenario

The lack of engagement causes everything to happen by rote: the same old stuff is delivered the same old way, classroom training doesn't stick, IT teams lock systems down so they are almost unusable, operating from a rulebook that justifies their actions but that few know about. Finally, some users try to make a go of it despite all this, but without the amplifying effects of having everyone on the same system at the same time, your enthusiastic user may ask why he or she bothers.

The result of this lack of engagement from the top leads to a lack of accountability.

■ **Note** I do *not* hate management: I have been painting an extreme picture of a management team that is completely disengaged. This is never entirely the case. The level of engagement falls along a spectrum from poor to excellent, and I have seen both ends of this. On average, there are engaged individuals—and even groups—who see the business value. However, they are not invested enough in the SharePoint project to devote the energy it requires.

Lack of Accountability

Another issue from the real world of SharePoint implementation is that people are not required to use it as they are with many software tools. Think about your expense tracking system or your timesheet system at work. In most cases those are just *awful* systems to use. User interfaces are lousy, you have to do way too much repetitive work, and they often just look ugly. Yet everyone in the company uses them on a regular basis: You see virtually 100 percent adoption. You have to use these tools or you won't get your expenses paid or your time approved, so you have no choice in the matter.

Now consider SharePoint. You as an employee are told there is a great new system for finding and sharing news, information, documents, plans, ideas, and so forth. All it requires is to change the way you do your normal day-to-day work. This type of change is quite painful for most people. As annoying and painful as the existing systems are, you at least know how they work and you can "get stuff done," even if it's really inefficient. You also need a critical mass of people who have bought into the new platform. If you put your documents into SharePoint and a colleague insists that you e-mail them to him, then you start to wonder why you bother loading them on SharePoint. If your site has poor information architecture so that people have too much metadata to enter, especially if they don't see the value of those metadata, then they will be unlikely to use it.

Very early in my career I learned about the power of leadership when it comes to SharePoint. I was working for a consulting firm that had a strategic planning meeting every Monday morning. The CEO would sit at the head of the table with a keyboard and mouse, and his computer would be projected onto the screen at the front of the room. All meeting notes were kept in SharePoint, along with links to key documents, which also were housed in SharePoint.

At one point in the meeting, the CEO asked me about how I was coming along with a particular proposal. I said it was 90 percent done. He wanted to see it and asked me where it was in SharePoint. I said, "Sorry, I have it saved to my desktop, I'll upload it after the meeting." He said, "No, we'll wait while you go and upload it now." From then on, everyone knew: Documents *must* be saved into SharePoint. I was held accountable for not following the company policy on documents: I never made that mistake again.

It is this type of top-down messaging that makes SharePoint a key component of the operations of a business and this type of leadership that makes people careful about their actions, because they know they will be held accountable for them.

The lack of accountability also affects the IT department. Because many IT departments are looking to avoid chaotic SharePoint growth, or are afraid of being overwhelmed with help-desk requests, they lock down SharePoint (in the name of governance) so users can't really accomplish many useful tasks. SharePoint becomes just a glorified file share (like the chaotic network shared drive), and most people don't really use it for much more than that. The lack of a clear mandate from leadership, indicating that the business needs to use this system to improve competitiveness or the bottom line, means that IT is not really motivated to solve these problems in partnership with the business.

■ **Note** I have worked with a lot of IT teams and found them to be willing to listen and be flexible up to a point. The issue is that they are usually overworked and understaffed, so they need to get their critical work done under difficult circumstances. It is precisely for this reason that leadership is important: Priorities need to be set and resources allocated if you are going to have a chance at getting the maximum value out of your SharePoint investment.

The final element where this all breaks down is with communication.

Lack of Communication

Another downfall for governance is that it is not well communicated within the organization. People do not know what they are allowed to do, they don't know what the system is for or what its capabilities are, and they don't really have anyone to turn to in order to obtain this information. The only thing they know is that when they try to do things with SharePoint, the features seem very limited because their environment is so locked down.

Change is difficult for most people. Even if the portal they are currently using is terrible, at least they have roughly figured out where everything is, or at least the most important stuff. If you change that on them overnight, no matter how good your solution is, they are not going to be happy. They need lots of warning about what's coming, how and why it will be different, and what benefits they will experience from the change. They also need to know what the rules are, and these rules can't be in a fat binder somewhere, they need to be instantly and easily available, in what Susan Hanley calls "consumable chunks." That means that there have to be good summaries of what the rules are in a form that anyone can read (e.g., brochures, quick reference cards, or easy-to-access sites on the intranet that present well written and relevant content).

Making It Work Anyway

So, if we've identified some of the causes of governance (and adoption) failure, what are some potential solutions?

The reality is that while you can try to get onto the agenda of senior leadership and try harder to convince them to get fully engaged in the SharePoint initiative, they may be difficult to sway. They are more interested in evidence of value than any argument you can make, and you won't be able to show value until after SharePoint has been implemented. As you saw in Figure 10-2, the idealized governance hierarchy model has a steering (governance) committee at the top. However, if you believe my argument that this committee is not engaged enough to force accountability onto the layers below, then *the answer lies in the self-empowerment of the operations team.* In most organizations, the SharePoint project starts out being owned by IT. The solution here is that enlightened IT teams look for partners in the business to create an operations team that becomes the de facto guiding body made up of representatives from the business. These are the people who are going to be stakeholders in the intranet, as they will be responsible for a lot of content. Because they don't have top-down power to make things happen, they will need to build their power from the bottom-up by evangelizing their vision and recruiting people who buy in to it. Michael Sampson, an author and an expert in collaboration and adoption (http://www.michaelsampson.net), calls these the "first wave people." If you can get these first wavers on board, then they will pull the largest chunk of the population, the "second wave people," along with them.

I have seen this work: If you can present a compelling case to the right people for how their work experience will be better and tell them how they will be empowered to make their own work better, many of them will join you for the ride.

Making this work takes some preliminary effort to create a starting point for a great information architecture with a core group. Having well-designed mockups and comps of how the new site will look is another huge selling point. Most corporate intranets are so abysmal that a clean, clear, and good looking new design that includes an easy-to-understand site structure and navigation can really motivate a lot of people to want to see this happen.

You will most commonly start with human resources and communications (internal and/or marketing) and, if the organization has them, library and knowledge management teams. Then you have key players from other divisions like QA, engineering, sales, and manufacturing.

When you have your core group, the ones who will be your operations team (and de facto governance committee), you can now put your governance planning tools into play to ascertain what the current state is and work on defining the aspirational future state. Once you have established what it is you hope to do, you will be able to work on how this will be accomplished. In the process of determining this, you will be able to establish who will have the power to make decisions, how new ideas will be heard, and how accountability will be assigned and enforced.

This is a daunting task, but don't let it intimidate you, the tools you have learned in this book will help you manage the process, and I have pointed you to great sources and content that have been proven to work in the real world.

Building a Community

There is a group of people outside your operations team who can help you succeed with your SharePoint project. Wherever I have gone, there is always a group of SharePoint enthusiasts out there. These are people who see the potential of SharePoint, and in many cases they have already started to harness it for their own needs (sometimes in a non-sanctioned way). If you can find these people and give them some recognition, such as private lunch-and-learns or a site for them to share information or answer one another's questions, or even a "sandbox" site to experiment on, they will be your champions, informal helpers, and evangelists throughout the company. This will help your second wavers to see the light and overcome their initial hesitations. Your community can be your secret weapon for success within your organization.

Now that we've discussed governance and adoption, the third leg of the table that your SharePoint project stands on needs to be addressed: training.

Training

In this section on training, I'm going to take a different, some may say heretical, tack from the normal emphasis on training for SharePoint deployments.

The training I am talking about here is for site owners and content creators, not end-user training. At the end of this section, I will address end-user training.

▦ **Note** In terms of 'above the line' and 'below the line', my comments below apply more strongly to 'below the line'. For above the line content creators, a short (2-hours) orientation and training session can be useful to get help them understand what the new portal is, how it works and what their role will be. After this initial orientation, I revert to my argument below about how to make them productive and useful in an efficient way.

I have been involved in SharePoint training on many projects, and I am here to tell you that a high percentage of that training investment is wasted. Let me explain why I say that by looking at the typical approaches to training: classroom and video.

Why Traditional Classroom Training Sucks

I have a lot of experience as a classroom trainer, and I have experienced firsthand the issues presented in the sections that follow.

Training Is Often Delivered Too Soon . . . or Too Late

Because of scheduling requirements, which require adequate notice so people can schedule one, two, or even three days into their calendars, training days have to be booked well in advance and at times that don't interfere with other business requirements. When you couple this with the sometimes uncertain timelines of software project delivery, you end up with training that happens weeks before the SharePoint site is ready for people to start working on it. The result is that by the time the site *is* ready for use, the training happened so long ago that no one remembers how to do anything anymore.

The other side of this coin is that sometimes the training doesn't happen until after the users are required to start loading it with content. So they muddle along, or need extra help. When they finally get around to training, a lot of time has already been wasted, pushing untrained users onto the system.

Training Is Not Relevant

The training material is often compiled from generic material that covers basic SharePoint content but does not address any of the specifics of this particular organization's customizations, branding, or even purpose. The training is therefore useful as background, but exercises bear very little resemblance to the work that will actually be done on the production site.

Training Is Too Time Constrained

Let's face it: It can be really hard to schedule a full day away from your regular work to attend training (let alone two or three days). So the training plan calls for cramming too much information into too little time, meaning that retention (and even understanding) may be quite poor.

Training Is Expensive

Getting classroom space with computers, getting a trainer on site, and—most of all—getting workers to the training center and removing them from work for a few days is very costly, especially given the next point.

Training Doesn't Stick

The sad truth is that I have seen smart people, trained by excellent trainers, with pretty good content who end up not having the faintest idea of what to do when they are handed the keys to their new site. And now I am just talking about the basics of adding or modifying content. When it comes to defining new elements, such as new lists or libraries, and defining new metadata or content types for those lists, the retention rate is just about zero.

The fact is that people who have regular jobs to do (outside of IT) are just not going to remember what a content type is and how to apply it to their new list. The time taken to teach them these concepts is completely wasted for the vast majority of trainees.

It turns out that fully grasping the concept of why content types are valuable is not easy. Then remembering how to implement them and how to pick the appropriate metadata and whether to use lookups or managed metadata—and what the caveats are of using certain types of managed metadata—it's just all too much. They don't see the relevance and they don't get the time to practice the skills, which is required to solidify these concepts.

Even if they were to get the right amount of practice, not everyone is suited to the logical process of determining whether a list or a library is the right approach for a particular problem, let alone select the appropriate metadata.

Because the concepts are not easy, and the material is not immediately applied to real-world solutions, there is just no way it will be retained by the people getting all this expensive training.

The Return on Investment for Training Sucks

The expense of running classroom training, coupled with the opportunity cost of taking people away from their regular work, is very expensive. If the result doesn't actually make your intranet or portal better, the benefit is very small, leading to an almost nonexistent return on investment (ROI).

Why Video Training Sucks

For some people, the answer is video training. I think that video can be a great supplement—and some people prefer to be able to manage their own pace of learning—but I think that as a solution, it has a number of limitations.

It Is Often Generic

Video training is often purchased in precreated packages that are not directly relevant to the particular organization. There are usually differences in look to deal with, as well as features in place that work differently from the out-of-the-box, generic platform that most training is based on.

If It's Not Generic, It's Expensive

Creating well-produced video content based on the design and features of your site is time consuming and expensive. The other problem is that your site may not be far enough along in functionality to be able to give the video producers a stable enough platform to build from.

Tricky to Find the Right Video to Watch, When You Need to Watch It

If the user is not fully familiar with (or can't recall) the name of what they are looking for, it can be difficult to find the right video to watch to help them solve the problem they are having at that moment.

Video Can Show Basic Functionality, but Can't Help with Creatively Applying SharePoint Features

The real power of SharePoint is that it is a very flexible tool that can be used to quickly solve business problems. Covering the features, even in some depth, in a video does not help the person watching figure out how to solve their problem.

It's Hard to Get the Granularity Right

Sometimes you need an overview that gives context for an overall approach, and sometimes you just need a one-minute segment that reminds you how to do that one crucial step. It can be hard to find a collection of videos that covers both ends of this spectrum and which apply to your specific environment.

The ROI of Video Training Sucks

Because it is so hard to find the right video for a particular purpose, all but the most dedicated may stop using them, making purchasing them a poor investment.

Doing No Training Sucks

If you don't train your users, there is no way they are going to figure out a tool as complex as SharePoint on their own. They will manage to get some work done and find some ways to get *some things* to work. The more dedicated will go out and buy a book. But the reality is that they will not learn to use SharePoint efficiently, and they'll be frustrated and unhappy. These people tend to say (loudly and to whomever will listen): "SharePoint sucks!"

Your untrained users will complain that SharePoint is unintuitive. They will revert to using nested folders, thus just moving the sins of the X-drive (or whatever you call your shared network drive) into SharePoint. They don't see any real way to build usable solutions, and so they'll wonder: Why did management ever agree to buy this load of junk? Is the Microsoft sales guy blackmailing the boss or something?

So, if people feel that SharePoint sucks so badly, why bother to invest in SharePoint as a platform? The answer is that SharePoint is very flexible, capable, and powerful, and it can provide great ROI (see Chapter 8 for examples).

The realization that must be arrived at is that of all the people you train in SharePoint, a vanishingly small percentage of them will be able to take advantage of the power it has to offer. This is not because they are stupid or lazy: In my experience, the vast majority of SharePoint users are people dedicated to doing a great job. The problem is that they don't have the time or interest to invest in understanding information architecture, knowledge management, or business-process modeling concepts. They have day jobs that consume the vast majority of their time and capacity. No matter how much of their time you waste training them, they often will not absorb and apply the concepts they were taught.

There are of course exceptions to this. Some people will really embrace the platform or may have experience with it from a previous job. But most of the time it takes a unique combination of time, talent, and training to create a SharePoint expert for your organization (and you have to find those people and bring them into your SharePoint community).

What Is the Strategy to Make SharePoint Not Suck?

The answer is coaching. When I use the term coaching, I extend it slightly from the sports metaphor. By coaching I mean training, mentoring, consulting, and assisting.

Coaching Instead of Training

Coaching is different from classroom training, because it is not curriculum based; it is practicality based. In a classroom, I would say: "Here is how you add a generic piece of content to a generic SharePoint site." A video will demonstrate the same generic content, but without even the option to ask any questions. In contrast, a coach would say: "Let's add some of your content to your site."

▓ **Note** It is possible to create custom classroom curriculum that shows the customer how to use their particular branded and customized site, but this approach often suffers from the "too soon/too late" issue discussed above. The training has to be created so far ahead of time that some of the planned functionality may still be under development and not be ready to use during course development, or there can be major changes between the time the curriculum is developed and when the site is rolled out.

As I mention in the introduction to this section, a short, introductory orientation session can be useful to get everyone up to the same level of understanding of what the new intranet will be about, what SharePoint is and basically how it works. This is *not* in-depth, technical training.

Coaching can be done one on one or it can be done in small groups. The people getting the training will be prompted ahead of time to gather the content they will be responsible for so they will have content to add.

The coaching is supplemented with lightweight materials, like a Microsoft Word or PowerPoint document with screenshots of the sequence to be followed. This material will exactly match the steps you follow during the coaching session. This is not a workbook exercise: You do not give this material to the trainees ahead of time because you don't want them to be following instructions in a book; you want them to listen to you and then think about what they are doing. In fact, I don't usually make the material available until after the training because there can be unexpected changes in content or processes that need to be accounted for: The content made ahead of time would then be slightly out of date and wrong. I am now also experimenting with capturing very short videos showing the process for the exact activity they are doing.

The thing about coaching is that it is also not a one-time activity. The coach has to be available, either on site or via screen-sharing tools, to help the trainees over hurdles once they are back at their desks and continuing to add content.

The objection to coaching over training is that it is perceived as being more costly: Having a trainer stand in front of 20 people for 8 hours is cheaper than working one on one or with small groups. But if the value of the classroom training is minimal, and people won't remember how to add their own content or they add it incorrectly, compromising the quality of the SharePoint site, then the "cost" of classroom training goes way up.

Coaching has two other major benefits: it helps with migration and with governance.

Coaching for Migration

When you work on SharePoint projects, you get the feeling that there is always this 16-ton weight hanging over everyone's heads: migration. Everyone knows that the site won't be done until it's loaded with content. When I refer to migration, I am not just talking about lifting content out of the old portal and moving it to the new one. I am talking about finding existing material and repurposing it for the new structure as well as creating new content. I am also talking about moving documents of all kinds from an existing older repository into the new system and putting it into the right locations with the right metadata.

■ **Note** There is a number of third-party vendors of migration tools that can substantially reduce the migration workload. These tools are great when you can apply patterns to the migration tasks. For example: All the documents in the folder called "Sales/France" will be automatically added to the SharePoint Sales Document Library using the "Sales Document" content type, and the "Geography" field will be set to "France." However, these tools generally won't be able to help you to create the pages that people use to navigate the site and that have the text that describes the purpose of the content you are looking at.

Everyone working on these projects knows that this has to happen. As SharePoint IAs, we keep reminding our clients that the project is going to create a great new structure for content, but that the content will have to be moved and created. Yet, in most cases, there is a mad dash at the end to get stuff in. By taking the coaching approach, you will be able to work with your content creation team to start getting real content into the system as early as possible. By focusing only on real content, not sample data, you will quickly find where the holes are—where content is missing or not in a format that is going to work for the new site.

The coach is not just a trainer; he or she is an active member of the team who understands the concept of how the site is structured. The coach can help content authors determine where to put certain content and how to apply the metadata appropriately. Truly coaching the users helps them to become more adept and confident at their tasks as they continue to actually build out the site.

Coaching for Governance

This is one of the most important aspects of the coaching approach. The phrase I used earlier in the chapter was: Governance without enforcement is just suggestion. In the section on coaching, I've mostly been referring to the initial process of getting people up to speed with a new intranet. The issue that I want to focus on here is the ongoing process of creating and managing collaboration sites—an area we have previously referred to as "below the line."

One of the most powerful—yet dangerous—aspects of SharePoint is how easily you can create sites for teams or projects. These subsites can be places for a team to store their key documents, communicate via discussions and blogs, keep track of vacations on a calendar, or announce news that is of value to the team. Each team has specific processes they follow and information they track. For example, the marketing team may have a list of samples they send to the press. They generally have a spreadsheet that tracks who has what, what date they were given, and when they were returned. The shipping department has a list of carriers, with contact information, route guides, and notes about which carrier is preferred for which type of cargo or which route. Accounts payable has a process to ensure that payments are properly approved and issued at the date the company policy dictates.

The purpose of these examples is to point out that SharePoint can be used to simplify and organize all of these daily business needs, but what is most likely to happen is that the same old methods and processes (spreadsheets and e-mails) are likely to be followed. If the value of investing in SharePoint is to be realized, these approaches need to change. I advocate coaching as the best way to achieve value from the SharePoint investment.

When a request comes in for a new SharePoint site from a manager, a team, a project lead, or anyone else, a process should be followed that includes capturing who the request is coming from, a brief description of what the site is to be used for, what the expectations for size and growth are, and who the main administrators of the site will be. At that point, a coaching appointment is made with a coach who is knowledgeable of the capabilities of SharePoint, who knows how SharePoint is organized at that organization, and who is familiar with the rules for collaboration sites within the organization.

The coach meets with the key stakeholders (owners and administrators) for an hour to get a preliminary assessment of what this team does and what they expect they will use the site for. Depending on complexity, there may be a follow-up meeting arranged to review specific content or processes that need to be looked at. The coach will then make recommendations for the site, including where to start, how to plan for the next steps, and what site template to use and how it could be modified.

When it comes to building the site, the coach works with the team (and this is where the coach definition is extended to include "assists") and helps to define the content types and metadata that will enable the team to efficiently meet its business requirements.

In my opinion, and based on my experience, training the site owners and administrators in the creation and use of content types just doesn't work. Only a very small percentage of them will ever apply these concepts on their own. Yet, without this, you have very little chance of "squeezing the juice" (value) out of SharePoint.

As important as getting the site set up properly in the first place is what comes afterward. How will the site grow? Will it continue along a roadmap that leverages the power of SharePoint's capabilities or will it go off the rails, either dying out due to lack of usefulness, or grow chaotically, diverging from company policy?

This is where regular follow-up with the coach is important. Every quarter, the site owners and/or administrators meet with the coach to go over the site, review its structure and content, and ensure that rules are being followed (this is the governance with enforcement part).

Leveraging coaching gives you a number of key wins:

- Ability to move from an organic, unplanned SharePoint growth model to a strategic model that takes advantage of SharePoint's power and capabilities;

- Ability to standardize your organizational approach and replicate a winning methodology;

- Ability to ensure SharePoint is being used consistently, avoiding rogue sites;

- Ability to more easily implement change management and encourage increased user adoption;

- Ability to avoid unnecessary cost and risk as teams find SharePoint to be a tool that can solve many problems, and therefore avoid spending on other software tools that your SharePoint infrastructure could have handled.

End-User Training

All of training discussed up to this point is for people who will be site owners and content authors. You also need to provide training for the users who will be browsing the portal and looking for content, but on a different scale.

You want everyone to understand why the portal was created and what its design goals are. You want them to know their responsibilities to watch for out-of-date or incorrect information and how to report that. You also want them to know how to use search effectively. Even these few things can make a huge difference in the success of your project.

The tools that make sense to use here are quick reference guides, lunch-and-learn meetings, auditorium presentations, and video training. Also, don't forget to let them know about the community program for enthusiasts; you'll be sure to get a bunch of recruitees who look forward to learning more and being helpful.

It is really important that your end users not be forgotten, so you must make sure they have opportunities to understand the system and how they can make the best use of it.

Summary

Getting to success with SharePoint is hard. It is a large and complex platform that can do almost anything. Like that old joke goes: "New Shimmer: It's a floor wax, and it's a dessert topping." Whenever you have something this powerful, and yet nebulous, especially when it has the potential to affect large parts of a business, you know you're going to be working on wicked problems.

This chapter discussed how deeply intertwined governance, adoption, and training are. At first you may have wondered, why are we talking about these topics in a book about information architecture? The answer is that all the pure IA work you do is not going to amount to much if people don't use it. The consideration of how and why people will accept your SharePoint solution into their daily lives is crucial. You need to be prepared to help build the political and operational structures that will lead to success, and you need to ensure you have a plan to help people understand what they are working with and why they should care.

I will close this chapter with the ideal governance training and adoption scenario, one that it is possible to achieve, as presented in Figure 10-5.

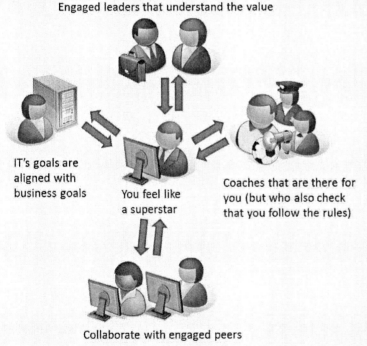

Engaged leaders that understand the value

IT's goals are aligned with business goals

You feel like a superstar

Coaches that are there for you (but who also check that you follow the rules)

Collaborate with engaged peers

Figure 10-5. The ideal scenario

It won't be easy or fast, and you'll have to help your client build a system that ensures the garden is watered, the new ground is tilled in logical and sustainable ways, and that everyone is engaged in keeping the landscape beautiful, but you can do it! In the next chapter we're going to look at how you can build your SharePoint knowledge as well as test ideas or demonstrate proofs of concept by creating your own SharePoint environment in the Cloud.

CHAPTER 11

Practicing and Testing in the Cloud

In theory there is no difference between theory and practice. In practice there is.

—Yogi Berra

As I am writing this chapter, I am in the middle of the first phase of a midsized SharePoint communication and collaboration portal project. A recent meeting brought me to again realize how crucial visualization is to so many people: They just can't look at your navigational and site structure mind maps and understand how their site will look and how it will work. At this point in the project, I could have opened up the Balsamiq mockups, but I had already shown the beautifully rendered comps of what the landing pages looked like. However, one member of the client team (an owner of the content in her corner of the intranet) could not visualize how her particular content would look on the site. Fortunately, we had an accessible SharePoint instance that allowed me to build out her landing page on the spot while she provided advice and feedback. At the end of a two-hour meeting, we went from "I have no idea what we are doing and what you want from me" to "Okay, this looks good—it's going to be a great improvement over the old intranet."

Another situation that I find myself in all the time is trying to remember exactly how a bit of SharePoint functionality works. Things like "Can I use the content query web part to display the data in that list really well?" or "Does metadata navigation work for lists, or is that just for document libraries?" Having a place to try out ideas and show them to stakeholders lets you quickly decide whether to expand on, or rule out, a particular idea.

This chapter will answer the question: How can I have access to my own SharePoint environment whenever I need one? I will very briefly mention a couple of possible non-Cloud options, and then I will delve into detail on three Cloud-based options for you to consider.

Virtual Machines on the Laptop

For some of you who have very powerful laptops, the answer to the question is to run a virtual machine (VM) on your laptop. While that can be a great alternative, there are issues. First is the need for some really heavy (literally and figuratively) iron to be able to run both your regular desktop functionality as well as the VM. The second is getting the right software running. You can't run Microsoft VMs on client operating systems (such as Vista or Windows 7), so you need to install a server product, which is not ideal for your day-to-day work.

■ **Note** The next version of Microsoft Windows (Windows 8) will be able to support Microsoft VMs.

An alternative is to use a third-party VM tool such as VMWare, but there is a cost for this, and your company may not support the installation of third-party software on their standardized desktop platforms. Finally, you can install SharePoint 2010 directly onto your Windows 7 laptop, but doing experimentation on a system that is deeply integrated with your production (i.e., important) machine can be scary. You need to have it working for all of your regular work: What if you want to try out a new third-party tool that breaks your installation? You have no easy way to roll back from that.

All of these are viable options, but you are then stuck with the reality that because SharePoint is running directly on your laptop you can't have anyone work with you on a project or give anyone else access to your SharePoint environment while you not there. I know people (mostly IT pros and developers) who do a lot of work on VMs running on their laptops, and they are happy with that, but I have not had the right combination of hardware and software to really make that work well for me.

The bottom line on VMs is that if your hardware supports it and your particular work-process fits with it, go for it: It is a great option with the advantage that you can use it anywhere, anytime (no need for Internet connectivity). However, I think that most of us in the world of IA don't have the appropriate hardware, and the inability to share your environment with others is a major limitation.

Using Your Own "Shop"

If you work for almost any sized organization, you probably have an IT department, and that department may have a mandate to make machines (or more often these days, virtual machines) available for staff to use. Even if you are working with a really talented and cooperative IT team, as I do, they are extremely busy. (Why are IT teams always *so* overloaded?) And of course, there are a few ~~hoops~~ standard procedures that you need to ~~jump through~~ follow: You must justify the reason for the machine, specify when you need it (for me, that's usually right now!) and how long you will need it, and what resources it needs (memory and disk). Then, if you need it to be accessible from outside the firewall, you have another set of issues to deal with because your IT team is going to hate you for increasing their security risk. Getting your IT team to open ports for you can be difficult to impossible.

Other issues I have run across are limited hardware resources for testing environments, so in order to get yours, you have to find someone who doesn't need theirs anymore so it can be archived or deleted, freeing up space for you. I have also run into situations where an e-mail goes out saying: "We have an important demo tomorrow, please shut down all your machines on the test servers so that we have good performance and no glitches."

Something else to take into account is what happens after you get your test environment? Will SharePoint be installed for you? Will you have to install it yourself? What if some of your projects require SharePoint 2010, some require MOSS 2007, and some require Foundation versus Server? It is expecting an awful lot of your IT team to make all of these options available to you.

Again, as with running a VM on the laptop, under the right circumstances—if your organization has the right infrastructure and support mechanisms in place—this can be a great solution that can really meet your needs very well. However, in my own experience, there have always been limitations that make it less than ideal. So, let's look at options that remove the limitations of your on-laptop or in-house resources; let's look at the Cloud.

Defining the Cloud

What exactly *is* the Cloud anyway? Like clouds themselves, the definition is a bit misty and hard to pin down. I mean, we've been using systems that have been hosted in external datacenters for decades; what is with all the Cloud hype lately? The difference can be found in an acronym that you may have seen bandied about in recent years: SaaS. SaaS stands for Software as a Service, which differentiates Cloud services from previous models of hosting. In the good old days you had your own hardware sitting in a datacenter. You may have owned the hardware outright or leased it from the datacenter, but it was yours and yours alone. You may have also outsourced the management of that hardware, but you were paying them to manage *your* equipment. If a server failed, you would have to find a way to divert the load or get it fixed in order to get back up and running again.

Under the Cloud paradigm, you are buying your software as a metered or monthly service from the provider. You have no ownership or control over any physical devices. If a server goes down, the provider is responsible for shifting your workload onto working hardware and getting you back up and running. Under these types of regimes, all the system monitoring, performance, backup, and disaster recovery are the responsibility of the service provider. One of the distinguishing characteristics of many definitions of Cloud-based services is multitenancy. This means that your service is being provided on shared hardware; one physical server may be hosting you along with a number of other of the provider's clients. The meaning of this is that if your workload is very light, there could be many other clients sharing the same hardware with you. If your workload increases, the operators of the service may need to move your workload onto machines with more horsepower or fewer competing clients (of course, this is within a range; if you really need more power, you'll have to pay more for the service). It also means that you cannot be allowed to install anything on your system that could affect the other clients. And you will of course never be allowed to do anything like access the server settings or reboot the physical machine. In exchange for giving up a certain level of control, you save money because your provider can take advantage of economies of scale to get lower cost hardware, and they can operate and maintain it at a lower cost than you can.

The definition of Cloud computing is not really fully agreed upon. There are lots of so-called "cloud services" that are really just tacking the trendy term onto a pretty standard service. A lot of the argument about the use of the term is that everyone has a different idea of exactly what it means. However, the lack of a strong definition is not going to stop us: In this chapter we are going to look at three different types of services from three different suppliers: CloudShare, Amazon, and Microsoft.

CloudShare

I am going to spend the most time and space in this chapter on CloudShare because it is the service that provides the best mix of capability for a great price. (In the interest of full disclosure, I need to tell you that as a Microsoft MVP, I have been provided a free one-year license of the base-level service from CloudShare. The value of this license is $490, at 2012 prices. I will gladly pay for it when my free license expires.) I will also cover its weaknesses, but I think that it provides the best option for people with some technical capability who are not system administrators and who need to be able to access the full capability of SharePoint without limitation (i.e., you, dear reader). Later, when I discuss Amazon's and Microsoft's offerings, I will discuss their strengths and weaknesses as well.

CloudShare Overview

CloudShare is a service that gives you access to a virtualized environment running SharePoint. One of its key advantages is that it has a number of prebuilt SharePoint configurations that you can select from and have up and running in minutes. However, if you need to mess around with the deepest levels of SharePoint, changing settings or splitting services across multiple machines, you have the power to do that. Another key (and unique) capability is that you can create a snapshot of your site and share it with others. Each person will get his or her own snapshot to use for free for 48 hours, allowing these individuals to try out the environment and make any changes they want. The changes that each person makes will not affect your master snapshot, but the changes will be lost at the end of the 48 hours. This can be a great scenario for training or sharing concepts. There is no cost for running these snapshot environments, and you can have as many of them as you need.

Getting Started with CloudShare

To get started with CloudShare, visit their home page at www.cloudshare.com and click the "14-day free trial" button. You can use your Google or Facebook accounts, or just register directly with the service. You will *not* need a credit card for the trial. As simple as that, you are ready to proceed with the creation of your SharePoint environment.

Creating a New Environment

The first screen will present you with a high-level overview of the service. It's quick to go through, but I thought the Next button in the wizard was pretty well camouflaged, so I've highlighted it in Figure 11-1. (Yes, I saw the arrow on the road sign, but still.)

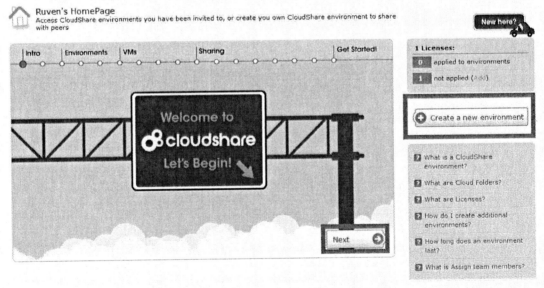

Figure 11-1. Getting started with the CloudShare setup wizard

As you can see, I have also highlighted the "Create a new environment" button, which is where we'll really get started.

Adding a Machine

The next step is to select from a cornucopia of possible options. In Figure 11-2 you can see some of your SharePoint 2010 options. Scrolling through this list, you will find not only a number of SharePoint 2010 configurations, but also Linux (CentOS) servers with options like Ruby on Rails. More from the Microsoft stack include MS-Exchange Servers, MS-SQL Servers, Oracle Servers, Windows XP and 7 workstations, Windows Server 2008 and Windows Server 2003 servers, and others. One of the most useful ones though is MOSS 2007 (SharePoint Server 2007), so that you can jump backward in time if you need to work on the previous version or if you want to look at upgrade scenarios. The other one that is pretty handy is the Microsoft Information Worker demo. This is a VM that Microsoft has put together that has a large collection of Microsoft technologies (Reporting Services, Communication Services, FAST search, etc.) all working together in one massive environment, prepopulated with mythical data and people from Contoso, Microsoft's made-up demo corporation.

The other thing you'll notice is that many of the SharePoint environments come preconfigured with Microsoft Office, SharePoint Designer, Visual Studio, and Adobe Reader, giving you all the tools you need to work with your environment.

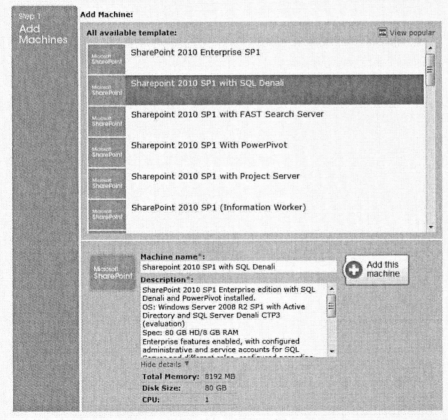

Figure 11-2. Selection of available machines in CloudShare

When you find the environment you want, click the "Add this machine" button to move on to the next step. The next screen will allow you to add another machine, but at this point, let's just click the "Continue to step 2" button.

Naming Your Environment

The next screen gives you the opportunity to name your environment and give it a description (Figure 11-3). This will be important if you decide you will be sharing your environment with others in the future. The figure is showing the default values that CloudShare automatically populates the fields with.

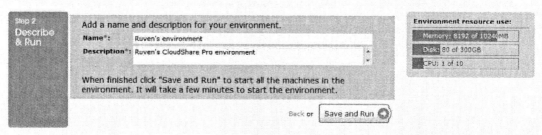

Figure 11-3. Naming the CloudShare environment

The other thing you can see here is what proportion of your available resources your environment is using. As you can see, we are using 8 of a possible 10GB of memory, 80 of the 300GB total available, and just one of the ten available CPUs. Later, we will see how we can modify this.

Running Your Environment

Clicking the Save and Run button will cause your environment to be created. As Figure 11-4 shows, you will see a progress bar showing you an animated update of the status of your environment.

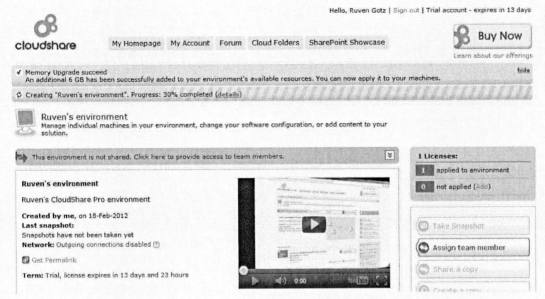

Figure 11-4. The environment creation screen in CloudShare

I have found that it takes about three to six minutes for the environment to finish creating (or resuming after being suspended). There is a YouTube video explaining more about the service that you can watch while you wait.

■ **Note** You will see a green bar in Figure 11.4 showing that there was a memory upgrade offered during the environment start-up. It offered "for a limited time" an extra 6GB of memory for free. I clicked the Accept button to take advantage of the offer.

Configuring and Viewing Your Machine

Once you have finished creating the environment, you will have access to some additional functionality, but there are also a number of important things to note, as shown in Figure 11-5.

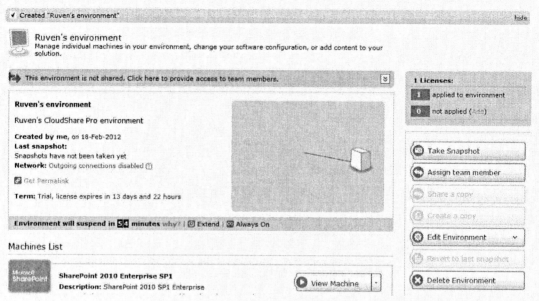

Figure 11-5. The CloudShare environment is now running

First, you will see that the progress bar is gone and the status at the top of the screen says that the environment has been created. Below that is a sharing status bar telling you that you have not yet shared this environment with anyone and giving you the option (via the icon) to add people. In the main status area, you can see the date that the environment was created and the date of the last snapshot (a way of capturing the state so that you can share it or revert to it later). The Network status says that outgoing connections are disabled. This is only the case for the 14-day trial. Once you have a paid account, you can browse the Internet from within your environment, allowing you to download and install additional software onto your virtual machines.

At the bottom of the status window is a notification that the environment will suspend in 54 minutes. This is because CloudShare attempts to reduce resources by closing environments that are not in use. They can't really tell if yours is in use or not, so it just suspends at that time. Don't worry, there is a pop-up warning ten minutes before this happens. When the pop-up appears, you will have the option to renew the time for another hour. You can also click the extend button, which gives you three hours before suspending; as you can see, I have just clicked it in Figure 11-6.

Environment will suspend in 180 minutes why? | ⊗ Extend | ⊗ Always On

Figure 11-6. Extending the suspend time in CloudShare

There is an Always On option as well that you can purchase for another $600 per year (in 2012 prices). If you use CloudShare extensively and frequently, this could be a worthwhile investment for you.

You also have the capability to adjust the hardware specifications of the machines by clicking the Edit Environment button on the right side of the screen. Note that this only works when the environment is running. Clicking the Edit Environment button adds a number of new options, as you can see in Figure 11-7. Clicking the Edit Hardware button opens an edit window (Figure 11-8).

Figure 11-7. Editing options for the environment in CloudShare

SharePoint 2010 Enterprise SP1
OS: Windows

Memory: 8192MB Disk: 80GB CPU: Single CPU

Figure 11-8. Hardware configuration editing in CloudShare

Let's say that I want to add a second CPU to the machine. Clicking the Edit icon next to the CPU allows me to change that option, as seen in Figure 11-9.

Machines List

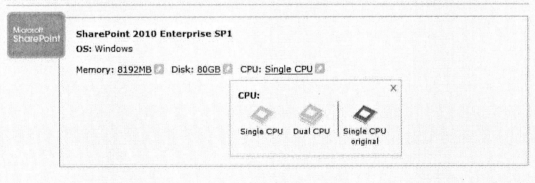

Figure 11-9. Selecting the Dual CPU option in CloudShare

Clicking the Save changes button causes a reboot, meaning the environment needs to be updated. You are sent back to the status screen with the active progress bar, showing you how far along you are with the reboot.

Once the environment has restarted, you can now get into it by clicking the View Machine button.

Working with Your Machine

In Figure 11-10 you can see how your running machine looks inside the browser. It takes a moment to start up, and then you will see a status and information area above the RDP window that gives you details about your environment and allows you to change various settings. The links across the top allow you to enable file sharing between your computer and the CloudShare environment, setting the resolution of your environment screen and, by clicking Fullscreen RDP, switching to full-screen mode.

■ **Note** RDP stands for remote desktop protocol. It is a Microsoft protocol that is used to handle the transfer of keyboard, mouse, and screen information from servers to "thin client" environments.

Internet Explorer automatically starts on the desktop, with two tabs, one with SharePoint Central Administration and one with the home page of the default portal home page. At this point you can click Fullscreen RDP and start working.

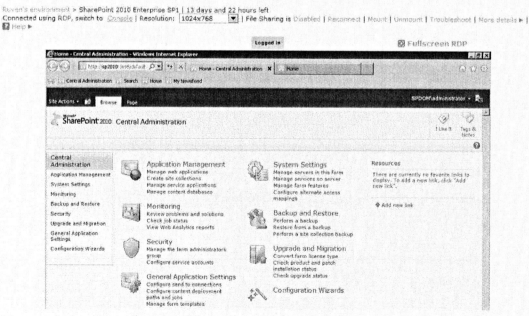

Figure 11-10. Working with your machine in CloudShare

When you switch to full-screen mode, you will see your environment taking over your screen. There is a blue bar at the top of the screen that shows you the internal IP address of the server (Figure 11-11).

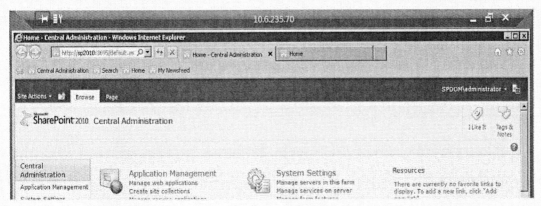

Figure 11-11. Managing the RDP screen in CloudShare

At the left edge of the blue bar is an icon of a push-pin. If you click it, the bar will become "unpinned" and it will disappear out of the way. Moving your mouse to the top edge of the screen will cause it to pop back down so you can access it again. Beside the push-pin is an icon of a wrench, which opens the management screen, while leaving the RDP screen open. On the right side of blue bar are the regular icons for minimizing, restoring, and closing the window. Typically, I use the restore icon to switch between the full-screen and management-screen views.

■ **Note** Licenses? Licenses! We don't need no stinkin' licenses!*: You may have noticed that I have made no mention of licensing SharePoint or any of the tools that we are working with in our environments. This is because CloudShare deals with licensing for you; your monthly subscription fee covers all the licenses you need.
*Faulty reference to the film *The Treasure of the Sierra Madre*.

At this point, you are ready to work in your environment: trying out new ideas, building out sample sites, customizing pages, testing third-party web parts, trying new SharePoint tools, or whatever SharePoint task your heart desires.

Snapshotting and Sharing

Before you can share your environment with someone, you will first need to take a snapshot. A snapshot captures the current state of your entire environment, right down to which windows were open. Capturing a snapshot is also like making a backup; if you mess up your system, you can revert back to the previous snapshot. In Figure 11-12, you can see the Take Snapshot button on the right side of the environment management screen (labeled with a 1). When you click it, you will be prompted to enter a snapshot name and description. The figure shows the default values. The next step is to click the Take Snapshot button (labeled with a 2 in the figure).

At this point you will, once again, see the active progress bar, captioned with "Taking a snapshot of Ruven's environment." This will take several minutes to complete.

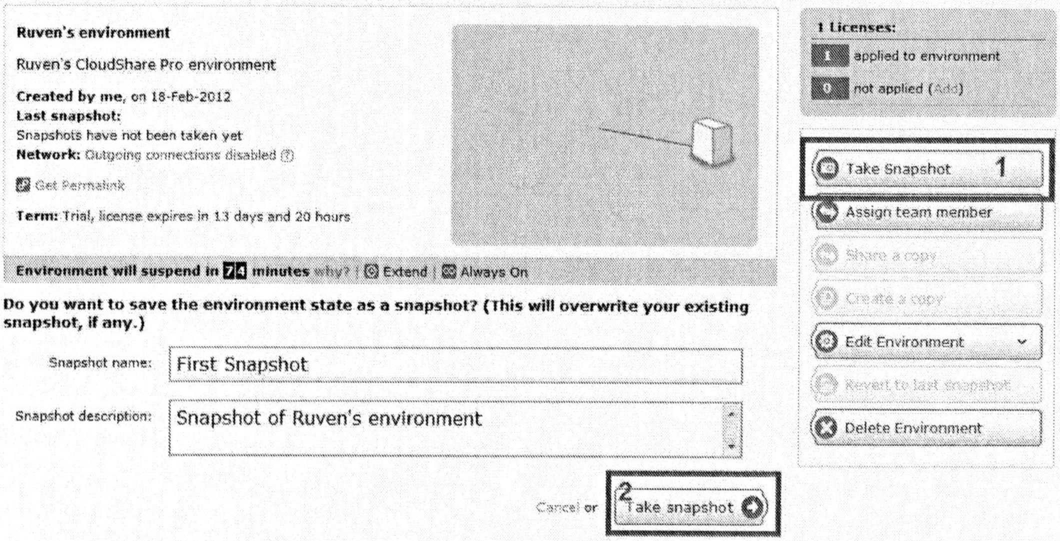

Figure 11-12. Taking a snapshot in CloudShare

Once the snapshot is complete, you will be able to click the "Share a copy" button on the right-hand menu, just below the Take snapshot button. A pop-up dialog box will ask you for the name and e-mail address of the person you want to share the copy with. Once you fill this out and submit it, the person you want to share with will get a link to a CloudShare environment that is an exact copy of your snapshot. That person can then navigate, edit, and otherwise use and change the environment in any way he or she sees fit. The person will have 48 hours from the time he or she first logs in to use the environment. If the person takes ownership of the environment, by signing up with CloudShare and paying for a subscription, he or she will be able to retain the snapshot and advance it from there.

Wrapping Up with CloudShare

I have been using CloudShare for about a year now, and I have found it to be just what I needed for doing quick tests, proof-of-concepts, trying out third-party applications, and otherwise spinning up quick instances of SharePoint for any reason. In fact, I used it to create my MultiMEGA portal that I use for the examples in this book.

There is one major downside, however. You can only take one snapshot (the latest one overwrites the prior one), and you can only have one environment in your account at a time. This means that if you are using your CloudShare account for one project, you can't temporarily put it aside and work on a different project. If you want to spin up a new environment, you will need to delete your current one first. There are a couple of solutions for this, but they cost more money: You could purchase more than one account. At $49 per month (in 2012 prices) it may be worth getting an extra account for a month or two, if you need it. The other alternative is to purchase their Enterprise account, which allows you to have a number of environments active at once.

In the next sections, we'll look at some alternatives to CloudShare.

Alternatives to CloudShare

My use of CloudShare has been sandwiched between two other alternatives: Amazon, which is the Cloud environment I was using before CloudShare existed, and Microsoft Office 365, which arrived on the scene after I was already using CloudShare. In this section I'll talk about each of them.

Amazon

I first thought about using Amazon's Elastic Compute Cloud (EC2) service in late 2009. I was tired of some hassles I was having with the virtual machines I was working with on my laptop, and I needed a more robust environment for testing SharePoint 2010. I was searching the Internet when I found a great blog post (www.czarzbon.com/2009/12/10/) by Marek Czarzbon that described the steps he followed to get SharePoint up and running. Following his blog, and with a bit of help from a friend, I was able to get my own instance up and running and I have continued to maintain it.

The amazing thing about the Amazon service is that you rent your virtual machine space from them by the hour. Amazon calls their VMs "instances." A large "instance" includes 7.5GB of memory, two virtual CPUs with two EC2 compute units in each core, 850GB of local storage all on a 64-bit x86 platform. You can see all of these options in Figure 11-13.

Request Instances Wizard

CHOOSE AN AMI	INSTANCE DETAILS	CREATE KEY PAIR	CONFIGURE FIREWALL	REVIEW

Provide the details for your instance(s). You may also decide whether you want to launch your instances as "on-demand" or "spot" instances.

Number of Instances: 1 **Instance Type:** High-Memory Extra Large (m2.xlarge, 17.1 GB) ▼

Type	CPU Units	CPU Cores	Memory
Large (m1.large)	4 ECUs	2 Cores	7.5 GB
Extra Large (m1.xlarge)	8 ECUs	4 Cores	15 GB
High-Memory Extra Large (m2.xlarge)	6.5 ECUs	2 Cores	17.1 GB
High-Memory Double Extra Large (m2.2xlarge)	13 ECUs	4 Cores	34.2 GB
High-Memory Quadruple Extra Large (m2.4xlarge)	26 ECUs	8 Cores	68.4 GB
High-CPU Extra Large (c1.xlarge)	20 ECUs	8 Cores	7 GB

Menu expanded.

Figure 11-13. Selecting an instance on Amazon's Elastic Compute Cloud

This "machine" is available for rent on demand for less than 50 cents per hour (in 2012 prices). And when you're done with it, you don't pay at all. The bandwidth charges are also quite small for the testing scenarios we are talking about here, and your storage requirements will be relatively small in the overall scheme of things.

If you forget to turn off your server, it could cost you $350 for the month (in 2012 prices). But in the time that I have been using the EC2 Cloud, I have hardly ever gone over $50 for the month, and most months have been under $20.

In Figure 11-14 you can see the display screen showing My Instances (both of which are stopped now).

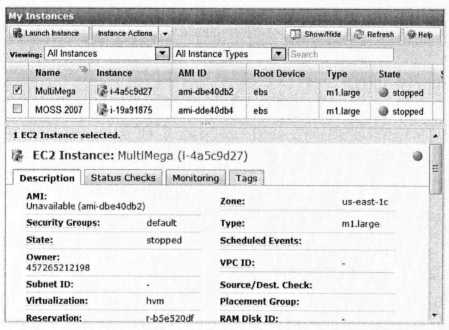

Figure 11-14. Amazon EC2 dashboard display screen for My Instances

If you are thinking of using a service like Amazon, you will have more power and flexibility than you would with CloudShare. You can choose your memory, processors, and disk space, and you can choose exactly how to set up your environment. You can also take snapshots of your environment and create copies that you can share with others, but you will need to run these environments on additional instances, which will incur additional hourly charges. You can also give anyone you wish access to your current instance, but it has to be running (incurring the hourly charge) whenever someone does this. Note that you would not normally give others access to the control panel that turns your virtual servers on and off, so they will have to be in touch with you to do that.

▓ **Tip** If you need to install SharePoint on your own, there is a really great tool to help you with that. It's called AutoSPInstaller and you can download it for free from CodePlex (www.autospinstaller.codeplex.com). AutoSPInstaller was created by Brian Lalancette (a coworker and friend of mine), and it has been downloaded over 30,000 times. How it works is that you set some parameters in a setup file and then, with one click it will download all the prerequisites you need, install SharePoint, configure the services, set the passwords, name the databases, and do all the dozens of things that you have to remember to do absolutely perfectly to do a clean and error-free SharePoint install. One interesting side note: CloudShare uses AutoSPInstaller to create its SharePoint instances. You can read more about it by following Brian on twitter @brianlala or on his blog http://spinsiders.com/brianlala/.

Amazon also has a large number of other services and capabilities for hosting giant sites. For example, FourSquare, Virgin Atlantic, Urban Spoon, and hundreds of other companies host their applications and web sites on Amazon. However, if you are looking for a quick and easy way to get set up, you need to be more of a technical expert if you want to get SharePoint set up properly. The other thing you have to think about is licensing. Your Amazon Web Service (AWS) instances include Windows licenses, but you need to obtain your own license for SharePoint. This may be a show-stopper for many of you. If you have access to Microsoft Developer Network Platforms (MSDN), then you can use those licenses for your setup.

Microsoft Office 365

Microsoft has been offering Cloud-based services since 2009. Their first offering was called the Business Productivity Online Suite (BPOS), and the collaboration platform at that time was based on SharePoint 2007. In the summer of 2011, Microsoft upgraded their offering, basing it on SharePoint 2010. The Office 365 package includes e-mail (Outlook/Exchange), Microsoft Office, and Lync (for messaging, voice chat, and screen sharing).

The Office 365 suite has different pricing and capability levels, but for our purposes of being able to work with as many of the capabilities of SharePoint as possible, you will need to sign up for the E1 plan for midsized business and enterprises for $10 per user per month (in 2012 prices).

The important thing to understand about SharePoint on Office 365 is that it is a true multitenant solution, as described at the beginning of this chapter. This means that you are not in control of your own virtual machines, as you are with CloudShare and Amazon. Because of the multitenant nature of Office 365, there are some severe restrictions to what you can do with it, and some differences in the way that it works. The first major clue that you are not dealing with regular SharePoint can be seen in Figure 11-15, this is the closest you will get to Central Administration.

Ruven Gotz ▾
sign out
❓

administration center

Manage site collections
A SharePoint site collection is a group of related Web sites organized into a hierarchy. A site collection often shares common features, such as permissions, content types, and consistent navigation, which can be managed together.

Configure InfoPath Forms Services
InfoPath Forms Services enables users to open and fill out InfoPath forms in a browser without requiring Microsoft InfoPath installed on their computer.

Configure InfoPath Forms Services Web service proxy
The InfoPath Forms Services Web service proxy enables communication between InfoPath Forms and Web services.

Manage User Profiles
The User Profile service provides a central location where administrators can configure user information, including user profiles, organization profiles, and My Site settings.

Manage Business Data Connectivity
Business Connectivity Services bridges the gap between SharePoint sites and other web services, databases, and external business applications. It enables SharePoint to create read and write connections to external data in lists, and to display external information in Web Parts.

Manage Term Store
A Term Store contains a set of related keywords (called managed terms) organized into a hierarchy of information, such as a well-defined product category or materials list, that you can then use to control the entry of list values. A Term Store helps improve the consistency, reliability, and discoverability of information within a site collection.

Manage Secure Store Service
The Secure Store contains credentials such as account names and passwords, which are required to connect to external business applications. The Secure Store provides a method of mapping the credentials, and associating them to an identity or group of identities.

Figure 11-15. The Office 365 SharePoint administration center

As you can see, you are dealing with a very much reduced set of controls and capabilities. Other limitations include the fact that you cannot install just any third-party add ons and components. Microsoft has designed the Office 365 SharePoint service to be very protective of applications that could hog all the resources on a server or that could interfere in any way with the operations of another instance of SharePoint running on the same box as yours. The only solutions that are allowed are what Microsoft calls "Sandboxed Solutions." These are applications that run in a secure, monitored process that has access to a limited part of the web farm (from MSDN). The system can shut down a sandboxed application that has used its allotment of resources (memory or processor cycles).

■ **Note** This is not meant to be a negative comment on the use of Office 365 as a potential client solution. There are use cases for Office 365 that make it a great solution to meet the needs of a business. In this chapter I am talking about using Cloud-based services as platforms for the information architect to test ideas, share proof of concepts, test third-party add ons, and other types of testing or trialing scenarios.

The results of these limitations mean that if you want to use Office 365 as your environment for trying new ideas, tools, and proofs of concepts, it would be best if your delivery platform is itself Office 365. If that is the case, then this is the perfect platform for you to use. Otherwise, you will need to tread with caution to make sure you aren't hampering your solutions with limitations that are not a part of the full SharePoint platform.

Summary

Having a great environment that you can access quickly, share easily, and obtain cost-effectively is a tremendous asset to any SharePoint practitioner (IA, BA, PM, IT Pro, developer, and others). Having the chance to stop talking about what you are going to do and actually showing your client can make the difference between confusion and clarity.

Over the past several years of my experience in the SharePoint space, I have tried various options, including local virtual machines, relying on my IT team, and Cloud-based solutions. Starting with Amazon, I finally found a solution that was under my control and allowed me to do what I wanted, exactly when I wanted it, at a reasonable price.

In the past year, I have come to rely on CloudShare, as it gives me most of what I had with Amazon but freed me from spending too much time in the nitty-gritty technical details. Its limitation on the number of environments and snapshots that I can have active at once is a bit painful. I wish they would allow me to snapshot and archive an environment so I could resurrect it at a later date. If your work requires you to constantly switch between multiple environments, then this may be a fatal flaw with CloudShare and you may have to look at their other pricing options or at Amazon. Finally, Office 365 has a very cost-effective platform, but I would recommend sticking to it for doing work that specifically pertains to Office 365 solutions; its limitations for testing real-world scenarios in the full version of SharePoint may otherwise cause you some problems.

CHAPTER 12

Conclusion: Putting It All Together

Things done well and with a care, exempt themselves from fear.

—William Shakespeare

Among my friends who do the type of work I do, we sometimes debate the question: Is it the practice or the practitioner? What we are trying to get at is, how much of the success we experience in our projects is due to our skill and experience in general and how much is due to the specific methods we use? We generally agree that the practitioner is a large component of the equation: It is difficult to work with both IT and businesspeople, understanding what they are really trying to say and proposing and building solutions that will really meet their needs. It takes a lot of experience and hard-won skill to do this job well. One of my favorite expressions is: Good decisions come from wisdom; wisdom comes from bad decisions. There's nothing like learning from your mistakes to make you wiser. However, I believe that at any given level of skill and experience, there are some basic things you can learn that will make you better at what you do: Getting shared commitment from your stakeholders and building from a good foundation of shared understanding are crucial to the success of any project. The way to make this happen is through the application of tools that will help get everyone onto the same page.

The techniques and tools I have presented in this book have made a big difference in the way I work, and I have seen them be tremendously helpful to others. However, there are no silver bullets. This means that even the use of these methods does not guarantee success. SharePoint projects are complex and often political; the stakeholders have other priorities and other projects and people who are seeking their attention. You may not have the level of senior management buy-in that you need, the project may be underfunded, or you might not be able to hire the right technical resources in time. In short, there are many things that can interfere with the success of the project. What I have covered in this book is not going to guarantee success. You will need to use these tools and combine them with your experience and skills as a facilitator and business problem solver to navigate the rocky shoals of potential shipwreck for your project.

On that cheerful note, let's take a high-level look at all the elements you have to put together for a successful project. As we walk through these components, you will see how to string together the skills and approaches we have discussed throughout the course of this book.

Kick-Off

Your project kick-off is where you get to set the course for the rest of the project. The old proverb "Well begun is half done" may not be literally true, but I'd say that "Badly begun means never getting done." This is your opportunity to get it right. If you are lucky, you've had the chance to be involved in the project from the earliest stages, and the vision and course are already well set. But often this isn't the case, so you need to nail a few things down.

Identify the Players

You need to know who the key stakeholders are. There are really two groups to get a handle on: who will be on the project team and who will be on the governance committee. These will probably be different individuals, though there may be some overlap. You want to know who the final decision makers will be both during the project and after delivery. You want to know who is going to make up the top two layers of the governance hierarchy (Figure 12-1).

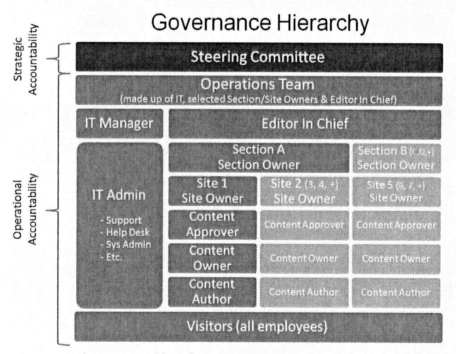

Figure 12-1. The governance hierarchy

The top layer of this stack is the trickiest one to get right (and the one you probably will have the least control over). Getting the buy-in and participation of the right people at this level can have a profound influence on the success of your project. If you can get key members of the organization leadership to see the value of the project, they can provide direction to others, which will greatly improve the chances of successful adoption.

Nail Down the Vision

This is where your IBIS skills will come into play. Making sure you are on the same page as the key stakeholders and, more importantly, that they are on the same page with one another. Figure 12-2 will remind you of one type of scoping exercise that can be done. This one is not definitive; you need to adjust it depending on the type and scope of the project you are working on.

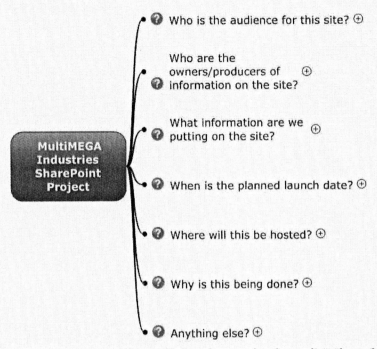

Figure 12-2. Build out the map that explores, and makes explicit, the goals and vision

You need to make sure you have the key players in the room when you do this exercise, because if you don't, you are going to eventually hit a roadblock with someone at a high level, and it's going to disturb, delay, derail, or destroy your project.

By the way, the vision can't be a bunch of platitudes like "improve collaboration" or "drive efficiency." Your vision has to include concrete goals that can be addressed with realistic actions and measured in some way (ROI is great, but not always an available option).

Personas

It's important to get a good understanding of who your users are. Create persona profiles representing the different groups that will be users of the intranet in your organization. Don't go crazy with this one. It's possible to do a lot of ethnographic studies and devote a lot of resources to building very detailed profiles for each persona. I think that this may be a worthwhile exercise for a public-facing e-commerce web site, I am not sure that it's worth a huge investment for a corporate intranet. But it is good to have a clear picture of who your users are and what they are expecting to get out of the site (Figure 12-3).

MultiMEGA – Personas

Persona	Group	Site Priorities/Goals	Details
	Everyone	Contact Information - Name/Role/Email Effective search Pulse of the company (news)	
	Member of the Board of Directors	Relatively limited use Collaboration space for meeting minutes and material to prep for next meeting	
	Manager	Pulse of company Creating the messages to lead the team Tools & Templates Human Resources - Staff Management - Hiring/Forms Project collaboration	
	Administrator	Team collaboration workspaces Policies Human Resources Easy to search material	

Figure 12-3. A simple persona analysis (top few items of a full page)

Creating these personas is something you can do in conjunction with your stakeholders. After you have conducted a number of discovery workshops, you will have a pretty good picture of many of the roles, but you will have to rely on the input of people who know the organization well to fill in the gaps in your knowledge.

Assess Current Maturity

If you are replacing or upgrading an existing SharePoint intranet, or just investigating where to start doing so, go to www.SharePointMaturity.com and download the "Maturity Model" (shown in Figure 12-4) developed by Sadalit Van Buren (with input from the wider SharePoint community). It is a great place to start, and it will help your stakeholders get a picture of the current state of the organization and to help them set targets for where they would like to be at some point in the future.

The SharePoint Maturity Model – 1 – Core Concepts
Maturation also occurs along this vector

Level	Publication	Collaboration	Business Process	
500 Optimizing	Content is personalized to the user. Content is shared across multiple functions and systems without duplication. Feedback mechanism is in place for pages and taxonomy. Automated tagging may be present.	Collaboration occurs outside the firewall – i.e. with external contributors. Automated processes exist for de-provisioning and archiving sites.	Power users can edit existing workflows to adapt them to changing business needs on the fly. Users leverage data from BPM to optimize process, simulate on real data, clear bottlenecks, balance work across workloads. Users have visibility into the process and can provide feedback to process improvements. Business processes extend to external users.	Us tag Pro w/r tag vol
400 Predictable	Content is monitored, maintained, targeted to specific groups. Usage is analyzed. Digital assets are managed appropriately. If more than one doc mgmt system is present, governance is defined. Mobile access considered.	Collaboration tools are used across the entire organization. Email is captured & leveraged. The system supports promotion of content from WIP to final. Mobile access considered.	Workflow is a component of SP-based composite applications with connectivity to LOB systems. Users have access to process analytics and audit trails. Collaboration happens in the context of a work item as part of a dynamic, nonlinear business process (the "case").	Co pro Ad ref cus ma
300 Defined	Site Columns/ Managed Metadata standardize the taxonomy. Custom content Types are created. Custom page layouts & site templates are configured. Approval process is implemented. Incoming email activated for some lists/libs. Site Map is present. Some content targeted to groups.	Collaboration efforts extend sporadically to discussion threads, wikis, blogs, and doc libs with versioning. Site templates are developed for specific needs. Incoming email activated for some lists/libs.	Process is considered as a whole, rather than as automating functional tasks. Transition from procedural document workflow to orchestration of dynamic business process. SharePoint is becoming the BP platform, w/the introduction of 3rd party BPM tool to support more complex business rules.	Se Be pro the
200	Custom metadata is applied to content. Templates standardized across sites. Lists	Mechanism is in place for new site requests. Collaboration efforts are	Business processes are designed; some custom, departmental "no-code" workflows (SP Designer, Visio.	Cu the

Figure 12-4. The SharePoint "Maturity Model"

Discovery Workshops

Running the discovery workshops with a broad spectrum of teams and roles is essential to the success of the project. Yes, you will learn a lot in the first few workshops, but the more important result is that you will have seeded your message throughout the organization that people are being listened to, their ideas are being taken seriously, and there is a competent team running this project that will give them a new solution to improve on what they had. You can see some of the workshop deck in Figure 12-5.

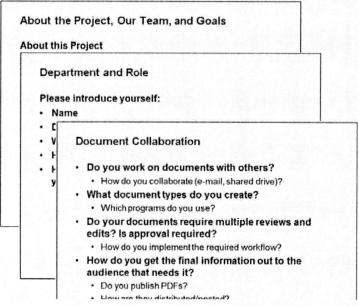

Figure 12-5. Discovery workshops

Having an assistant to act as a scribe to help record the meeting is not absolutely required, but it makes it easier to facilitate if you can concentrate on the people without having to note the words.

Managing Content

No matter how much work you put into designing a great information architecture for a project and doing all the other things that need to be done, you will not have anything of value unless the structures you build are filled with content. You may be surprised at how often there is a mad scramble near the end of the project to obtain or migrate content. If you want to avoid this mad scramble, you need to have your ducks in a row well in advance.

Inventory Content and Identify Content Owners

There is usually a ton of content already in existence. Your goal is to migrate content of value, create new content where it is needed, and remove ROT (redundant, obsolete, and trivial) content. To do this properly, a content inventory needs to be taken and the content owners found. For each item of inventory, determine if it is to be migrated to the new site, archived, or deleted (according to the organization's records management policies).

■ **Tip** When in doubt, *don't* migrate that content. If you can't find an owner who can determine whether something should be moved to the new intranet, or if the owners themselves are not sure whether anyone uses the content, don't move it. Later, if anyone squawks, you can bring it over. This is usually better than expending effort on moving things that no one cares about. My favorite saying here is: Don't move boxes from the old attic to the new attic when you move.

Writing for the Web

When creating new content for your site, you have an opportunity to improve overall quality by creating concise, useful, well-written content that is written to be displayed on a web page. In many cases, you will not be able to hire professional writers to create your content, so you will have to train your in-house content creators to create better material. You need to teach them about how people read on the web, and you have to educate them on the "voice of the firm" so there is a constant tone to all the writing on the site.

One of the best resources for this is Jakob Nielsen's blog (www.useit.com/papers/webwriting). His "Writing for the Web" articles (Figure 12-6) give you the research-based answers on how to write effectively so people will read and be able to absorb your content.

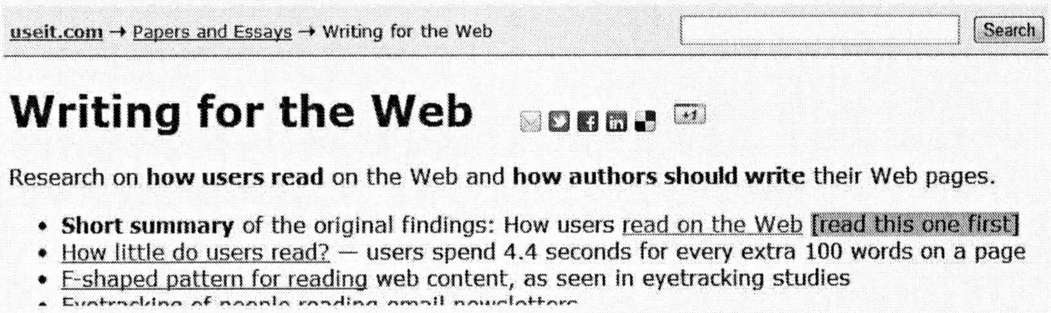

useit.com → Papers and Essays → Writing for the Web   [   ] [Search]

Writing for the Web ✉ 🐦 f in ⚫ ⊕

Research on **how users read** on the Web and **how authors should write** their Web pages.

- **Short summary** of the original findings: How users read on the Web [read this one first]
- How little do users read? — users spend 4.4 seconds for every extra 100 words on a page
- F-shaped pattern for reading web content, as seen in eyetracking studies
- Eyetracking of people reading email newsletters

Figure 12-6. "Writing for the Web" by Jakob Nielsen

Don't let the very plain design of the useit.com web site fool you. It is widely recognized as a top resource for intranet and web design and writing. The bottom-line message of his articles is that people don't read web pages the same way they read articles on paper. Everything has to be much shorter and to the point, and key items or concepts need to be highlighted.

Creating and Approving Content as Early as Possible

Some organizations have internal communication departments whose mandate is to create content for internal use. This team will be responsible for creating content such as news stories and also for working with business teams to create content that goes on to the pages that make up the site. However, in many firms there is no such resource, and no person or group is directly tasked with the role of intranet content creator. Because you are going to need to have new content created (and in some cases translated) and you may have to get people who are already doing other jobs to write it, it is crucial to start as early as possible to get people assigned to be the content creators and to get them to start thinking about what they are going to create and where they are going to source their material. The approval workflows will also have to be established. Who is going to approve this content? Will it be the business owner, the site owner, or the intranet owner?

One of the most contentious and difficult content tasks is finding the images you are going to use. In some organizations, the desire is to avoid generic stock photography and to make sure all the pictures are of "real people" who work at the firm. At other companies, this is strictly forbidden; they don't want pictures of any staff on the intranet except in the case of news stories that include people doing specific things that are relevant to that story. In this case, it is important to have a library of preapproved stock images that can be made available for authors to use.

One of the things you need to do is to create an editorial calendar that will govern the launch of new articles, stories, and other content after the original site goes live. For example, if you have a news display on your home page, you need to have a collection of stories written, edited, and ready to go, so that you can have fresh content appearing on a regular basis. Of course, your news content will contain some actual "news" when it happens, but much of this content can be prewritten. The editor-in-chief of the site should be in control of this calendar and ensure that there is enough good content in the pipeline to keep the site fresh and interesting.

Navigation Workshops

Designing the site navigation is one of the most critical elements of building a new site. Although it is possible to change a site's navigation after it goes live, this is very costly in terms of user confusion and frustration. This task has added complexity due to political forces that can impact the process: People want *their* content to be easier to find or more prominent. In Chapter 4 we covered a couple of ways to mitigate these challenges. The most important one is to use a mind mapping tool to interactively build out the map with your stakeholders (Figure 12-7).

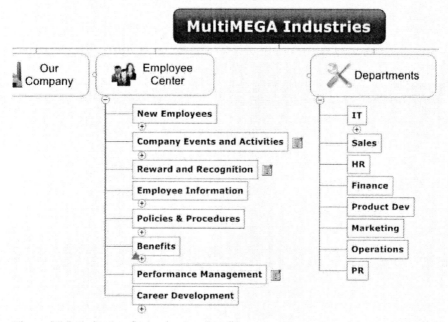

Figure 12-7. Designing the navigational architecture

By working interactively, you can try ideas and instantly see what benefits and problems the changes cause. The process of using a visual system enables everyone to see the choices and understand the options. Even if you cannot get agreement among all the stakeholders, everyone knows what decision was made and why. By the time they get back to their desks after the workshop, they will have a PDF of the map in their inboxes (or on the SharePoint site being used to manage the project) that they can review and share with other members of their team.

Another useful and important technique is the use of card sorting to get input from your users on the terms they use and understand their logical relation to one another. It's important that you don't take the card-sorting results as the only input for the structure of the new site, as your users may be influenced by the structure of the site they are used to or by the organization chart they are familiar with. Following up the new structure with usability testing, where you ask users to look at your new IA and then ask them where they think they would go to find certain content or perform certain actions, is an important follow-up step that can save you from delivering a navigational structure that is difficult for your users to work with.

Collaboration Strategy

It is very important that your stakeholders understand what the difference is between the portal areas and the collaboration areas. The use of the pyramid (Figure 12-8), with the "above-the-line" and "below-the-line" concept, is a very useful way to communicate this.

Above the Line vs. Below the Line

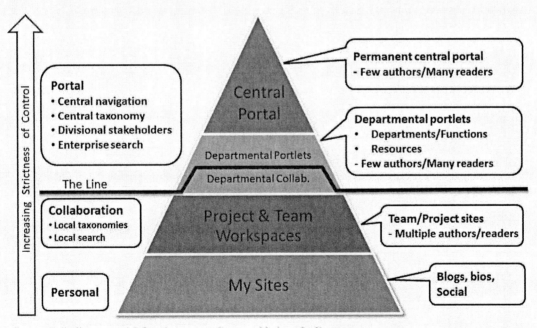

Figure 12-8. The pyramid showing areas above and below the line

The portal areas are ones that require tight control because the content on display there is meant for broad consumption and therefore needs to be vetted for accuracy and to ensure it reflects the voice of the firm. The collaboration sites that exist below the line are places where people work together and potentially have many authors. The fact that these sites are meant for teams to work together more freely does not allow you to abdicate your responsibility to plan, communicate, and enforce a strategy. Simply giving users full rights to as many subsites as they want is a recipe for chaos, information silos, and loss of content integrity.

It is *very important* that you create and communicate your collaboration strategy before you start releasing team sites in the wild. You need to know what kind of branding you will be applying, how much power you are going to give the owners, and what kind of training or coaching you are going to supply. This is discussed a little bit further in the governance section below, but I think that governing your collaboration is one of the toughest things to do well and also one of the most important things to do well. When people talk about SharePoint adoption strategies, they are most often talking about weaning people off using e-mail and shared drives for getting their day-to-day work done. If you make it too hard for them to get to a site when they need one, or lock it down too severely, they will not use SharePoint and will try to find ways around it whenever they can. I think that lack of resources (time/people/money) to support collaboration is one of the biggest sources of SharePoint project failure.

Although we tend to think of the portal as the most important part of the intranet, because it is most widely viewed and is the communications and information authority within the organization, it is the ongoing life of the collaboration areas that really provides the greatest value over time. You will see some team sites grow into large repositories of information that are specialized yet of value to a large number of people and teams across the organization. Many of these team sites will benefit from time spent designing their own internal information architectures that will mesh well with the overall site. This is also the place where you can get huge benefit by exploring business process automation. The ROI from automating simple, but "soul crushing, spirit destroying" work (as Sarah Haase calls it in Chapter 8) can help pay for a lot of the value provided by doing a good job at making sure that collaboration works well.

Infrastructure

Building your SharePoint infrastructure is a crucial part of the process of building out or upgrading SharePoint. The problem is often one of timing. In order to meet project timelines, the infrastructure components have to be designed, budgeted, signed-off, ordered, installed, and configured according to a set of project milestones. The pressure is often high to get the design finalized as soon as possible because of hardware-ordering lead times. The problem is that this is asked for before the business problem is fully defined, leaving your technical team in a quandary: They will have to make guesses and estimates before they really have all the information they need. This is another reason to get the key decision makers involved early and to use the mapping techniques discussed earlier to ensure that everyone has a shared understanding of what is required so that reasonably accurate infrastructure plans can be made.

In addition to the physical infrastructure, your technical team will have to design the architecture of how SharePoint will be installed and configured. Issues to consider will include how the site collections are laid out, which services will run on which servers, how many databases are required, and how the site collections are mapped to them. These decisions will have to be made in conjunction with hardware decisions to support reliability and recoverability and be made in a way that balances cost, potential downtime, and performance.

Finally, there will have to be a systems and infrastructure governance plan developed that covers service-level agreements for all of the above (reliability, disaster recovery, etc.) as well as server maintenance and backup procedures, patching and update processes, and all the other information required to keep SharePoint running smoothly and well. If everything goes as planned, a lot of people are going to be trusting SharePoint to store and manage their crucial documents and information; you have to be sure the infrastructure does not let them down.

Search Strategy

The single most important thing that SharePoint can do for your organization is to improve information findability. The concept of findability encompasses both browsing and searching. One of the best lines I've heard about SharePoint search, when implemented poorly, was that it is a "random document generator." This person meant that the results he or she received when searching within SharePoint were essentially useless. SharePoint search can be extremely powerful, useful, and fast (even without Microsoft FAST technology). Following a detailed search strategy, as discussed in Chapter 9, will take you a long way toward having a world-class intranet platform.

Wireframing and Branding

Getting the page layouts right is where wireframing comes in. With an easy-to-use tool (like Balsamiq, covered in Chapter 5) and easy-to-change page layouts, you can work with your stakeholders to come up with a set of layouts that will work with their different types of content. These wireframes can then be used for quick and relatively inexpensive usability tests to see if people can perform the tasks they need to accomplish. In Figure 12-9 you can see the original wireframe that led to the final SharePoint page seen beside it on the right.

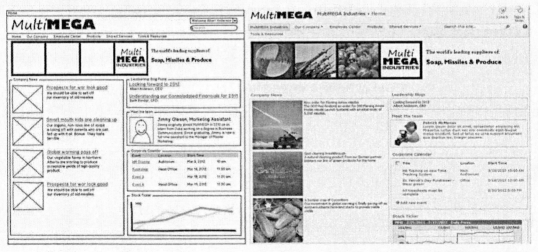

Figure 12-9. From wireframe to implemented page

The way the site's pages actually look is a surprisingly large factor toward successful implementation. Many of us—especially those from a technical background—believe that the function and architecture of the site are the most important parts. But having a site that *looks* good is very important as well. Having a site comp based on the home page layout is something your stakeholders can use to communicate to others what is coming and why. Having a great looking home page can drive a lot of enthusiasm, making the communication and subsequent adoption process just a little bit easier.

Creating a style guide that tells content creators how their work should look, including font colors and sizes, picture sizes, and so forth, can help maintain the site's visual consistency across all areas. Consistency makes it easier for users to understand what a page is about and how it is to be used. A good, well-applied style guide will help the site maintain this consistency throughout its lifetime.

Communication Planning and Community Building

I attended a presentation about four years ago (I wish I could remember who presented it) where the message was: If you've had your project kickoff meeting and you haven't started your communications strategy yet, you're late!

As much as people generally dislike their current intranet, they've at least figured out where the stuff they need is. If they arrive on a Monday morning to find a brand new, super well-designed, and beautiful intranet waiting for them, chances are they'll hate it. People generally don't like surprises at work. So, getting the word out that something new is coming is very important. A great way to pave the way for this is to do a survey first, asking what people think of the current intranet: what works and what doesn't.

Some people will be involved in card-sorting exercises and some in usability testing. Although usually the actual numbers of participants will be quite small, they should be drawn from across the organization. Their participation will start to seed the idea that something new is coming.

When the comps are signed off, sharing them widely or even doing a road show will really start the juices flowing. This is the time to identify your community of gurus and champions. These are the people who have an innate interest in technology in general or SharePoint in particular. They can be your core team of support; and the best part is that they are already in the trenches, so they understand what their coworkers are going through.

■ **Tip** It is very worthwhile to recognize and reward your SharePoint IT Super Stars. Give them a private site where they can share information or ask each other questions. Get them together over pizza once a month. Really, whatever it takes, you should work hard to keep this group engaged and happy.

Training, Adoption, and Governance

In Chapter 10, I explained why I think that training as a classroom exercise is less than optimal. However, I realize that my coaching manifesto may be too much too soon for some organizations. If this is the case with your organization, then yes, send your content owners and authors on training, but you *must* make sure they have enough support once they get back to work, otherwise they will have to just do their best with whatever parts of the training stuck. For some of them, this will be great stuff; for others, they'll head way off course and just figure out whatever works, and some will just give up and use whatever archaic systems they can—or find outside services to host their content. These outcomes—chaos or adoption failure—are closely aligned with governance and training. As I said in Chapter 10, governance without enforcement is just suggestion. You have to stay on top of your owners and authors to ensure they are building a system that has value to the users and that meets the company's goals and implements company policy. The most effective form of training is coaching people on how best to use the new system as they learn to add their own content to it.

Summary

And that is how I want to conclude this chapter and this book, with the bookends that are the most important success factors for a SharePoint project: good planning at the start with shared understanding of business goals, outcome alignment, and an understanding of the complexity facing the team; and then proper support at the end of the project through the application of coaching and governance that carries the project from the build phase through deployment and maturation, while ensuring that the initial goals set by leadership continue to be met.

Index